National Children's Bureau series

Editor: Ronald Davie

This series examines contemporary issues relating to the development of children and their needs in the family, school and society. Based on recent research and taking account of current practice, it also discusses policy implications for the education, health and social services. The series is relevant not only for professional workers, administrators, researchers and students but also for parents and those involved in self-help movements and consumer groups.

Combined Nursery Centres
Elsa Ferri, Dorothy Birchall,
Virginia Gingell and Caroline Gipps

Growing Up in Great Britain
Ken Fogelman (editor)

Children in Changing Families: a Study of Adoption and
Illegitimacy
Lydia Lambert and Jane Streather

Caring for Separated Children
R. A. Parker (editor)

A Fairer Future for Children
Mia Kellmer Pringle

The Needs of Parents: Practice and Policy in Parent Education
Gillian Pugh and Erica De'Ath

Unqualified and Underemployed: Handicapped Young People and
the Labour Market
Alan Walker

Also by Gillian Pugh

Shared Care: support services for families with handicapped children

Preparation for Parenthood (editor)

Parents as Partners: intervention schemes and group work with parents of handicapped children

Perspectives on Preschool Home Visiting (editor)

The Needs of Parents

Practice and Policy in Parent Education

Gillian Pugh and Erica De'Ath

MACMILLAN

First published 1982
Reprinted 1985

Published by
MACMILLAN EDUCATION LTD
Houndmills, Basingstoke, Hampshire RG21 2XS
and London
Companies and representatives
throughout the world

Printed in Hong Kong

British Library Cataloguing in Publication Data
Pugh, Gillian
The needs of parents
1. Child welfare—Great Britain
I. Title   II. De'Ath, Erica
362.7'0941   HV751
ISBN 0–333–37326–X
ISBN 0–333–37327–8 Pbk

Contents

List of Tables and Figures

List of Abbreviations

ACE	Advisory Centre for Education
AIMS	Association for Improvement in the Maternity Services
APNI	Association for Post-natal Illness
ATW	Active tutorial work
BAECE	British Association for Early Childhood Education
BBC	British Broadcasting Corporation
BFUW	British Federation of University Women
BMA	British Medical Association
BON	British Organisation for Non-parents
CACE	Central Advisory Council for Education
CAP	Calderdale Association for Parents
CASE	Confederation for Advancement of State Education
CEDC	Community Education Development Centre (Coventry)
CERI	Centre for Educational Research and Innovation
CETHV	Council for the Education and Training of Health Visitors
CDT	Community Development Trust
CHAT	Contact Health and Teaching
COFACE	Confederation of Family Organisations in the European Community
CHSC	Central Health Services Council
CSE	Certificate of Secondary Education
CSV	Community Service Volunteers
CTVC	Churches Television Council
CWLA	Child Welfare League of America
EOC	Equal Opportunities Commission
EPA	Educational Priority Area
FLEEP	Family Life Education Ecumenical Project
FPA	Family Planning Association
FSU	Family Service Units
FWA	Family Welfare Association

GAFL	Gloucester Association for Family Life
GCE	General Certificate of Education
GP	General Practitioner
HEC	Health Education Council
HMI	Her Majesty's Inspectorate
HMSO	Her Majesty's Stationery Office
HVA	Health Visitors Association
IBA	Independent Broadcasting Authority
IFPE	International Federation for Parent Education
ILEA	Inner London Education Authority
INSTEP	In-service Training and Education Panel
IUFO	International Union of Family Organisations
LEAs	Local Education Authorities
MAMA	Meet a Mum Association
MSAC	Maternity Services Advisory Committee
MSC	Manpower Services Commission
NAMCW	National Association for Maternal and Child Welfare
NAWCH	National Association for the Welfare of Children in Hospital
NAYPCAS	National Association of Young People's Counselling and Advisory Services
NCB	National Children's Bureau
NCDS	National Child Development Study
NCH	National Children's Home
NCOPF	National Council for One Parent Families
NCPTA	National Council of Parent Teacher Associations
NCT	National Childbirth Trust
NCMA	National Childminding Association
NCVO	National Council for Voluntary Organisations
NCVYS	National Council for Voluntary Youth Service
Newpin	New Parent-Infant Network
NFCA	National Foster Care Association
NHS	National Health Service
NMGC	National Marriage Guidance Council
NNEB	National Nursery Education Board
NSPCC	National Society for the Prevention of Cruelty to Children
NUS	National Union of Students
NUT	National Union of Teachers
OECD	Organisation for Economic Co-operation and Development
OPCS	Office of Population Censuses and Surveys
OPUS	Organisation for Parents under Stress
OU	Open University
PACT	Parents Children and Teachers
PET	Parent Effectiveness Training
PMS centres	psycho-pedagogical-medical-social centres
PPA	Pre-School Playgroups Association

PTA	Parent Teacher Association
RCGP	Royal College of General Practitioners
RCM	Royal College of Midwives
RCOG	Royal College of Obstetricians and Gynaecologists
SCHEP	Schools Council Health Education Project
SLS	social and life skills
TACADE	Teachers Advisory Council on Alcohol and Drug Abuse
VCHC	Voluntary Council for Handicapped Children
YFDCA	Young Family Day Care Association
YOP	Youth Opportunity Programme
YSDC	Youth Service Development Council
YTS	Youth Training Scheme

Reports

Usually known as	*See reference under*
Albemarle report	Ministry of Health (1960)
Court report	Committee on Child Health Service (1976)
Crowther report	Central Advisory Council for Education (1959)
Hunt report	Youth Services Development Council (1967)
Latey report	Lord Chancellor's Office (1967)
Macnaughton report	Royal College of Gynaecologists (1982)
Miles report	National Council for One Parent Families (1979)
Milson-Fairbairn report	YSDC (1969)
Newsom report	CACE (1963)
Peel report	Central Health Services Council (1970)
Plowden report	CACE (1967)
Short report	House of Commons, Social Services Committee
Skeet report	House of Commons, Youth and Community Bill
Taylor report	DES and Welsh Office (1977)
Thompson report	DES (1982)
Warnock report	Committee of Enquiry into the Education of the Handicapped

Acknowledgements

Many people have contributed to the development of this book, by discussing their thoughts on parent education with us or by attending one of the seventy or so conferences set up during the course of the Bureau's parenting project. Some of the main groups and organisations we have consulted are listed in Appendix 1, and we are grateful to them for their time and their ideas. Particular thanks go to those who served on the working party which produced *A Job For Life*, a document which has guided our thinking throughout the project: Kate Torkington and Joan Kidd with whom the booklet was written and Brenda Crowe, Ken David, Gill Feeley, Heather Hyde, Jill Manning Press, Lin Poulton and government observers Rachel Lockwood, HMI (DES), and Dr Barbara Ely, Hilda Kell and Daphne Learmont (DHSS).

Colleagues to whom we are grateful for their constructive comments on all or part of earlier drafts of this book include Ron Davie, Dorothy Birchall, Elsa Ferri, Dorothy Henderson, Richard Ives, Lydia Lambert and Christine Such (from the Bureau); and, from outside the Bureau, Dorit Braun, John Coleman, Bernard Davies, Shirley Goodwin, Margaret Harrison, Janet Paraskeva Hunt, Lesley Rimmer, Sheila Shinman, Lesley Smith, Willem van der Eyken and, in particular, Kate Torkington. Many helpful comments were made, but the responsibility for the final manuscript is entirely ours. Our thanks, too, to Ian Vallender and Biddy Cunnell for laboriously checking through our numerous references.

Neither the book nor the project would have been possible without the hard work and commitment of our secretary, Margery Geoghegan, and we wish her a happy and well-deserved retirement.

And finally our grateful thanks go to the late Mia Pringle, who sought and obtained funding for the project on which the book draws, and to the Department of Health and Social Security who responded to her request for funding.

GILLIAN PUGH
ERICA DE'ATH

Introduction

This is a book about being a parent in the 1980s. It looks at the kind of society in which parents are bringing up their children, and at the types of families in which children are growing up, but its chief concern is with what could be done to make being a parent and bringing up children easier, more enjoyable and more satisfying than it is for many parents at present. Parenthood today is a demanding and at times stressful, lonely and frustrating experience; and if society continues to put high expectations on parents, then it must also provide sufficient support to enable them to fulfil their obligations with knowledge, understanding and enjoyment.

How this support might be defined and, more importantly, provided are examined in the pages that follow. The evidence upon which we draw has been gathered during the course of a three-year development project, based at the National Children's Bureau, which has looked at preparation, education and support for parents on a national basis. This has been an exercise in gathering and analysing information and promoting discussion, rather than a detailed study of individual schemes, and in order to illuminate the position from which the book has been written, the following paragraphs include a brief description of the Bureau's involvement in the field of parent education with particular reference to this parenting project.

The material in the book is presented with three main objectives in mind. It attempts to present for the first time an overview of what help parents and prospective parents in Britain might find in their local schools, clinics and communities under the general umbrella of 'parent education and support'. It hopes also to encourage the many people who are working with parents and their children, whether as professional or voluntary workers, to re-examine what their own contribution might be to the network of supportive and educative services, and to question the nature of their relationship with parents. It contributes to the current debate on parent education by presenting for discussion a framework for examining the skills of parenting, the needs of individuals if they are to develop to their full potential as parents, and the way in which these needs might be met.

The National Children's Bureau and parent education

The Bureau's contribution to the parent education debate grew from the strong commitment of the late director, Mia Kellmer Pringle, to the needs of children and her views on the importance of preventive work in the child-care field if children were to develop to their full potential. She argued that parenthood, and particularly motherhood, has been undervalued for far too long; children are our future and their upbringing and care is a skilled, responsible and demanding job in which the community as a whole should invest considerable resources (Pringle, 1975, 1980a, 1980b, 1982). She campaigned tirelessly for parenthood to be a deliberately chosen role, undertaken with the full understanding of what it involved – 'warts and all' – and she stressed on many occasions the importance of the quality of care during the early years of life. Parenting was, she said, too demanding and complex a task to be performed well merely because we have all been children, and she was one of the first to argue for a compulsory 'core' element in the school curriculum of all young people which would include human psychology, child development and preparation for parenthood.

The project on which this book draws for its evidence was funded as the result of a joint DHSS/DES initiative early in 1979. As a continuation of earlier discussions (DHSS, 1974a, 1974b) the two government departments invited a small group of experts together to discuss 'what action can and should be taken by public authorities, voluntary organisations and others to help raise the standards of parenting in this country?' In order to provide an informed basis for these discussions the National Children's Bureau prepared a brief paper for this seminar, illustrating the range of practical initiatives already in progress in the field of preparation for parenthood (as it was then called) and raising issues for discussion at the conference. This paper was published, together with papers by speakers from the Bureau, the DES and the DHSS, and a summary of the resulting discussion as *Preparation for Parenthood: some current initiatives and thinking* (Pugh, 1980).

Both the background paper and the seminar itself showed how difficult it was to obtain an accurate picture of schemes and services available to young people and to families. The piecemeal and unco-ordinated way in which such services as there were had grown up, made it difficult for families to know about and thus use these services, and for many parents there appeared to be nowhere to turn for support. Despite – or perhaps because of – this lack of co-ordination, there was considerable interest in sharing experiences with others working in this field, and providing better and more co-ordinated services within each local area. It was therefore recommended that a national clearing house be established to promote discussion about parent education and support and to publicise currently available resources and 'good practice'.

The Bureau's parenting project

On the strength of these recommendations, the DHSS agreed to fund a three-year development project from September 1980 to August 1983. Its brief was a wide one: to establish a national clearing-house for the dissemination and interchange of ideas and information on schemes and services in the field of preparation for parenthood and support for parents with young children. The remit was to include the role of schools in preparing young people for family life; relevant work in youth and community services and in further education; antenatal preparation; support services for families within the community; and the role of the media, particularly radio and television, in parent education. The approach was to be two-pronged: to find out what was happening in both the statutory and voluntary fields in different parts of the country and what research was in progress; and to promote discussion of some of the key issues through the dissemination of information and through working parties, seminars and conferences at both local and national levels.

Building up a comprehensive picture of the schemes and services available in different parts of the country was not easy, for, as we shall show, definitions and approaches show considerable diversity. However, through the Bureau's extensive network, contact was made with local authorities and health authorities, with all the main professional associations and voluntary organisations concerned with child-care and with many universities and colleges. All directors of education were approached (in association with the DES/Aston University project on preparation for parenthood in the school curriculum – see Chapter 3). Personal contacts were also made with as many of the statutory and voluntary organisations working in this field as time allowed. A full list of these is given in Appendix 1, and reference will be made to their work in the chapters that follow.

With limited resources, it has been important to work closely with colleagues who have specialist knowledge in their fields, and a number of working groups have thus been convened. A key group was that which guided the publication of *A Job For Life*, a short discussion document which attempts to identify individual needs and clarify what forms of preparation, support and education should be available at each stage of a person's life. Published jointly with the National Marriage Guidance Council and National Children's Home, *A Job For Life* (Pugh *et al.*, 1982) is now being used in several parts of the country as a basis for planning better co-ordinated and more appropriate services for parents and prospective parents. For example, it has provided a framework for working parties and conferences; it has been used in curriculum planning in schools, colleges, adult education and antenatal classes. Elsewhere it has inspired health visitors and other workers concerned with children under five to rethink their work with families. Its potential as a guide for training and development has been welcomed, and as the current stage of the work draws to a close, further in-depth work is planned in order to set up and evaluate in two or three parts of the country, parent education initiatives at each stage of the life cycle.

Another group has brought together over a period of two years some eighteen pre-school home-visitors, from both the educational and voluntary fields, all of them with many years experience behind them, but all wanting a forum where issues could be discussed and clarified at a national level. Accounts of their individual home visiting schemes, together with a discussion of the development of home visiting and some of the issues which face home visitors today can be found in *Perspectives on Pre-school Home Visiting* (Aplin and Pugh, 1983).

The initial seminar which gave rise to the project described the media as 'potentially one of the most important and powerful means of influencing the general public and increasing standards of parenting', and a further working group was thus set up to examine how those working in the media might increase their contribution to parenthood education and work a little more closely together (Pugh, 1982f). A workshop in June 1981 pointed to the need for a 'contact' group which could provide a two-way channel for information-flow between groups of parents and programme-makers. Although the additional funding required to set up such a group was not forthcoming, the project has been able to provide this two-way contact in an informal way.

There were two stages of the life cycle which were quickly identified as receiving very little in the way of education or support. These were parents of teenagers, and teenagers themselves, other than through provision within the school curriculum. In both these areas seminars were convened to bring together those who were doing some work in the respective fields. In the area of adolescence representatives of youth and community work organisations were invited to identify relevant projects and some of these are discussed in Chapter 4 (see also De'Ath, 1982). Schemes and projects involving parents of teenage children are included in Chapter 7.

A final working group was set up in response to the increasing number of people who were asking for help in evaluating their parent support groups. Evaluation of groups whose principle aim is often to increase individual self-confidence or parents' enjoyment of their children, is not easy, but a number of researchers with experience of evaluating such groups were brought together to see whether the publication of a basic 'guide' to evaluation might be feasible. With the help of this group, and in particular of Sheila Shinman and Willem van der Eyken, *Evaluating Parent Groups* was published as Parenting Paper 7 (De'Ath, 1983b).

An additional small-scale study linked to the project was a three-month survey of family centres undertaken by Dorothy Birchall as part of her work on the Bureau's research team. Some thirty-three centres were visited, and a short report was published in *Concern* (Birchall, 1982) Family centres are considered in more detail in Chapter 6.

We have in addition organised or spoken at nearly seventy conferences in all corners of the United Kingdom and in Paris, Dublin and Japan. Twelve of these have been organised by the project under the umbrella title of 'Parenting in the Eighties', six of them in London and one each in Hull, Lewes, Leeds, Nottingham, Tredegar and Glasgow. These conferences have been multidisciplinary gatherings, bringing together parents, para-professionals and professionals from all the services working with children. In order to share with a wider audience some of the more interesting approaches to parent education and support, the edited papers from six of these conferences have been published as Parenting Papers 1–6 (Pugh, 1982a-e; De'Ath, 1983a). Finally, a number of discussion papers and articles have been published in an attempt to spread the notion of parent education beyond the limited contacts of two part-time workers.

How the book is organised

This book attempts to synthesise and analyse the experience of the Bureau's wide-ranging study of parenting. The material is presented in three parts. Part I examines what it is like to be a parent in the 1980s, at a time when family structures and roles are changing quite rapidly. Part II draws on the project's experience of parent education schemes throughout the country to present an analysis of what is currently available to parents and prospective parents, and looks at some of the key issues at each stage of the life cycle. Part III summarises the evidence presented throughout the book to suggest a coherent approach to parent education and support. We make a number of specific recommendations and look at the implications of these for policy-makers and practitioners alike.

We conclude this preface with four points which have a bearing on the parameters within which the material is presented. First the book does not on the whole single out those with special needs or from different ethnic backgrounds, for all parents whatever their age, class or creed, need access to resources and to information, contact and communication with other parents, and the confidence that they can do the best for their children. Britain is a multicultural society, and cultural diversities, which are expressed through different child-rearing patterns and attitudes to family life need to be taken into account in any support for parents. In addition there are some families who may have special needs – for example, single parent families, 'reconstituted' families (through remarriage or adoption) families who have a handicapped child and families in which both parents are unemployed. There are many different types of family in Britain today and in recognising this diversity we have tried to avoid labels and the stigma that so often attaches to them. Just as there are many single parents or handicapped families who cope well, so there are 'normal' families who find bringing up children particularly fraught with difficulties. Schemes and services for specific groups of parents have not therefore been considered in detail although reference is made to such schemes.

Second, when the word 'mothers' is used it is because most schemes attract mainly mothers, but not only is the closer involvement of fathers essential for their own and their children's sake, but so-called 'mothering' can equally well be done by fathers, or indeed another full-time career. In addition to biological parents, a growing number of adults are caring for other people's children, whether as stepparents, foster parents, members of the child's extended family, childminders or other professional child care staff. The skills of parenting and the support services are thus relevant to a wider group than just those who are looking after their own children. As Schaffer says in his study of mothering 'The ability to rear a child, to love and to cherish and care for him, is basically a matter of personality' rather than a blood bond (Schaffer, 1977).

Third, although the book's main focus is parent education in Britain, the project's work has involved contact with colleagues from all over Europe, North America, Australia, New Zealand and Japan. References to similar approaches and problems overseas have thus been included where relevant, although constraints of space of necessity make these very brief.

Finally a word on terminology, for the schemes and approaches in this book have variously been described as preparation for parenthood, family life education, parentcraft, parent training, mothercraft, parent education, education for parenthood, education for family life and parents as educators. It is a broad canvas, but in that the book is principally concerned with parents, both those of today and of tomorrow, the term '*parent education*' has been used to encompass all these approaches. We define parent education as 'a range of educational and supportive measures which help parents and prospective parents to understand themselves and their children and enhance the relationship between them'. A more detailed discussion of the aims and objectives of such a programme is presented in the final chapter.

Part I

WHY PARENT EDUCATION?

1
Parenting in the 1980s

WANTED: Responsible person M/F to undertake twenty-year project. Candidates should be totally committed, willing to work up to twenty-four hours daily, including weekends (occasional holidays possible after five years service). Knowledge of health care, nutrition, psychology, child development, the education system essential. Necessary qualities: energy, tolerance, patience, a sense of humour. No training or experience needed. No salary but very rewarding job for the right person.

Good Housekeeping (1981)

Introduction

The notion that being a parent in the second half of the twentieth century is demanding and at times a difficult and lonely experience, has been the focus of increasing attention in the last decade. Whilst many parents have brought up their children over the centuries in conditions of considerable hardship, they have not always done so in the isolation of today's nuclear family, nor against a backcloth of rapid technological, social and economic change such as we are experiencing in the 1980s. Young people are having to make choices about how to live their lives which did not face their parents, and there are many who feel that in this complex and ever-changing world the traditional ways of transmitting parenting skills from one generation to another may no longer be adequate. As a comprehensive review of research on parenting concluded 'many ordinary families are in trouble . . . not so much because of the older problems of poverty, poor housing and sanitation, but because they have inherited conceptions of family life that are inadequate to cope with the requirements of modern living' (Rapoport *et al.*, 1977).

There are other factors, too, that are putting increasing demands on parents. The first of these is our ever-developing knowledge and understanding of children's physical, intellectual, social and emotional development, and of the importance of growing up in a secure yet stimulating environment, especially during the early years of childhood. Research brings us a steady stream of new insights into the development, behaviour, feelings and capabilities of infants and young children, causing us constantly to review our perceptions and our knowledge of the needs of children and the ways in which these might best be met. At the same time, there are still considerable gaps in our knowledge and many ways of interpreting what we do know.

Secondly, there is the growing awareness of the crucial role that parents play in their children's development and, as a result, the high expectations that society places on parents to bring up their children adequately. The Newsons summarise well the tensions and demands that this brings when they point out how comparatively simple it was for a parent to satisfy society's demands when the emphasis was upon hygiene and affectionate firmness, and when the parental ethic included the dictum that 'mother knows best'. 'It is much more difficult when parents are asked to recognise the child's emotional and egotistical needs as valid while still giving him a moral framework of principles – and moreover to present the whole in a democratic context which acknowledges that mother might *not* know best' and they quote Johnson and Medinnus on the modern mother 'Her feelings of inadequacy are matched only by her undying efforts' (Newson and Newson, 1976).

Few parents can be unaware of the enormity of the responsibility placed upon their shoulders, but at a time when the media are devoting ever more column-inches and air- and viewing-time to conveying to parents images of life in the perfect family, many parents find themselves in the isolation of their homes, beleaguered with anxiety and guilt and unsure of which way to turn as they are deluged with conflicting advice. The Rapoports, writing in the mid-1970s, found a number of central concepts prevalent in the child-care literature, many of them reflecting the lasting influences of psycho-analysts such as Bowlby (1953) and Winnicott (1964). Amongst these were the notions that children are society's most valuable assets and their needs must therefore be paramount; that the experiences of the early years are crucial and that mothering is crucial to this experience, with fathers playing a secondary role as protector and provider; that being a good parent comes naturally, and so on.

The growth of interest in parenting over the last decade and a number of research studies have certainly begun to question some of these assumptions. Schaffer's study of mothering, for example, dispels the myth of good parenting as an inherent quality:

> We can be certain that mothering is not an 'instinct' in the sense of an inherently determined behaviour pattern that will manifest itself blindly and automatically irrespective of circumstances. It is rather, a set of abilities and feelings which, though based on the mother's inherent propensity to interact with others, will manifest itself only under particular social conditions. (Schaffer, 1977)

There is evidence too that some recent child care books and comments in the press and on television and radio, have begun to acknowledge the existence of different styles of parenting and the need to provide support rather than dictates based on a powerful and implicit value position.

Never the less, attitudes are slow to change and mothers, in particular, are often made to feel entirely responsible for the optimum development of their children, and yet may have little access to facilities that would help them in their task. One of the major problems is the sense of isolation experienced by many mothers, particularly those with young children. A recent study points out that modern motherhood has become separated from every other aspect of life, and that not only are children excluded from places of work, but also from many places of leisure as well – the pub and the sports club for example (Dally, 1982). The separation that keeps mothers in their homes, also separates fathers from their children, for men tend to spend their longest hours at work during the years when their children are young (Moss and Fonda, 1980).

A third issue as we look at the pressures being brought to bear on parents is the relationship between parents and the considerable number of specialists and experts in the field of child care and development and family support. A recurring theme in talking to groups of parents and reading research reports and accounts of group discussions is that the attitudes of many professionals are tending to undermine parent's self-confidence and their belief in their own parenting abilities. In the account of the conference that led to the establishment of this project, we reported the need for professionals to work with parents on their (parents') terms in their homes or groups rather than in offices and consulting rooms (Pugh, 1980) and this need was reflected too in the Court report:

> The growth in the number and variety of professions connected with child rearing, however necessary in our kind of society, has in some measure undermined the self-confidence of parents. . . . Professionals tend to gather a mystique to themselves which can be predatory on the proper role of the layman . . . There is a case to be made at this stage in the development of our society for stating the true relationship that should exist on behalf of children between their parents and other caring adults who affect the child and the family. Besides doctors and nurses, this applies to teachers, especially as nursery education develops, and to social workers. We feel especially keenly that services for the very young child must not be allowed to become over-professionalised: instead they should seek to work through the family, encouraging its strengths and helping in its shortcomings. There is overwhelming evidence that measures that do not involve parents achieve only short term gains. (Committee on Child Health Services, 1976)

Fourth, a difficulty for many parents as they struggle to cope with what Wallerstein and Kelly (1980) have described as 'diminished parenting capability' is how they can attempt to reconcile their own needs as adults with those of their children, especially if their life has been disrupted through separation, divorce, bereavement, illness or unemployment. As the debate continues to pit the needs of children against the rights of parents, for many parents the fear of not being seen as 'good enough' and the anxiety that their children might be taken into care, may prevent them from seeking help until a crisis overtakes them.

Finally, there is a pressure for prospective parents of a rather different sort, and this is the dilemma of whether and when to have children. The wide availability of contraception has presented women in particular with a difficult choice. Those who have enjoyed several years of a job and financial independence are often finding it hard to decide what is the most appropriate moment to give up work and start a family, and reliable contraception makes the possibility of a mistake (and the decision being taken involuntarily) less likely.

Increasing numbers of couples are deciding, for this and other reasons, not to become parents at all. Non-parenthood, or voluntary childlessness is still subject to much negative social pressure however, and has led some of those who believe in the right to choose not to have children, to form the British Organisation for Non-parents (BON). BON argues that:

> not everyone is cut out to do the job [parenting] happily. Responsible parenthood, like any profession, demands special attention, special skills and special inclinations and can be limiting in certain ways. Being a parent does not guarantee a full and rewarding life; fulfilment can be gained in many other fields than in reproduction.

For others, childlessness is a painful reminder of 'failure' and of the inability to conceive or bear a much-wanted child. Whereas alternative routes to parenthood used to be limited to adoption or fostering, modern medicine and technology has now produced a bewildering choice of possibilities: artifical insemination, 'in vitro' fertilisation and embryo transfer, surrogate motherhood, womb-leasing and fertility drugs. These recent developments and their potential implications have become sources of concern and investigation for scientific, legal, social, moral and ethical reasons. Whilst they have brought hope and happiness to some, there are still many for whom parenthood remains an unfulfilled dream.

The tasks and skills of parenting

Many of the tasks traditionally inherent in family life, such as teaching specific skills, preparing for a trade, and passing on cultural and social norms, are now shared with other groups, notably schools and many of the influences shared with other groups, notably the peer group. Despite this, the family still provides the main basis for bringing up succeeding generations of children, and it still falls to parents to help children develop into complete adults and take their place in the wider world outside the home. In outlining some of the conditions which offer parents and children emotional security, learning opportunities and a system of values which provides for a creative relationship with society at large, Joan Cooper (DHSS, 1974a) suggests that a family home may be thought of as functioning effectively when it:

offers adequate shelter, space, food, income and the basic amenities which enable the adults to perform their marital, child-rearing and citizenship roles without incurring so much stress that anxiety inhibits a confident and positive performance;

secures the physical care, safety and healthy development of children either through its own resources or through the competent use of specialised help and services;

acknowledges its task of socialising children, encouraging their personal development and abilities, guiding their behaviour and interests and informing their attitudes and values;

offers the experience of warm, loving, intimate and consistently dependable relationships;

assures the mother of support and understanding, particularly during the early child-rearing period, and provides the child with a male/father/husband model which continues to remain important through adolescence;

offers children (2–6 years) an experience of group life, so extending their social relationships, their awareness of others and intellectual development;

responds to children's curiosity with affection and reasoned explanations, and respects children through all developmental stages as persons in their own right, so securing affection and respect for others within the family circle and wider social network;

co-operates with school, values educational and learning opportunities and encourages exploration and a widening of experience;

supports adolescents physically and emotionally while they are achieving relative independence of the family, personal identity, sexual maturity, a work-role, relationships within society and the testing out of values and ideologies;

provides a fall-back supportive system for the young marrieds during their child-bearing period. (DHSS, 1974a)

What do parents require if they are to perform their parenting tasks as well as possible? The work with parents (presented in

Chapters 6 and 7) suggests there are four main areas in which support and guidance may be needed.

The first is what Rutter (DHSS, 1974a) has called 'permitting circumstances' or necessary life opportunities and facilities. The interaction that takes place between economic, social and educational deprivation is a complex one, but many parents find it extremely difficult to bring up their children when basic personal and family needs are not taken care of first. As the British Association of Social Workers said in its submission to the 1973 DHSS consultations:

When a family is suffering multiple deprivation . . . then intervention aimed at only one of the factors at work is unlikely to be successful. It cannot offset the downward spiral. There is a much better chance of helping families to mend defective emotional relationships and to escape from social isolation if at the same time they can be cushioned against money problems. (DHSS, 1974b)

Margaret Harrison points out from her experience of 'Home-Start' (see p. 161) that some parents may themselves need parenting before they can respond to the needs of their own children (Harrison, 1982). Parents who as children were brought up in care, or who experienced inadequate parenting, may have unrealistic expectations of an idyllic family life and it is 'an insensitive farce' to try to promote better verbal or physical contact with a child or the need for positive reinforcement before first working with some of the parents' personal and social problems.

Second, parents require information and knowledge about sources of help within the community; about welfare rights and benefits; about common childhood ailments and how to cope with accidents; and perhaps most important of all, about human health and development and particularly what to expect at the different stages of child development and what part parents might play. Although professionals working with families and the many child-care books on the shelves testify to the extent of current knowledge on the different stages of development, the DHSS consultations on preparation for parenthood in 1973, suggested that there was still a surprising amount of ignorance among parents of all social classes about what can be expected of children of different ages and what their real needs are (DHSS, 1974b). In a survey undertaken by the authors in association with *Mother* magazine, in answer to the question 'with which of the following would you most like help now that you are parents?' the majority of both mothers and fathers put 'stages of development' at the top of their list, with behavioural problems coming second. Unrealistic expectations of behaviour at each age and stage is frequently a major source of frustration, anger and disappointment and is often a key factor in cases of child abuse (Franklin, 1977; Gorell-Barnes, 1979).

A better understanding of children's development must include awareness of social and emotional factors, as well as physical and intellectual. In *The Needs of Children*, commissioned as a response to the DHSS discussions, Mia Pringle suggests that children have four basic emotional needs which have to be met if they are to grow from helpless infancy to mature adulthood: the need for love and security; for new experiences; for praise and recognition; and for responsibility. She argues that we do now know enough about children's all-round development to take action:

> If even half of what we know were accepted with feeling and applied with understanding by all who have the care of children, then the revolution brought about in children's physical health in the past forty years might well be matched by a similar change in their psychological well-being. (Pringle, 1975)

Third, parents need certain skills, many of them acquired over a life-time. These will include a core of social skills which all adults need if they are to function adequately, for example:

   the ability to love and undertake relationships, to care, to support and nurture other people, and to be sensitive to their needs;

   flexibility of mind and thinking, the ability to respond and to adapt to changing needs and demands;

   consistency of attitudes and behaviour, a reliable and dependable behaviour that provides a stable and secure environment where responses can be anticipated and rules are clear;

   the ability to communicate, through active listening, giving appropriate non-verbal and verbal messages, reflecting on feelings, and negotiating;

the ability to make decisions and to accept responsibility for them;

the ability to cope with stress and deal with conflict;

the ability to apply the knowledge and information, for a theory on how to cope with temper tantrums is no use unless it can be put into action.

They will also include practical skills such as those required to provide a home, manage the family's finances, produce a balanced diet and combine work with family life.

Fourth, parents need understanding of themselves as parents and as people, and of their values and of how these affect the way in which children are brought up. The emphasis on understanding and responding to children's needs has sometimes obscured the fact that parents have their own needs for personal development and fulfilment. These needs have to be understood too, and the almost inevitable conflicts of interest within a family group faced up to and resolved.

The schemes described in Part II respond in their different ways to these four areas of need – for 'permitting circumstances', for information and knowledge, for skills and for understanding.

Factors affecting the way parents bring up their children

These tasks and skills have to be examined in the light of the many constraints and influences within families, for the ways in which parents bring up their children cannot be seen in a vacuum. What are these factors? Some are personal and family characteristics, whilst others reflect social and environmental constraints.

Assumptions about the effect of childhood experiences on one's own ability to parent were central to the thinking behind the DHSS consultations in 1973, when Sir Keith Joseph suggested that disadvantage was transmitted from one generation of a family to the next, and argued that more preparation for parenthood might help to break this cycle of deprivation (DHSS, 1974a and 1974b). The consultations themselves and Rutter's subsequent review of the research (Rutter and Madge, 1976) showed that whilst there are likely to be *indirect* effects on parenting behaviour through influences on personality development, and the acquisition of social values and attitudes, there was little systematic information on connections between personal childhood experiences and methods of bringing up one's own children. Indeed, such links as could be found tended to illustrate the point that many parents deliberately wanted to avoid doing to their children what they had gone through when young themselves. The factor most consistently associated with happiness, stability and satisfaction in marriage was the quality of their own parents' marriage. There is however, a much stronger inter-generational link with abnormal parenting. A high proportion of parents who abuse their children have experienced serious neglect and abuse in their own childhood, and mothers who have been separated from their own parents during childhood have been found to have marital problems and difficulties in child rearing (Frommer, 1973). Rutter (1972) also makes the point that a child's ability to form good inter-personal relationships in adulthood may be based upon bonds that he forms in the first three years of his life.

The style of parenting will also vary according to whether mother or father is the chief care-giver. Although traditionally parenting has tended to be synonymous with mothering, with the father's role seen principally as supportive and fairly distant, men are now spending more time with their children. One of the chief influences has undoubtedly been the shifting balance between the worlds of home and work as women increasingly seek to combine a job outside the home with bringing up a family, and rising unemployment keeps many men at home during the day. There is no reason why women should continue to bear the principal responsibility for their children's upbringing. Even Spock, in the latest edition of *Baby and Child Care* (1979), introduces a new section on 'The father as parent' in which he states:

> There is no reason why fathers shouldn't be able to do these jobs [home and child care] as well as mothers, and contribute equally to the children's security and development ... It will be a great day when fathers consider the care of their children to be as important to them as their jobs and careers.

Although it has become fashionable to talk about role reversal and shared parenting, the increasing number of research studies into fatherhood show that although fathers' involvement with their children has increased, (Beail, 1982; McKee, 1982) the majority of fathers do still principally see themselves in terms of their work first and their families second, while even women who work full-time see their primary responsibility as being to their families. Whilst most men do regard marriage and babies as an inextricable part of their adult career patterns (McKee and O'Brien, 1982) the development of gender identity and expectations regarding traditional roles are still deeply ingrained.

The quality of the relationship between the parents and their supportiveness to each other as parents are particularly important. The reason for having children will also affect the way in which these children are brought up, particularly when it is related to this relationship. A child can be seen as a symbol of unity or disunity, conceived to demonstrate love, to provide a common interest, to 'complete' a marriage or to end a disagreement, to 'save' a marriage, to tie a husband down or keep a wife at home, or to increase distance in the partnership. Reasons given by parents for having children often focus on what they hope the baby will give them, rather than what they will provide for the child (Hoffman and Hoffman, 1973; La Rossa, 1977).

Parents will need to balance their own needs for personal fulfilment as adults with those of their children, a potential conflict which has not always been recognised and certainly not resolved amidst the child-centred values of contemporary society.

In recent years we have also begun to accept the notion that children influence and shape parent's behaviour right from the day of birth, and that even small babies have an inborn ability to interact with others. Parents are often surprised to find how different each child in the family is and how differently they feel towards them, and studies have shown that parents' responses differ according to whether the child is a boy or a girl, and where he or she comes in the family (Rutter and Madge, 1976; Beail and McGuire, 1982).

The parents' social class is another determinant, as is so well illustrated by the Newsons' longitudinal study of child-rearing in Nottingham. The involvement of fathers, for example, or attitudes towards breast- and bottle-feeding showed considerable differences between the social classes. Perhaps the most marked contrast was in different styles of disciplining seven-year-olds (Newson and Newson, 1976) where the higher social groups used highly verbal democratically-based means of control, while the unskilled group used highly authoritarian and mainly non-verbal means of control, using words to threaten and 'bamboozle' the child rather than help him understand. These two styles, they argue, were adapted to their social position: privileged children are equipped to use the system, the disadvantaged children expect and get nothing. 'The child in the lowest social bracket has everything stacked against him, including his parents' principles of child upbringing.'

Different ethnic and cultural backgrounds will be an important influence on how children are brought up. There are now about three million immigrants and immigrant-descended people in Britain, and whilst some have been assimilated, others have remained culturally distinct, with their children being brought up in two sometimes conflicting cultures. In the Asian community, for example, arranged marriages are still a strong part of the cultural and religious tradition and can present emotional, economic and social difficulties for young girls born and educated in this country who do not want to marry young, and, in opposition to their parents, may want to pursue their education and a career.

Social and environmental factors are also crucial determinants of parenting styles. We have looked at the 'permitting circumstances' which are essential to good parenting and at the complex interaction between economic, social, educational and emotional deprivation. Whether one parent has a job; who is caring for the children if both parents are working, and the adequacy of that care; the housing conditions and financial position; whether family and friends are near enough for regular contact; the strength of community support; the extent of isolation – all these factors have a bearing on how parents manage. The Newsons' study of mothers of one-year-old children in Nottingham illustrated how basic differences in living conditions can affect the attitudes and methods of infant-care and child-rearing: 'Any woman who has an automatic washing machine will testify to the dramatic affect it has upon her ability to show equanimity when her toddler continues to wet nappy after nappy; the mother who has to wash everything by hand, in water she has heated on top of the kitchen stove, is likely to be far more emotionally involved in toilet-training' (Newson and Newson, 1963). While fewer mothers today have to heat water on the stove, many families without washing machines live on isolated housing estates with no access to launderette facilities. They are also likely to be living very close to neighbours and thin council house walls will affect both the general irritability of the mother and whether and for how long baby is left to cry.

It is evident that the number of variables involved within the relationship of even one parent and child militate against an exact definition of a 'good parent' and it is neither possible – nor desirable – to produce a blueprint. We could all make a list of qualities and our lists would all be different. We might include sensitivity, empathy, stamina, patience, tolerance, persistence, self-control and a sense of humour, and the various social skills already mentioned. One study which attempted to identify what qualities were present in optimally-functioning families concluded that there was no right way or one way of parenting. Rather, there was an inter-relationship of a number of variables: leadership was provided by a clear parental coalition, power was not exercised in an authoritarian way, children had opinions that were considered and negotiation was common. Communication was clear, differences were tolerated, there were high levels of personal autonomy and an acceptance of personal responsibility for each individual's own feelings, thoughts and actions. In their conclusion the authors state 'that the skills in relating and communication which the optimal family demonstrated are teachable and learnable' (Lewis and others, 1976).

Changing family patterns

Bringing up children cannot be seen in isolation from the wider patterns of family life and of changes in society as they affect families. This chapter concludes therefore with a brief description of this broader backcloth. Although the family life-cycle is still frequently portrayed as an early marriage, early child-bearing, and a small number of children with a compact period of parenthood into the mid-adult years and then an extended period without children until the death of one or both spouses, this is no longer an appropriate generalisation. Only 5 per cent of households at any one time consist of a married man who is working, with a wife not in paid work and with two dependent children, and although the majority of children are still living in households with both their parents, the structures and patterns of family life in Britain today are characterised by their diversity. The family is, as one commentator has put it, 'simply what you find behind the door' and variation, whether by chance or choice is now the norm.

Family structures are changing as divorce, cohabitation and remarriage are experienced by growing numbers of people; family patterns are changing as parents have fewer children, but four or even five generations may be alive at the same time; and roles within families are changing in response to changing employment patterns and greater equality for women.

Marriage

Current trends indicate that the vast majority of women (92 per cent) and men (86 per cent) will marry (Rimmer, 1981), and indeed marriage appears to be retaining its popularity, with the majority of those whose marriage breaks down marrying again within five years. Marriage is still seen as an important goal in life. In the Bureau's National Child Development Study, of some 15 000 young people, at the age of 16, only 3 per cent said they did not want to get married, and only 4 per cent did not want children (Fogelman, 1976).

While marriage remains popular it has also been affected by two significant trends – cohabitation and divorce. Efficient contraception, economic independence and individual rights have altered public attitudes and both are now more acceptable. The 1979 General Household Survey suggested that 20 per cent of women in the 20–29 year age group are currently cohabiting. For some this is a prelude to marriage and planned parenthood, but it is more likely to precede a second or later marriage where one of the partners involved is often unable to marry.

Divorce

The rapid rise in the divorce rate is one of the most marked changes in family life. Over the last twenty years in this country there has been a 600 per cent increase. One in three marriages is now likely to end in divorce, and over 60 per cent of all divorces involve children under sixteen. A recent estimate suggested that about one fifth of babies born in 1982 are likely to experience a separation of the parents before they reach school-leaving age (Richards, 1982).

Divorce dissolves the legal bonds of marriage but not of parent-hood, for parental obligations remain. For many parents and children the adversarial nature of the divorce courts only brings increasing conflict over custody, support and access to the children. A conflict-ridden divorce also affects the attitudes with which individuals enter a second marriage, and family courts and conciliation services, designed to reduce such conflict and help parents recognise their continuing parental responsibilities are widely welcomed. As second marriages are currently twice as likely to end in divorce as first marriages, a minority of children may be involved in two or more divorces and a growing number of stepparents.

The notion of a 'good marriage' where the husband was provider and the wife a housewife and mother is changing. Many couples now enter marriage with high expectations of emotional and personal fulfilment with complete sharing, affection and understanding – a partnership based on equality. Many young couples marry to experience independence and freedom from their own parents. They expect an idealised perfection that is unrealistic and are unable to deal with the conflicts and complexity of roles within marriage. Given the almost universal experience of marriage, it is not surprising that many fail to reach such high expectations and would rather divorce than tolerate a painful or disappointing marriage. Although studies have failed to isolate any one, or several, dominant variables which distinguish those marriages which end in divorce from those that continue, they have indicated a number of high-risk factors. Teenage marriages are particularly at risk of breakdown with a bride in her teens twice as likely to become divorced than in marriages where the bride is 20–24 years old, and four times as likely as those in which the bride is 25–29 years old (Haskey, 1983).

One-parent families

One of the most obvious consequences of the increase in marital breakdown is the rising proportion of one-parent families. In 1981 the National Council for One Parent Families estimated that there were 975 000 one-parent families with the care of 1.5 million children. It is extremely difficult to obtain reliable estimates of the numbers of families and children involved, and any current figure underestimates the impact of divorce on family life. The number of children now estimated to be in step-families illustrates that a far higher proportion of children actually spend a part of their childhood in a single parent family than a single snapshot count can indicate (Ferri, 1976). Within these households there are different structures and variations, (see Figure 1.1) all of which may have implications for the present and future well-being of the parent and children involved. There are slightly more families of West Indian origin and very few families of Asian origin headed by a lone parent (Hansard, 1981). Geographically there are important variations with a particularly heavy concentration of lone-parent families in certain inner-city areas, for example, in Inner Newcastle, 11 per cent of households are lone-parent households whilst in Inner London the figure is nearly 33 per cent. This has obvious implications for provision of services at a local level.

Remarriage and step-families

For many children the lone-parent family is one of several stages in the family life-cycle. Today one in three new marriages involves a remarriage for one or both spouses. On the basis of current trends it has been estimated that 80 per cent of those divorcing under the age of thirty will remarry within five years, and that one person in five will have been married at least twice by the year 2000. Divorced women with children under ten years old, are more likely to remarry than those whose children are older or who have no children. The increasing number of marriages and remarriages involving divorced people, particularly divorced women who are more likely to have custody of any children of the marriage, has led to an increase in the number of families in which one of the parents will not be the child's natural parent. As with lone-parent households, there are different types of step-parent households. In many cases only one partner brings children to the new household; a single mother marries; a bereaved parent remarries; a divorced custodial parent remarries; or two divorced parents marry and the newly-formed unit combines his and her children, although usually his children remain with his former spouse. All these step-families may also produce natural children of the new marriage.

While society continues to idealise the two-parent family and regard it as the norm, there is a danger that remarriage and step-families may be seen as part of the 'solution' to lone-parent

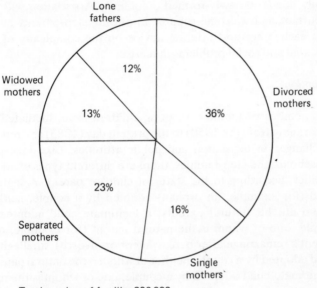

Lone fathers

12%

Widowed mothers

13%

Divorced mothers

36%

23%

16%

Separated mothers

Single mothers

Total number of families 890 000

FIGURE 1.1 *Different types of lone-parent families in Great Britain, 1979*

SOURCE House of Commons, *Hansard*, 23 July 1981, col. 225

households. Not only is there a lack of research evidence to support this view but it has been argued that many children do better remaining in a single-parent family than in having to make further adjustments to a third form of family life – the new step-family (Richards and Dyson, 1982). One of the consequences of presenting the step-family as a new 'normal' family is that step-parents receive virtually no form of support, advice, or recognition of the differences between the natural family and a 'blended' family (Maddox, 1980). Since marital breakdown is a primary reason why many children acquire step-parents, they are likely to have experienced already a series of changes in their family situation prior to the new family formation (Ferri, 1984). The current relatively high rate of breakdown amongst step-families indicates that they are not immune to stress and conflict, and that particular support and advice is required if substantial numbers of children are to be prevented from experiencing a frequently changing and disruptive family life. The newly-formed Stepfamily Association will be an important and welcome support in putting step-parents in touch with each other and offering advice on the complexity of legal, custodial and social problems that arise.

Adoption

The number of families adopting children have fluctuated quite remarkably from the 1950s to the present day (1983) as a reflection of changes in legislation and public attitudes. Like lone-parent households and step-families, there are different types of adoptive families, according to the status of child or parent. A legitimate child (for example, an orphan) adopted by a couple, neither of whom are his natural parents; a legitimate child adopted by a couple, one of whom is the natural parent (for example, on the parent's remarriage after bereavement or divorce); an illegitimate child adopted by a couple, neither of whom is the natural parent; an illegitimate child adopted by a couple, one of whom is the natural parent (for example, when an unmarried mother marries a man who is not the father of the child). The rise in illegitimate births in the 1950s together with an emphasis on placing children in family homes rather than in institutions saw a peak of 25 000 adoptions in 1968. Since then the number has reduced by more than half as a result of more efficient contraception, easier access to abortion and more young people keeping their babies. The number of step-parent adoptions has also halved since the Children's Act of 1975. In 1980 a total of 10 609 children were adopted, almost half of them under five years, and three quarters under ten years of age.

Family size

Families are also changing in size and shape, and in particular they are now smaller than they were. There are fewer childless marriages but also fewer large families. The one- or two-child family has become quite common, with less than 20 per cent of married couples having three or more children. The actual numbers of births are declining and recent figures show that fewer babies are born in each year than is necessary for population replacement. As a result, fewer youngsters grow up as part of a large family or have much experience of babies and young children before starting their own family. However, since life expectancy is greater, many more families now span four generations as grandparents live on to become great-grandparents. This has particular consequences in view of the changing family patterns we have traced, for it increases the possible permutations when divorce and remarriage occur within one or more of the age groups. Will step-children be as willing to look after newly-acquired elderly relatives, or step-grandparents to help out with the instant grandchildren?

Where are the children?

We began by noting the changes and the increasing diversity of family structures and patterns, but when we look at Table 1.1 and see where children are actually being brought up, we see that the broad elements of family life continue despite the changes around them.

TABLE 1.1 *Children by age and where currently living, Great Britain, 1979*

Children aged 0–15 of women aged 18–49*

	Age of children			
	0–4	5–9	10–15	Total
Current whereabouts of children	%	%	%	%
In the household:				
Living with both natural parents				
parents married	88	84	80	83
parents cohabiting	2	0	0	1
with natural mother and stepfather				
mother remarried	2	4	7	4
mother cohabiting	1	2	1	1
with lone mother	7	9	9	9
Outside the household:				
living with father				
(marital status not known)	0	1	1	1
Adopted or fostered, by relatives or				
non-relatives	0	1	1	1
At special school or home	0	0	1	0
Base = 100%; N =	1887	2174	2781	6842

* Includes 5 married women aged 16 or 17.

SOURCE Adapted from *General Household Survey 1979*, HMSO, 1981, Table 8.23.

The family is still very much alive in Britain, for most young people get married (only 8 per cent of women and 14 per cent of men at present, do not); most marriages do survive (two out of three still end naturally); most married couples will have children, and most children will be brought up by two parents, with some 84 per cent of children under fifteen living with their natural parents. However a snapshot picture cannot reflect the diversity of families nor the number of stages in the family life-cycle. Whilst the majority of parents, children and families do still follow a fairly traditional pattern, the minority who do not is growing and this diversity may not be evident from the cross-sectional pictures which do not reveal the constant ebb and flow as children move between families.

Changes in society as they affect family life

The diversity of contemporary life not only creates opportunities for challenge and change but also increases anxiety, insecurity and instability in family life. Social acceptance influences patterns of behaviour such as cohabitation and pre-marital sex. Changes in legislation endorse such social changes and divorce, abortion, illegitimacy, equal rights and opportunities become an accepted part of modern life. Values and attitudes are influenced by changes in technology, from contraception to computers. Being older or being a parent no longer necessarily means being wiser, and it can in fact, mean knowing the 'wrong' outdated information. Economic and employment trends can alter the expectations and patterns of family life. It may become easier for wives and daughters to obtain employment than it is for husbands and sons. Social welfare provision may encourage disillusioned unemployed school-leavers to see parenthood as a career with more status and with the added benefit of council accommodation for themselves and financial independence from parents.

Three issues are particularly relevant to a discussion on parent education and to the debate on the relationship between family life and the wider society and these are the changing role of women; patterns of work and unemployment; and the role of the welfare state.

The changing role of women

As women have fought for – and to some extent won – greater equality and independence, the dilemma of combining their dual roles of worker and mother has placed them in an often intolerable position. Widening educational, employment and social opportunities after the Second World War encouraged women to expect the same things from life as men. Yet as men returned to their jobs after the war and Bowlby published his influential report to the World Health Organisation (Bowlby, 1953) on maternal care and mental health, social pressures were already being exerted to encourage mothers to stay at home and subordinate their new-found role for the sake of the family. The debate is a complex one beyond the scope of this chapter, but the current political climate, the economic recession and high levels of unemployment make it as relevant today as it has ever been.

It is evident from a number of surveys that many more mothers would take up work if adequate child-care facilities were available (Bone, 1977; Hughes, 1980; Haystead, 1980). Many of these mothers work – or would work – because they want to do so. For women in a variety of occupations, employment offers an identity and independence, as well as enjoyment and companionship, for self-esteem and self-confidence may be as important as cash benefits. Other studies have reinforced the findings of Brown and Harris (1978) that employment can reduce a woman's vulnerability to depression, in bringing relief to both parent and child if adequate child-care arrangements can be made.

A considerable number of mothers work because they have to. A recent paper from the Central Policy Review Staff (1980) for example, estimated that if married women did not go out to work, the number of families living in poverty would increase fourfold. Women's employment was found usually to compensate for low pay rather than for male unemployment. Some of these working mothers would prefer not to work, if they could afford not to, and this has led to suggestions that mothers should be paid a 'salary' to stay at home looking after their children (Pringle, 1980b). Others, particularly those with young children, would like to be able to work part-time. The important points appear to be that few mothers feel that they have a real choice – if they want to work who is to look after the children, and if they do not, how are the bills to be paid?

Whichever choice they do make they are made to feel guilty.

A recent discussion paper suggests there is no inherent conflict between the rights of women and the rights of children. A family policy could offer support to families and choice for parents if the government ceased to base its policies on the male breadwinner and dependent female model of the family (Coussins and Coote, 1981), but it is not just young children who are dependent. Greater life expectancy means that more and more people are now living beyond their three-score years and ten, and women are increasingly finding themselves looking after frail elderly relatives. There is too a move towards community – often home – care for the physically and mentally handicapped. Whilst social policy emphasises the need for care within the family it will be impossible for women both to work to keep their families out of poverty and to remain at home to look after dependent relatives, be they young, old or disabled.

Patterns of work and unemployment

The relationship between work – or lack of work – and family life shows itself in a number of ways but for many families the two are not easily compatible. A woman may be unable to work because of the demands of home and children for example; a father may be unable to see much of his children or to help his wife because of long working hours or periods away; parents may rarely find time together as a family, while they work on shifts to ensure an adequate standard of living and share the care of their children. Some families are regularly moving through a succession of houses, schools and communities as a result of the father's promotion; whilst others move to more depressing, isolated and dilapidated accommodation as the price of unemployment or lone-parenthood. The structure of the work environment, working hours, conditions of employment, career patterns, mobility and travel are rarely planned with the family's needs in mind.

Few employees are seen also as parents. Work and the family are seen as separate areas by different government departments, and while for example, maternity leave may be introduced as part of employment legislation, there is no complementary provision of child-care services. Although women may improve their rights to better maternity leave, sick child leave or crèche facilities, this is seldom extended to include fathers. Current employment and wage policies and practices often appear to be anti-family. Many fathers undertake most overtime and shift work when their children are young because of the increased costs of parenthood. For low-paid workers, shift work or overtime is essential to lift themselves above the poverty line. The shape of the traditional working week with its rigid hours is not conducive to family life, for hours of work usually conflict with school opening and closing times and many working parents rely on a complicated routine of school, child-minder, friends and neighbours, or on children with a key round their neck returning to empty houses.

Conflicting demands of work and the family affect not only the parents of young children. Although adolescents need less physical care and supervision than very young children, 'being there' is important to maintain some form of equilibrium and guiding influence during the turmoil of adolescence, exams or the debilitating effects of unemployment and rejection. Problems also arise when children are ill, for whilst there is now paid post-natal maternity leave for up to six months there is still no general parental leave to care for sick children or to attend school medicals and other functions, as there is in some other countries. In Sweden for example, either parent may take up to six months paid post-natal leave and there are additional provisions to care for sick children. Norway also allows either parent to take paid post-natal leave of twelve weeks. The Federal Republic of Germany allows up to five days leave a year when a child is sick and in France some occupations allow up to two years unpaid leave to care for a young child. The case could certainly be argued for attempting to devise alternative patterns of employment to take account of the different needs of families at different stages of family life – for example through working at home, flexi-time, job-sharing, more part-time posts, and better retraining opportunities. A guaranteed minimum income or a home responsibility payment would allow parents to choose to stay at home if they so wished, while better child-care facilities could ease the strain for those who chose to work.

With unemployment at the level that it is at present (1983), the problems for many families are of a different order. The loss of income and of self-respect concomitant with unemployment clearly has a particularly debilitating effect on families, the more so because workers who are already in low-paid and unskilled manual jobs are particularly at risk of losing their jobs and remaining unemployed for long periods (Rimmer and Popay, 1982). Figures in 1980 showed that one in three unemployed men have dependent children, but that the number of children affected by unemployment is greater than the number of families, for fathers with three or more children tend to experience higher unemployment rates than men with smaller families. There is a growing body of research to suggest that unemployment is associated with an increase in ill-health, emotional disturbance and family breakdown. Behavioural disorders, poor educational attainment, increasing admission to hospital and an increase in family violence, particularly child abuse, have all been found to be associated with unemployment (Madge, 1983). A number of local authorities have also found that an increasing number of children coming into care have no breadwinner in the family.

The family and the welfare state

One of the assumptions behind the establishment of the welfare state was that parents required certain economic and social conditions in which to raise their families. In particular, suitable housing; access to medical facilities and appropriate day care; an adequate income; and the opportunity for continuing education and training. Yet despite considerable expenditure (some 45 per cent of Gross Domestic Product) and an overall improvement for most families in the standard of living, there are still considerable inequalities between families. The Black Report (DHSS, 1980b) for example, showed marked differences in the mortality rate and in the use of health services and preventive services between families in different social classes and in different parts of the country. Many families are also still living in inadequate housing, with cramped and over-crowded conditions and lack of play facilities. The Bureau's National Child Development Study found that by the age of 16 one in five children had lived in homes which lacked the basic amenities of a bathroom, hot water supply and indoor lavatory (Essen and Fogelman, 1979) and this study was amongst the first to point to the link between inadequate housing and such problems as poor school performance, school truancy and poor health. As a report of the disadvantaged teenagers in this study concluded:

> The combination of poor housing, low income, uncertain health, insecure employment, coupled often no doubt with limited know-

ledge of parenting skills, offers a prescription for low achieving, poorly behaved, disenchanted or alienated young people. It represents a 'prescription for anti-welfare' for children. (Wedge and Essen, 1982).

Social services departments represent State provision for some of the most vulnerable families, and a recent report on the role and tasks of social workers distinguished three approaches to the relationship between the State and those of its citizens whose social and personal needs cannot be met from their own resources: (i) the *safety net* approach, which assumes that individuals, families and local communities should be the primary source of social care, with minimum state provision; (ii) the *welfare state* approach, which holds that the State has an obligation to provide comprehensive services to respond to the problems of poverty, old age and disability whatever their cause; and (iii) the *community* approach which assumes that lay people have more potential and commitment to care for each other than is assumed by the welfare state approach (Barclay, 1982). Current reductions in public expenditure suggest that families are likely to be increasingly dependent on their own resources as they bring up their children.

The picture of family income also reveals that families have not on the whole fared well over the last decade. Figures released in mid-1983 revealed that one in five children are living in families with incomes around the poverty line and that seven million people in Britain – approximately one in eight – are now dependent on supplementary benefit, a benefit originally devised to protect families, and particularly single-parent families, against extreme poverty. There is also an anomalous position whereby some benefits are paid out by the DHSS and taxed by the Treasury.

The value of child support, formerly the combined value of the family allowance and the child tax allowance, now child benefit, has also fallen. Families have suffered both from a reduction in child benefit and from paying a higher proportion of tax, for whilst the real value of child benefit for a family with two children decreased from the equivalent of £9.00 in 1956 to £7.60 in 1982, the amount of income tax increased more for families than other households. Between 1960–1 and 1982–3 income tax paid on average earnings increased 74 per cent for a single person, but it was a staggering 696 per cent for a couple with four children.

Although it is unrealistic to expect the same wage to serve the diverse needs of a single man, a married man with children or a divorced man with two families, there is still no national minimum wage (Department of Employment, 1982). The relative earnings of the lowest-paid men were lower in 1982 than at any time during the 1970s. Only a thorough reform of the taxation system would redistribute income to those millions of families currently living in poverty. One suggestion that has gathered wide support is for the abolition of the married man's allowance, which would release £3000 m. for redistribution to familes with children. This could be achieved through an increase in the child benefit, a home responsibility allowance or a parental allowance.

2

Parent Education

Being a 'good parent' is not simply a matter of having the right knowledge, or even the right skills. So much also depends on the personal characteristics of the child (and other children) and parents involved; their social and economic condition; their abilities to cope with stress; their relationships with one another; their sensibility to the aspirations and needs of others. Thus, even if there were an agreed body of knowledge about parenting to be transmitted (and there is not) and one could work on the assumption that knowledge always changes behaviour (which one cannot), it would still be necessary to bear in mind how much the inter-personal relationships and integrity of the parents affect their ability to be successful. So many previous well-meaning programmes aimed at changing behaviour for the benefit of health have fallen short of their objectives that we urge that any programme of education for parenthood should be based on principles rather than prescriptions. (Committee on Child Health Service, 1976)

Historical perspectives

Advice to parents on how to bring up their children has been offered by those professing to have some superior knowledge and experience since time immemorial. All societies, however primitive, have their rules about family life; and philosophers such as Plato, Aristotle, Aquinas, Locke and Hobbes, made known their own views on the rights and responsibilities of parents and children. From Rousseau's 'back to nature' philosophy which idealised motherhood as 'the most enviable and delightful activity a woman could hope for' (1762) to the self-effacement of continual mothering implied by James and Joyce Robertson (1982), a barrage of advice has issued from the pens of philosophers, doctors, psychologists, psychoanalysts and child-care experts. Much of this advice has reflected not so much the needs of parents, as the social and cultural norms of society and the influence of successive groups of professionals.

The most enduring influences of the last two hundred years have been traced by the Newsons, from the religious and moral overtones of the eighteenth and nineteenth centuries when child-rearing was 'clearly linked with the expectation of death rather than the hope of a balanced and integrated life'; through the 1920s and 1930s, dominated by the morality of aseptic rationalism, in which the 'evangelical concern to eradicate the devil' is echoed by the advent of the hygienist movement, and the all-powerful Truby King; to the 1930s where the impact of psychoanalysis and nursery educators such as Susan Isaacs put the child and his needs firmly into the centre of the stage; and on to the flexibility and individualism of many of today's writers (Newson and Newson, 1974). As the author of a recent review of child-care manuals from 1850 to today points out 'while babies and mothers remain constants, advice on the former to the latter veers with the winds of social, philosophical and psychological change' and we should see the advice in the books we use today as a temporary crutch, not as eternal verity (Hardyment, 1983).

The theoretical exhortations in the literature were matched with a more practical approach during the late nineteenth and early twentieth centuries, when in an attempt to combat infant mortality and childhood ill-health the first health visitors were appointed and 'schools for mothers' were established, forerunners to a comprehensive system of maternity and child welfare. As an historian of the infant welfare movement writes

> Evidently the capacity to bring up a baby successfully through the first years of life was not an innate feminine characteristic, with which all women were endowed at birth . . . it was proved to be a skilled job requiring a technique which, like any other kind of technique has to be acquired. (McCleary, 1933)

During the second half of this century the contributors to the debate and to the provision of parent education have been many and various. It is interesting that these approaches, whether in schools, in the health service or in local communities, have tended to evolve separately and that we have not, in this country, adopted a more coherent policy. In 1960 Stern published the first – and only – international survey of parent education in which he concluded that 'in Great Britain parent education has not yet been the subject of serious study. Yet practical measures are not altogether absent; but they have remained half-hearted, sporadic and, on the whole, ineffectual' (Stern, 1960).

In the same survey Stern commented on the widespread interest in parent education in the countries that he visited, with similar problems being expressed but little formal organisation in attempts to set up parent education programmes. In the decade since his survey was published, the interest in parent education has increased considerably, but whilst many national and international bodies have joined the debate during this time, the co-ordination of programmes is still far from complete.

In 1964 twenty-five countries came together to form the International Federation for Parent Education (IFPE), a voluntary, non-profit-making organisation working for the advancement of education for parenthood and family living throughout the world. Based in Paris, the IFPE took its inspiration from the *Ecole des Parents* which had been active in France since 1929. Since its foundation it has organised a number of international conferences and information exchanges. Britain has never joined the IFPE, and indeed attempts to set up a British Association for Parent Education in 1973 failed because of lack of support. Our only contact with the international body is through individual representation from the Health Education Council and from the Calderdale Association for Parents (see Chapter 6). The worldwide interest in family life and parent education is evident in the many other international and European organisations which have become involved in the debate over the last decade, amongst them the International Union of Family Organisations; the Confederation of Family Organisations in the European Community (COFACE); the Council of Europe's project on Preparation for Family Life (Schleicher, 1982); and the OECD/CERI project on the educational role of the family (OECD/CERI, 1982).

It is possible to identify many similarities between issues with which parent education in Britain has been concerned and those of quite different countries elsewhere in the world. There is widespread concern, for example, at the changing nature of social and family structures, at increasing rates of divorce and growing numbers of single-parent families, and at the considerable degree of both isolation and uncertainty. Although the United States in particular has pioneered a number of fairly structured parent education programmes, a general trend can be detected which rejects the didactic approach associated with the rapid rise of the child-care 'expert', in favour of an approach which recognises parents' own skills and abilities. The OECD/CERI project on the educational role of the family for example, summarised a number of principles which reflected not only work in Britain, but also schemes elsewhere in Europe, North America, Australasia and Japan:

1. a concern for quality and cohesiveness in family life;
2. the effectiveness of programmes which help people discover their own parental capacities;
3. parent education as following the individual life cycle;
4. the need for non-intrusive preventive approaches;
5. the importance of the 'setting' in which parent education takes place;
6. multi-dimensional approaches, using the media, group work, etc.;
7. the need to retrain professionals working with parents. (OECD/CERI, 1982).

In Britain, the systematic approach that Stern was seeking is still conspicuously absent, and the Bureau's parenting project supports his view that while a spontaneous approach built on an individual enthusiasm does have a certain appeal, it is also ineffective in either reaching a wider audience or in pooling expertise and resources. However, whilst much remains to be done, particularly in terms of policy development and the commitment of resources, there has been considerable progress in the last two decades. At central government level much of the thinking in the early 1970s grew from the proposition put forward by Sir Keith Joseph, then Secretary of State for Social Services, that there existed within society 'a cycle of deprivation' whereby personal, emotional and social problems persisted from one generation to another. This led to a considerable body of research into aspects of transmitted deprivation and much discussion about the causes and nature of disadvantage (see Rutter and Madge, 1976). Sir Keith also set up a series of consultations and seminars jointly with the Department of Education and Science, which focussed on preparation for parenthood as a possible method of improving parents' attitudes to relationship with their children, thereby breaking, it was hoped the cycle of deprivation (DHSS, 1974 and 1974b).

A succession of other reports has been published by select committees and government departments. The Court report on the future of the child health services (Committee on Child Health Services, 1976) for example, had a clear view on what schools might do to prepare young people for family life and what their overall objective should be:

> Attention to improving an individual's general ability to cope with life is the chief issue and should in any case be a primary objective of schools ... Emphasis should be placed on skills in interpersonal relationships, in communication and in helping children to understand themselves and the world around them.

The Select Committee on Violence to Children also expressed the view that:

> Much more should be done in the school curriculum to ensure that all pupils receive some education in the skills of parenthood. By this we do not mean simply abstract instruction in the physiological mechanics of conception and childbirth, but learning about what children are really like ... we recommend that the government, whether through the DHSS or DES, should ensure that education for parenthood is available for boys and girls of all levels of intellectual ability. (Select Committee, 1977)

These and other reports such as *Marriage Matters*, from the working party on marriage guidance (Home Office, 1979), and the report from the joint working party on pregnant schoolgirls (NCOPF, 1979) have all contributed to the debate on education and support for parents. The Bureau's parenting project, the research project at Aston University on preparation for parenthood in the school curriculum (Grafton *et al.*, 1983b), and research on the transition to parenthood at the Thomas Coram Research Unit (Moss, 1981,

1982a and 1982b), have also been funded by the government as a further contribution to this debate.

These expressions of concern and recommendations on the way ahead – seldom if ever matched with the resources to implement them – have both reflected and inspired some movement amongst statutory and voluntary agencies working with families and young people. New national bodies have been established: the Study Commission on the Family, now replaced by a family research unit, which aims to stimulate and contribute to debate and discussions related to family life and family policy in Britain; and Family Forum, which was launched in 1980 to bring together the many organisations and individuals concerned with families and to exert some pressure on policy-makers. Existing pressure groups have continued to campaign for better maternity grants and child allowances; for a fairer tax system for families; for a better deal for single parents; for more day-care for children of working mothers; and for the greater involvement of parents in the schools their children attend. There has been a very considerable increase in the range of support services available for parents, through informal groups, intervention schemes, home visiting, crisis telephone services and a vast array of printed, audio and visual information, and since Stern's survey there has been the evolution and development of two major contributors to parent education in Britain – the playgroup movement and the Open University's parent education courses.

The case for parent education

Being a parent and bringing up children is probably the most important job that most people ever do, yet it is one for which they receive virtually no preparation, no training and precious little support. There are those who feel that parenting is best learned 'on the job' or that it is 'caught' rather than taught. Common sense, intuition and the model of childhood experiences of being parented certainly appear to be widespread influences. The thousands of telephone calls received by Family Network for example led the organiser to conclude that 'most people felt that they had received no guidance about the overall skills of parenting other than through the examples they had been subjected to as children themselves' (Kidd, 1982b). Yet as we have seen, the world in which many of today's parents are bringing up their children is a very different one from that in which they themselves grew up; many parents are lonely and isolated; and for many their own experiences of childhood simply serve as a reminder of how they would not wish to bring up their own children.

Whilst most parents manage very well most of the time, parenting can be a difficult and lonely job, and it can be argued that society has a responsibility both to help youngsters develop some understanding of what is likely to be involved in bringing up children *before* they decide whether or not to become parents; and to provide parents with information, support and education as and when it is needed and particularly at critical periods of the life-cycle, such as the birth of a first child. The way in which this is provided is the key issue in this field and the subject of constant debate. There is not always agreement as to what information and skills are the most appropriate and how they should be offered to parents. British approaches to preventive work and family support are tentative compared with some programmes in America and elsewhere, although there is a tendency to intervene at times of crisis and take over from parents rather than work with them. Never the less, the dilemma is well summarised by Weikart:

> Society is concerned about the ways families are rearing children, and the situation appears to be rapidly approaching the juncture when the State will be assuming increased responsibility for children. Thus the stage is being set for massive conflict between the right of self-determination of families who desire children and of the responsibility they entail and goals established by the State through family policy decisions for all children. Ultimately conflict will be between the State's need for a healthy and productive citizen and the family's right of self-determination. (Weikart, 1980)

This dilemma reflects different political and ideological viewpoints and inspires the kind of reaction that led one journalist, referring to social workers making decisions on parents' abilities to care for their own children, to talk about 'armies of professionals who are a threat to the privacy of the castle which was once the Englishman's home' (Kenny, 1981). On the one hand parent education can be seen as a means of social control, and of encouraging conformity to a particular type of socially acceptable or desirable behaviour, for example reinforcing role-stereotypes by preparing men to be breadwinners and women to be primarily homekeepers and rearers of children; or focussing programmes on the role of parents in preparing their children to perform well and adjust quickly to the educational system. On the other hand, and at the other end of the spectrum, it can be seen as a means to social change, whereby individuals are given encouragement and increased self-confidence to take greater control over their lives, to break out of traditional roles, and to question the status quo.

Few programmes will be neutral in their value position, and it is interesting to speculate where the schemes outlined in the following chapters fit along this spectrum. The debate surrounding the teaching of child care and development in secondary schools (a subject which is taken at present mainly by girls), has led one critic to argue that 'the root notion of the family to be used in these subjects is patriarchal or of unequal sexual relations, in which fathers rule the family and women are subordinate' (David, 1982). The debate on parent education within the adult education field has also questioned whether stereotypes are being reinforced by concentrating on women's needs as mothers and some have asked whether it might not be more appropriate to focus on issues relating to the women's personal health and development.

The quotation at the start of this chapter links the discussion on the tasks and skills of parenting and the social and economic conditions of families' lives, with our current concern with how these needs might be met, for as the Court report pointed out, the importance of relationships within the family and of individual characteristics and abilities, suggest that any approaches to parent education should be based on principles rather than prescriptions. From the various approaches reviewed in the following chapters, it has been possible to draw up a number of principles upon which parent education and support might be based:

> that there is no single right way of parenting, no blueprint for a perfect family, and that it is important that diverse family patterns are acknowledged and respected;
>
> that parenting is a continuous process. The development of a parent starts at birth and goes on through early childhood, schooldays, early relationships, committed partnerships, pre-

gnancy, birth, parenthood and grandparenthood. There are likely to be different needs at different stages and these can be met in different ways;

that the ability to parent reflects each individual's level of self-confidence and sense of worth. This has implications for work in social and personal education in schools; and for work with parents and prospective parents, where support should acknowledge, value, and build on their own skills, experience and abilities rather than inducing dependency or guilt;

that parenting is not simply a matter of child-rearing; it is a constant interaction between parents and children, both of whom are continually developing;

that parenting involves (usually) mothers and fathers and that any approaches to parent education are therefore relevant to boys as well as girls, men as well as women;

that if parenting is a sequential process, concerned with the development of the whole person, this has implications for all those working with young people and parents throughout the life-cycle, who may need to see their own involvement as part of a wider network of support;

that because Britain is a multicultural society, cultural diversities which are expressed through different child-rearing patterns and attitudes to family life need to be taken into account in any support for parents, and those undertaking such work will require knowledge and understanding of these different cultural backgrounds;

that schemes and services planned in close co-operation with parents and based upon their own needs, are likely to be more acceptable and more widely used;

that bringing up children has to be seen in the wider context of adequate employment, financial provision (through equitable taxation and sufficient income maintenance) housing and day care.

But how are these principles to be turned into practice and who is to provide this support? A major difficulty is that whilst many professionals and para-professionals see parent education and support as a part – often a small part – of their brief, for very few it is the main thrust of their work. The initial review undertaken before the project started (Pugh, 1980) showed that whilst in some areas very little was available, elsewhere quite different programmes may be in progress, often set up at the instigation of one or two enthusiastic individuals working in health and social services, education, the youth service, churches and voluntary organisations and by parents themselves. In the last three years the extent of these schemes and the range of professional workers involved has increased, yet many are still working in isolation, unaware of similar schemes a few streets away, rather than offering families a co-ordinated service.

A life-cycle approach to parent education

If parent education is seen as a life-long process, it may be appropriate to consider what contribution it could make at different points in a person's life. But first a word on the terminology used, for as we indicated in the preface, the schemes and approaches described in this book are known by many different titles, from preparation for parenthood and education for family life to parent training and parentcraft. The term *parent education* which is used throughout this book encompasses all these approaches and is defined as 'a range of educational and supportive measures which help parents and prospective parents to understand themselves and their children and enhances the relationship between them'.

Work with prospective parents before the birth of a child has traditionally been called preparation for parenthood and has focussed on understanding physical changes during pregnancy and preparation for the labour and birth. For many this is the first contact with professionals concerned with parents and their children, and the evidence presented in subsequent chapters indicates that for many it has come too late. A more appropriate approach, it is suggested, would be to enable youngsters during their adolescence to have access to a programme of *family life education* or *preparation about parenthood* which could be made available through schools, further education colleges or the youth service. This could have a number of strands. The first of these is based on the notion that good parents are first and foremost coping, caring adults and that young people both at home and in school and the world outside, need to be able to grow up in an environment in which they can love and be loved; respect and be respected; trust and be trusted; develop self-confidence and self-knowledge, establish good personal relationships, both within the family and with their peers and make balanced decisions about how they wish to lead their lives.

The second element of this 'programme' concerns the need to present young people with a more realistic and less romanticised picture of parenthood in general and motherhood in particular. As families become smaller, many young people embark on parenthood with very little experience of what babies and young children are really like. A central theme of research studies on marriage and parenthood is of the discrepancy between the expectations of the sense of fulfilment that a wife, husband and children will bring, and the reality of an exhausting twenty-four-hours-a-day commitment amidst which one's own sense of identity seems to diminish. (Oakley, 1980; Mansfield, 1982; Clulow, 1982). As Mia Pringle has said:

> A more realistic and perhaps even daunting awareness needs to be created of the arduous demands which child rearing makes on the emotions, energy, time and finances, as well as of the inevitable restraints on personal independence, freedom of movement and indeed, one's whole way of life. Babies should be presented 'truthfully', warts and all – sometimes fretful and demanding, often wet, smelly, crying at night and 'unreasonable' – rather than with a permanent angelic, dimply smile and sunny temper. (Pringle, 1975)

The picture of course is not all black, and it would be dangerous to swing the balance in the opposite direction and to overstate the difficulties at the expense of the many joys and rewards. Indeed, some youngsters and prospective parents show a commendable caution in embarking on parenthood, with a considerable awareness of how they feel their lives will change (Mansfield, 1982; Prendergarst and Prout, 1980).

The third element is to make whatever courses are offered as relevant to boys as they are to girls, so that bringing up children is seen as parenting rather than mothering. And finally it is important to provide young people with sufficient knowledge and understanding of contraception and of options open to them that they can make a genuine choice as to whether and when to have children. As Schaffer (1977) has said 'There can be no better way of improving motherhood than making it genuinely a matter of choice'.

Once pregnancy has been confirmed, whether or not it was a voluntary choice to start a family, *preparation for parenthood* adopts a more practical and immediate importance. There has been a growing emphasis in recent years on the need for pre-conceptual care and on the importance of being as fit and healthy as possible when planning and embarking on pregnancy (Wynn and Wynn, 1981). This is important, for most classes are offered during the latter stages of pregnancy when potential damage from smoking, alcohol, drugs or an unbalanced diet may already have been done. Preparation classes are now widely available and, as is shown in Chapter 5, they offer information on physical changes during pregnancy and help with managing the process of labour and birth. However, the appropriateness of the content of these classes has been questioned and few have been found to be entirely adequate. Becoming a parent involves much more than the arrival of a new baby, yet few classes seem to be tackling the broader issues of emotional, physical and economic changes with both prospective parents. Whilst it is clearly not possible to anticipate adequately the transition to parenthood, research has pointed to the value of providing opportunities for discussion with other new and prospective parents; and of building up a supportive network of friends, family and health professionals which will also provide continuity from early pregnancy to the first months of parenthood, and may well be of more use in coping with major life changes than a series of classes.

The final and longest stage of the life-cycle starts with the birth of the first child. The needs of individual parents and their children will vary from one to another, as will the needs of any one family from month to month and year to year. The evidence presented in Chapter 6 and 7 suggests that at this stage a wide range of *support for parents* is needed in every local community, offering information, advice, support and education as and when it is needed.

To categorise approaches to parent education, or to attempt to draw boundaries between them, is a difficult and often pointless semantic exercise. When does information about welfare rights turn into a broader-based support for example? Is an informal mother and toddler club offering a learning situation or simply mutual support? Is home visiting an interventionist strategy or an opportunity for education and support within the home?

It may be helpful to look at a few definitions, for there are those who fear that the umbrella term 'parent education', which has grown considerably in popularity in the past few years, may be heralding the way for the kind of behaviour-modification programme and parent-effectiveness training so popular in parts of North America, Australia and Europe. One American volume describes parent education as 'a systematic and conceptually based programme, intended to impact information, awareness or skills to the participants on aspects of parenting' (Fine, 1980). Another spells out the aims of parent education as 'to effect change in parent role performance and upgrade child care practices of parents in the home' (Harman and Brim, 1980). These and other American commentaries reflect the influence of two main programmes, one based on the work of Adler and Dreikurs (Dreikurs and Soltz, 1970 Dinkmeyer and McKay 1976); and one on Gordon's Parent Effectiveness Training (1970). PET has been particularly successful, claiming back in 1976 to have trained 8000 instructors and 250 000 parents. Commentators however remark on the lack of a theoretical framework, of little evidence of discipline or rigorous thought and on the limited amount of research into methodology and effectiveness (Harman and Brim, 1980). The critics point out that such programmes tend to raise in parents, feelings of dependency, self-consciousness, guilt and anxiety with their stress on the importance of acquiring specific techniques and attaining high levels of perfection. One critique of PET, for example, speaks of it demonstrating 'a degree of certitude which verges on moral fanaticism' (Doherty and Ryder, 1980).

The approach in this country, reflecting perhaps a national tendency to be wary of expert advice or to expect instant returns from a series of evening classes, is rather more tentative and informal. The early parent education programmes, particularly those with families whose children were under-achieving, focussed exclusively on the parents' capacity for helping the child to do well in school. This placed an often intolerable burden on parents who were made to feel that their child's future success – or failure – lay entirely in their own hands and the emphasis has now shifted to some extent in an attempt to help parents understand and meet their own needs as well. Writing in 1960 when few of the approaches outlined in this book were in existence, Stern said 'Parent education should assist parents in the natural process of thinking, understanding, communicating and deciding on matters of child care. It should inspire confidence and encourage in parents a sense of independence and responsibility' (Stern, 1960). Subsequent developments have been in line with those sentiments, for the emphasis has been as much on the personal growth and development of parents, on increasing self-confidence and self-awareness, on improving communication skills, on reducing isolation and on helping people gain some control over their lives as it has been on instruction in the basic elements of child-development. Work with parents has also tended to evolve from the groups and meeting places with which they are already familiar, rather than by setting up classes in adult education institutes. Perhaps it is for these reasons that so many schemes have their roots in the strong community networks that have given us so many voluntary and self-help organisations.

The Pre-school Playgroup Association for example is concerned 'to help parents to understand and provide for the needs of their young children . . . to promote community situations in which parents can with growing enjoyment and confidence make the best of their own knowledge and resources in the development of their children and themselves'. Scope, a network of parent support groups in Hampshire is also interested in the growth of parents as individuals:

> The groups aim to reinforce the role of parents as educators of their own children; to encourage the personal growth of group members, particularly in relation to their self-esteem in the parenting role, through shared experiences in the accepting, non-threatening atmosphere of a neighbourhood group; and to encourage members to utilise resources and services which should be available. (Poulton and Couzens, 1981)

This emphasis on learning rather than teaching is crucial in attempting to base parent education on the abilities and the needs of parents, and it is evident too in the work of organisations which are perhaps more overtly 'educational'. A working group of adult education tutors in the Inner London Education Authority, for example, defined parent education as aiming:

to help people take more control over their part in the parenting relationship, to shape and value their own knowledge and experience and to understand a variety of options, thus broadening their perspectives. This is done by encouraging the questioning of adopted attitudes, by making available relevant knowledge and information (physical, emotional and environmental) and encouraging the learning of appropriate skills. (ILEA, 1983)

The education officer of the National Marriage Guidance Council, uses the term education:

to describe work which provides people (parents) with access to as much information as possible; offers them opportunities to consider and discuss the information in relation to their own needs, desires, life-styles, personal characteristics and potential; encourages them to have confidence to make their own decisions and choices; and accepts the choices they make. And when I talk of information in this context, I am imagining the small informal group situation, where much of the marriage guidance education work takes place, and where information is multi-way, from parent to parent, from parent to group leader, and certainly never only one way – from leader to group. (Torkington, 1982)

The parent education courses run by the Open University, which are used in a wide range of informal groups but which provide specific tools for teaching parenting skills are also relevant here. They aim:

To encourage learners to value their own and others' experiences; to provide information to assist personal and collective decision making; and to help learners to review their own experiences, values and resources and the information provided in making and implementing personal and collective decision making. (Wolfson, 1982)

All these examples acknowledge that the experience and knowledge brought by parents to the groups is in itself valuable and show that education is not the exclusive province of the educators. The South American educationalist Paulo Freire has defined real education as 'the practice of freedom – the means by which men and women deal creatively with reality and discover how to participate in the transformation of the world' (Freire, 1972). It is not just the acquisition of skills and knowledge, but a concern to help people understand themselves and their relationships with each other and the world they live in. Concepts of choice, of freedom and of control are central to parent education work with families who may feel that there is no way in which they can alter the circumstances of their own lives, and this has been a focus of many of the adult and community education approaches discussed in Chapter 6 (see also Liffman, 1978).

Perhaps the most overtly educational approaches, and certainly those closest to the structured American programmes, are those based on parent counselling and behaviour modification. Parent training in behaviour modification has received considerable attention in this country, in the first instance mainly in the treatment of children with behavioural disorders. Here studies have shown that parents from diverse backgrounds can learn to use behavioural methods effectively with their children of all ages, abilities and problems (Yule, 1975; Callias, 1980). More recently a number of schemes have been developed for use with parents of mentally handicapped children, notably the Portage project and derivations from it (see Pugh, 1981; Cameron, 1982). The techniques are obviously available for any parent experiencing quite normal difficulties in managing children's behaviour (Westmacott and Cameron, 1981), although many parents find such programmes difficult to initiate and maintain without support, whether professional or informal.

In the therapeutic field many clinicians and psychiatrists have moved away from individual casework to family therapy. This has inevitably led to a focus on family life and parenting, and an increasing awareness of the stresses placed on parents. These include the conflicting demands of work and family, the growing incidence of depression, loneliness, isolation and unemployment. Family therapy is concerned with all these aspects of family life and particularly with helping families to cope with the different stages of the life-cycle and the many different family structures outlined earlier (see Barker, 1981).

These are some of the many approaches sheltering under the umbrella of preparation, education and support for parents. Their labels conceal a wide variety of aims, objectives and methods of working and these will be taken up in the chapters that follow. None of the schemes would profess to present any definitive answers, but each in its own way goes some way towards increasing the under-standing and pleasures and easing the isolation and burden of parenting. Some, however, do raise a number of questions. As one American educationist points out, parent education programmes encourage parents to be excessively cerebral and self-conscious, and as a result they may lack confidence and get bound up in what she describes as 'analysis paralysis' (Katz, 1982). Technique-based parent education may yield positive effects in the short term, but feelings of failure and guilt in the long run. This is perhaps why approaches in this country have focussed on encouraging and supporting parents in their own competence and life-styles, for self-confident parents will surely be better and more effective parents.

Methods of parent education

Parent education covers a wide range of information, skills, aware-ness and understanding. There are different ways in which parents choose to seek help and guidance and a variety of ways in which parent education can be offered. The three main ways of reaching parents are through the mass media, through group work and through individual approaches. Table 2.1 shows what such ap-proaches might include.

Mass media

The principal features of this method of parent education are the potential breadth of the audience that can be reached, and the fact that there is usually no direct contact between the educator and the audience. There is certainly no shortage of books, articles and television and radio programmes beamed at parents, and although figures have not been compiled in this country, it was estimated that in America in 1977 some nine million child-care books were sold annually, with an average of 200 new titles each year (Harman and Brim, 1980). Pamphlets and leaflets too are widely available, particularly those issued by the Health Education Council, the

TABLE 2.1   *Methods of parent education*

Mass media	Group work	Individual approaches
Books	Casual drop-in centres	Information and advice services
Pamphlets and leaflets		
	Informal post-natal and mother and toddler groups	Counselling
Magazines and journals specifically for parents		Family therapy
	Playgroups	Radio phone-in programmes
Newspapers and general articles	Semi-structured parent education groups	24-hour crisis phone services
Television and radio		
	Structured therapeutic groups	
Films, film strips, slides		Individual professionals (health visitors, GPs, teachers, pre-school visitors, social workers, etc)
Meetings and lectures	Group discussion in schools	
		Voluntary one-to-one schemes

Scottish Health Education Group, the British Medical Association and the Health Visitors Association to all pregnant women. One study for example, found that 99 per cent of all prospective mothers had received and read copies of the BMA publication *You and Your Baby*.

Traditionally most women's magazines and journals have included articles about family life or advice on particular aspects of parenting, and several have regular columns or sections contributed by child-care experts. In the last few years a number of monthly publications specifically on child-rearing have also appeared, and *Parent* and *Mother* magazines have an annual readership of over two million copies. Television and radio, and now video, provide vicarious learning through the images and portrayal of family life in entertainment and drama series, through the advertisements, and through series such as *Coronation Street* and the *Archers*. There are also an increasing number of documentaries and special interest programmes which deal with many aspects of family life, from general programmes on pregnancy and birth, and child-care and development to special programmes on handicap, single-parenting, child abuse, parents and teenagers, working parents and so on. There are also the very popular pre-school programmes such as *Rainbow, Playschool* and *You and Me* which parents and children can often enjoy watching together. Schools broadcasting and adult education programmes have also begun to make a useful contribution to parent education, and the Open University parenthood series discussed in Chapter 6 also includes radio and television programmes that have been watched by many more than those who are enrolled on the courses.

One difficulty in keeping up with this increasing number of programmes has been knowing what is available and when it is to be transmitted. There is also little co-ordination between different departments involved within the BBC and IBA, nor indeed between the BBC and IBA. A further difficulty has been that parent education is not always a very high priority with programme schedulers, and many of the programmes are thus transmitted at times not always convenient to parents with young children.

As a means of reaching potential consumers, the mass media are clearly reaching large numbers of people. One survey of how parents prepared for parenthood, found that 99 per cent of mothers and 83 per cent of fathers read appropriate books or pamphlets during pregnancy (Moss, 1982a) whilst others have found that the majority of women watch appropriate television programmes (Draper *et al.*, 1981; Perfrement, 1982). Many parents however, have criticised the often contradictory nature of the material – particularly the literature distributed by the health services. When looking at clinic booklets as a help or hindrance to parent education, Perkins (1980) found that there were sometimes completely different approaches appearing in similar publications. In some the quality of the information was suspect and in others frankly inaccurate. Little evidence was given to support the advice or to help mothers make decisions. The image of family life was far removed from the conflicts, contradictions and difficulties of the real world. There were no single parents, all were well-housed and fed, employed and delighted with the new arrival. All these points have been substantiated by parents in a number of other studies. Television and magazines were said either to give a romantic and idealised picture of parenthood or to dwell on the abnormalities and sensational issues of pregnancy and childbirth. Many mothers found the advice either irrelevant or inappropriate to their own circumstances (Graham and McKee, 1980) or too brief to be of value (Draper *et al.*, 1981). For some parents the books made no impact either on their level of knowledge or state of preparation, whilst for others it caused anxieties or worry (Moss, 1982a).

One way of improving on the value of media approaches might be to use them in association with one of the other methods, for example, using a book or film as the focus for a group discussion. Another approach might be to provide opportunities for feedback and questions to the maker of the programmes or writer of the book, for example through the use of a phone-in programme from a local radio station.

Group work

Group discussion has become a popular method of parent education, and is particularly valuable for the opportunity it presents for drawing on the personal experiences of members of the group, and relating any educational input directly to those experiences. Groups vary considerably in their size and their composition; the frequency and context of their meetings; their purpose; the methods they use; and the nature of participation and leadership. The following chapters include many examples of the range of groups listed above, from work in social education with secondary school pupils, through antenatal groups, mother and toddler groups providing company for isolated mothers to more highly-structured parent education groups focussing on the Open University parenthood courses or perhaps developing specific skills through the use of games, simulations and role-play. Studies of such groups show that in their various ways they are providing parents with somewhere to meet, share their experiences, build up a network of friends and resources, and increase their understanding and enjoyment of their children.

Whilst the group method is able to provide an approach to parent education which is sensitive, responsive to individual need and respects the experience brought by each member of the group, this method is not without its problems. Groups have been found to need a certain homogeneity in order to 'gell' and are not able to cope with acute personal problems (LeRoy, 1982; Palfreeman 1982). A study of antenatal groups found that they were less successful when group members were anxious about particular problems – such as the impending birth – and that at such times consultations with individual professionals were of more value (Clulow, 1982).

Some of the evidence in the following chapters points to the difficulty in finding people who are suitably qualified to lead groups, with both an appropriate knowledge base, the skills required to handle difficult and sensitive issues within a group and the ability to respect attitudes which may be at variance with their own. One evaluator comments on the skills of low-key leadership:

> It would be all too easy for sessions like this to become lectures rather than discussions, or for conversation to become out-of-hand and hurtful or embarrassing to some participants. The style the discussion leaders used was semi-directive. It is rather like a teacher gathering her pupils together for an environmental studies walk in the country, but having taken them there, following their enthusiasms and interest, and only occasionally drawing their attention to things they had not noticed. Superficially this method can appear non-directive, but it would be destructive if the two methods were confused. With the semi-directive approach, leaders do establish the core of the agenda, do limit the boundaries of discussion, although in contrast with directive leadership, they are open for the group to be drawn to the issues raised by particular participants and believe that creative ideas and perceptions can come from anyone in the group. So long as these three styles do not become confused this semi-directive approach has much to recommend it in this kind of project. (LeRoy, 1982)

Further difficulties related to leadership arise when the leader is invested with an 'expertise' by the group which may increase rather than diminish parents' dependence. The prospective parents in Clulow's study for example, were perplexed by the open-endedness of the discussion and actually asked for more structure.

Individual approaches

The methods employed here vary considerably in the intensity of the contact, ranging from straightforward information to extensive counselling or therapy to help ease a particularly acute personal problem. The telephone has become an important instrument for reaching people who might otherwise not seek information or guidance, and local and national phone-ins on both radio and television have become particularly popular in discussing current issues of child care. These can have a double value as parent education, in that they respond to the individual caller and also highlight the areas of concern which can be explored more fully through complete feature programmes aimed at a mass audience. Many of the parents who call do not feel they have a 'problem' and would not consult a professional worker, but they do often express relief at being able to ask their question and learn from other people's experience or hear another point of view. Crisis telephone lines and off-the-air local radio help-lines have been recognised as an important means of giving information and support to parents who need immediate help with their own particular problems and are not able or willing to seek help from the statutory services.

The individual service offered by such professionals as health visitors, doctors, social workers, pre-school home visitors and by those who offer counselling and family therapy, is the only way in which specific worries can be discussed personally, and as such is extremely valuable, but apart from the one-to-one help offered by volunteers as in Home Start, it is also costly and time-consuming, and is limited by the individual experience and expertise of the professional concerned.

Choice of method will largely depend on whether the overall objective of the programme is to provide information to parents, to develop skills or to help with the development of understanding and identification of values. With these purposes in view, the methods could be grouped as in Table 2.2.

These various approaches to parent education raise three further questions which cannot be ignored: (i) what personnel are involved in parent education? (ii) what training do they receive? and (iii) has the effectiveness of different approaches been evaluated?

Personnel in parent education

Whilst in the United States parent education has developed into a separate educational profession, with degree courses available for

TABLE 2.2   *Methods in relation to objectives*

To provide information	To develop skills	To increase understanding
Books and articles	Social skills training (eg. exercises in problem solving and decision making)	Small group discussion (structured by leader but drawing on group experience)
Television and radio		
Films, videos etc.		Discussion groups using audio-visual material
Information leaflets	Games and simulations	
Formal lectures	Role-play of social situations	Using methods in skills column
Information and advice services	Use of OU materials	
	Home visiting schemes	

OU = Open University.

family-life educators, in Britain there is no one group of professionals who could claim to have a monopoly on parent education. The Bureau's original survey of parent education showed that quite different programmes were being undertaken by personnel in health, social services, education, the youth service, churches, voluntary organisations and by parents themselves. Teachers, psychologists, counsellors, social workers, health visitors, playgroup leaders, doctors, nurses, midwives, priests, youth workers, physiotherapists, educational welfare officers – all were involved (Pugh, 1980). The current project has shown that whilst these are amongst the many professionals and volunteers working with parents, the skills required to work in small groups in these sensitive areas are not always very evident.

In 1960 Stern recommended that there should be three categories of worker in parent education: (i) all those who have regular professional contact with children and families whose training should include an emphasis on family and parenthood; (ii) specialists in parent education recruited from medicine, education, social work, psychology etc. with extra training in group leadership; (iii) parents, trained and supervised as 'lay leaders' – preferably happily married with three children. So what progress has been made in the last twenty years?

Training

A detailed examination of the training of professionals working with families and with young people has been beyond the limited resources of this project. However, a number of points do emerge from studies to which we refer in the following chapters, and from observations on initial and in-service training. The most important of these are that most professional training still tends to include little on family life or parenthood, and there is still no explicit training for specialists in parent education. However there has been the recognition amongst some family workers that individuals are usually part of a family unit, and some professionals who have hitherto worked almost exclusively with the individual who is exhibiting the problem (for example, a child truanting, an anorexic daughter, a depressed or alcoholic mother or father) are now beginning to adopt a family approach and work with the family as a whole. There have also been attempts to introduce the concept of 'healthy families' into training which has hitherto tended to concentrate on pathology, deviancy and distress. But there are many instances – the training of teachers is a case in point – where the main concern is with the client group and the family is often forgotten or ignored. The evidence in Chapter 6 suggests for example that those who have been trained to work with young children are experiencing some difficulty in adjusting to work with parents as well; and studies on parental involvement in schooling conclude that teachers have no training or role-definition for working with parents.

Recent reports and initiatives suggests that there is an acceptance of the need to focus on the family and particularly to work with the parents, if any education or support is to have more than a short-term benefit. There has also been an awareness of the need for more inter-disciplinary training and sharing between professionals in order to encourage a more co-operative and better co-ordinated service. The possibility of a common core in the training of social workers and teachers has been discussed and a recent joint statement from the four national bodies responsible for the education and training for district nursing, general medical practice, health visiting and social work highlights the difference between 'joint training' and 'training for joint operations'. As the following chapters show, there are a great many different professionals who have different knowledge, skills and understanding to contribute to parent education.

The methods of parent education outlined above suggest that the training of professionals working with young people and families should cover three main areas – relevant *knowledge* (of child and human development, family patterns, local resources, etc.); the development of *skills* in working with individuals and with groups in often very sensitive areas; and the ability to examine their *attitudes, values* and *feelings* in respect of family life, and a sensitivity to others' point of view. While the training of education, medical and health care personnel in particular has focussed on the acquisition of knowledge, there is far less attention given to the development of group work skills or to awareness or sensitivity training. Teachers are increasingly finding themselves working in small discussion groups with pupils, and yet the teacher-training schemes outlined in Chapter 3 relate to specific approaches, such as active tutorial work, and are not part of either initial or general in-service training for teachers. Health visitors too have often found themselves setting up groups, and their training is only just beginning to explore the use of role-play and group exercises in order to make them more familiar with group work skills.

Demands for in-service training tend to be greater than the supply and the cut-backs in education, health and social services are equally severe in the area of training. Courses developed during the seventies for example, to help teachers in the development of their pastoral and counselling role have now been cut. It is ironic that many of those whose training does suit them for this kind of work – notably social workers, youth and community workers and marriage guidance counsellors – are not often in a position, or do not choose, to use them in relation to parent education.

In respect of parents leading groups, considerably more progress has been made, although with reference to Stern's caveat, the quality of their marriage and the size of their families is not revealed. Many of the approaches discussed in Chapters 6 and 7 show that with appropriate training and support parents in even fairly adverse circumstances are well able and willing to lead groups.

Evaluation

Given the increasing interest in the field of parent education there has been relatively little research on the effectiveness of different approaches to working with parents, and not even very many evaluation studies of individual schemes. It is not difficult to see why. Many of the schemes outlined in Chapters 3 to 7 are as much concerned with developing self-confidence and the enjoyment of being a parent as they are with increasing knowledge, and it is a difficult and time-consuming business to measure changes in attitude and behaviour.

Reference is made in the following chapters to such studies as have been mounted, whether in schools, in the antenatal field or in work with parents in the community. Most of these studies have simply attempted to assess the extent to which individual schemes are meeting their own objectives, whether these be to provide a meeting-place for lonely mothers or to increase specific skills. To the best of our knowledge there are few, if any, attempts to assess the comparative effectiveness of different types of approach, nor to see whether different kinds of family respond to different kinds of programme, nor to study in detail what individual parents need – and use – at different stages of the life-cycle. There have also been no long-term follow-up studies of parents, or prospective parents, who have been involved in specific programmes. There has however, been a growing interest amongst grass roots family workers to assess their own progress and question their own objectives (see *Evaluating Parents Groups*, De'Ath, 1983b).

Part II

PARENT EDUCATION IN PRACTICE

3

Family Life Education: The Role of the School

Introduction

If parent education is to be a life-long process it must begin in one form or another during childhood. Views of what schools can and cannot achieve are perhaps more realistic today than they were in the 1960s and 1970s. Little more than 15 000 hours, or 17 per cent of a child's time awake will actually be spent in school (Rutter, 1979) and the principal and most enduring influences, particularly in the early years, will undoubtedly be his own parents and close family. Nevertheless school does have an important role to play for social, educational and pragmatic reasons:

> education in this country has been traditionally concerned with the whole person. Understanding what is involved in preparing for, having, and looking after children is an important aspect of emotional development and personal responsibility;
>
> school is the only place where all future parents can be reached with certainty;
>
> parenthood is a topic which can offer educational material which pupils of all abilities find relevant and motivating, and can contribute to the development of skills in several important areas. (Verdon, 1980)

There are many ways in which schools can support parents in their parenting role. A closer working relationship between parents, teachers and children and increased involvement of parents in school is one way, a topic with which we deal in Chapter 7. This chapter examines the contribution that primary and secondary schools might make and, in some cases, are making to the development of their pupils as family members and probably, as parents. The terminology of the studies and approaches quoted is again varied and confusing. The term 'family life education' has therefore been adopted as reflecting the broad aims of work at this stage of the life cycle, for whilst not all young people will become parents, they are almost all part of a family.

Although the level of debate has increased in the last twenty years, family life education is no new phenomenon. The first parentcraft courses in schools date back to the early 1900s, and were principally directed at girls. Many were inspired by local medical officers of health in an attempt to combat high infant mortality and were taken up by teachers of domestic science and the vigorous campaigning of the National Association for Maternal and Child Welfare. Books for teachers dating from this period reflect this pioneering spirit and the preoccupations with hygiene, sanitation and infant mortality that accompanied it:

> The prevailing ignorance of mothers in the feeding and care of infants should be combatted. As future mothers all schoolgirls should receive intelligent instruction in hygiene, the care of infants and cooking. (Tucker, 1907)

Nationally, courses developed slowly, however, despite circulars from the Board, the then Ministry of Education. For example, the further education circular *Homecraft* (1946) encouraged local education authorities to set up appropriate courses and at the same time an adviser in parentcraft was appointed to the Ministry of Health.

Despite a survey of 1179 boys and girls between the ages of twelve and eighteen which showed that they would welcome family life education (Heron, 1952), a pamphlet on *Health Education* in 1956 (Ministry of Education) warns against 'prematurely elaborate teaching of this kind', whilst continuing to recommend school activities which prepare young people for parenthood. This led Stern to conclude in his survey that:

> preparation for family life in any organised form through schools has remained tentative beyond the more practical aspects of

housecraft. This caution need not be interpreted as merely due to inability or narrow-mindedness on the part of teachers. The restraint is likely to result from a certain diffidence in attempting to make a school subject of something that may not be amenable to a systematic form of teaching under school conditions. (Stern, 1960)

Today, whilst for perhaps these very reasons there is still no one government report providing authoritative guidance to schools on the place that family life education might find in the curriculum, there has been a veritable deluge of reports commissioned by governments of different political persuasions and from different departments, which have included amongst their recommendations some advice to schools on the need for preparation for parenthood and family life. It can only be advice, of course, for the curriculum of British schools is jealously guarded by the LEAs and heads and teachers of individual schools. Apart from a statutory requirement for some teaching in religious education, there are no compulsory elements, no core curriculum and no ways in which change can be enforced. The Crowther (1959) and Newsom (1963) reports were still preoccupied with future mothers, and Newsom in particular stated the case for a curriculum which would prepare less able girls for marriage and motherhood. It is not until the consultative document *Education in Schools* (DES, 1977) that more specific recommendations are made:

> Attitudes towards sex, parenthood, smoking, drinking and exercise, for example, will be set in these years; and schools should co-operate with parents in preparing young people for adult human relationships. . . . Both sexes should learn how to cope with domestic tasks and parenthood.

But here an important warning note is added: the curriculum has become overcrowded, the timetable is overloaded and 'essentials' are at risk.

Subsequent reports have developed this theme more fully, and have begun to turn their attention to how family life education might fit into the personal and social education of pupils. Three reports on health education (DES, 1977; HMI, 1978; Scottish Education Department, 1979) included preparation for parenthood as a major theme and in the latter case urged co-ordination between the various subject departments involved. In the broader-based *A View of the Curriculum*, HMI put forward the proposition that:

> schools need to secure for all pupils opportunities for learning, particularly likely to contribute to personal and social develop-ment. Religious education clearly has a contribution to make here and the study of personal relationships, moral education, health education, community studies and community service all provide one range of contexts in which such development may be furthered. (DES, 1980)

The following year the government circulated *The School Curriculum* (DES, 1981) to all schools in the country, a document with the most explicit advice to date on the need for and place of family life education, which it described as an 'essential constitutent of the school curriculum':

> Health education, like preparation for parenthood, is part of the preparation of the individual for personal, social and family responsibility. Health education should give pupils a basic know-ledge and understanding of health matters, both as they affect themselves and as they affect others, so that they are helped to make informed choices in their daily lives. It should also help them to become aware of those moral issues and value judge-ments which are inseparable from such choices. Preparation for parenthood and family life should help pupils to recognise the importance of those human relationships which sustain and are sustained by family life and the demands and duties that fall on parents. (DES, 1981 para. 25)

Several other major reports on trends and problems in society and family life also have a contribution to make to the debate, seeing relevant work in the classroom as a preventive influence in their own area of concern. Some of these were noted in the previous chapter (for example, DHSS 1974a, 1974b; Committee on Child Health Services, 1976; Home Office, 1979, Select Committee on Violence in The Family, 1977 and NCOPF 1979). Because schools work with young people near the beginning of the life cycle, it is often a temptation to cast them in the role of preventer and healer of all social ills. This is clearly impossible, for not only is curriculum change a long slow process, but these demands must take their place among many others.

Family life education has also become closely involved in the debate on political ideologies, and will doubtless become more so as the Conservative government develops its family policy. A key issue in this debate is whether the current level of family education work in schools is reinforcing sexual stereotypes and expectations, as current levels of unemployment rise and expenditure on public services fall. One study of school-based preparation for parenthood noted, for example, that the way in which child-care and development options were presented to pupils, such that very few boys were encouraged to take the course, extended and confirmed the traditional view of women within the family, as housewives and mothers, with prime responsibility for childrearing (Grafton *et al.*, 1983a). At the other end of the political spectrum the government's Family Policy Review Group is reputed to be recommending that schools should reinforce the idea that mothers should stay at home to look after their children (*Guardian* 1983); and some MPs and pressure groups have sought to prevent the Family Planning Association and the Health Education Council from publishing sex education material for use in schools.

It is clearly a controversial area in which value judgements and moral issues are open to criticism from those of very different political and other persuasions. Thus it is all the more important for schools to be clear about where they stand and what their contribution might be.

Aims and approaches

The reports quoted above provide the school with a long shopping list of what society would like for its future parents. But what of the young people themselves? Several studies now provide evidence that the youngsters would welcome more courses dealing with aspects of family life. Findings from the Bureau's National Child Development Study (NCDS) a longitudinal study of some 15 000 young people in England, Scotland and Wales born in one week in March 1958, show that when questioned in 1974, 66 per cent were satisfied with information received in school on reproduction and conception, but less than 50 per cent were satisfied with information on the growth of children, less than 33 per cent on the care of babies, and less than 25 per cent on family problems (Pearson and Lambert, 1977). Farrell's study however showed that 58 per cent of teenagers said that they had no sex education in school, and that as one in five teenagers were sexually experienced before sixteen, she suggests that it is too late to leave it until the fifth year (Farrell, 1978). Other smaller studies have produced similar results. In a survey of 4000 school-leavers in Scotland, nearly half the girls put child care or social education at the top of a list of subjects they would like to have studied at school (Docherty, 1978); and a study in Exeter of fourth-year girls' attitudes to health topics, found that sex education was the most important and child care the most interesting (Balding, 1979).

As teachers know, a course based on young people's current needs, interests and occupations stands a better chance of involving them than one concerned with remote possibilities – such as, for some adolescents in their mid-teens, parenthood. The Open University *Education for Family Life* course points to the importance of looking at current comics and girls' magazines, for example, which show how much more sexual freedom young people are facing today than twenty years ago. As one writer put it 'The agony columns, like the stories, reflect all the complex miseries of a generation being hurried into emotional situations that it is far too young and immature to handle'. It is often assumed that youngsters have hazy and unrealistic perceptions of parenthood, but recent research of how girls see future motherhood suggests that their knowledge directly contradicts this stereotype (Prendergast and Prout, 1980). The researchers are currently testing their hypothesis that children play an active role in the construction of their own views and futures, by examining the relationship between pupils' existing knowledge and the teaching they receive in parent education. This should provide some useful guidance for future curriculum planning.

In as diffuse an area as this, approaches in different schools will vary considerably. Very broadly, the way in which teachers have described their overall aims can be grouped into five main areas:

breaking the cycle of deprivation and preventing bad parenting;

raising the level of knowledge about child development;

educating about similarities and differences in families;

improving the quality of individual and family life through health education;

educating for personal and social development.

Family life education is thus very much broader than simply the introduction of a course on child care. But what should it embrace? A number of voices have contributed to this debate. Cowley (1981) for example, playing devil's advocate in an attempt to help teachers define their objectives more clearly, has argued that parenthood education *cannot* be justified because we are unable to predict future patterns of family life and parenting; that knowledge of parenthood can be learned more effectively at other critical periods; and that parenting skills cannot – one hopes – be systematically practised in school. It is questionable how much school can in fact affect the attitudes and behaviour of future parents, for the pressure of circumstances at the time (loneliness, exhaustion, anxiety for example) may well be stronger than the knowledge of the 'right' behaviour. It may however, be appropriate to challenge the notion of 'right' behaviour, by encouraging pupils to look critically at the advice offered by child-care experts and the media, and begin to exercise judgement about what might be right for them and their family at that time.

Others suggest that schools should concentrate on developing those skills which are needed not only by parents but by all adults in their relationships with each other (Rice, 1979). Lockwood (1982) has stressed the need to help young people understand just 'being': more responsible for themselves and others; more confident; more able to understand the choices open to them; more responsible for their own actions; more able to look after themselves; more able to cope with their feelings; and more aware of and accepting others' values and opinions. Developing an understanding of ourselves and others may well be facilitated through a study of child development, which provides useful opportunities for discussing values and attitudes and, as Perkins and Morris (1979) point out, the desirability of maintaining an open mind on some issues. 'We can do more for young people by encouraging positive attitudes towards change, than by attempting to prepare them for a new role in a highly specific way.'

A national perspective

In attempting to chart the extent of family life education in British schools, there are immediately two problems. The first is the extent to which schools are responsible for their own curriculum, so that even directors of education in local authorities are often not in a position to provide detailed information on individual schools. The second is the all-pervasive nature of the subject, and the difficulty of defining the extent of teaching even within one school. The overview presented here draws on published research, on reports from local authorities, on contact with individual schools and on replies to a brief questionnaire sent jointly by the Bureau project and the research team at Aston University to all directors of education in England and Wales in 1980. The Aston project, directed by Professor Richard Whitfield, was funded by the DES from 1979 to 1982 and has looked at preparation for parenthood in the secondary school curriculum. In addition to the authority-wide research it has worked in detail in five schools, one in each of five local authorities, and has also looked at the provision in other schools within those authorities (Grafton *et al.*, 1982a, 1982b, 1983a, 1983b).

A few general points are worth making before going on to look at the main areas in which work is developing. The first is that no responding authority reported having an official *policy* on parent education, although one had looked at education for parenthood in infant, primary and secondary schools (Hampshire) and several had set up working parties and produced guidelines on health education, social education or education for personal relationships (Gloucestershire 1971, Devon 1978, Wiltshire 1978, Somerset 1980, Waltham Forest 1980, Nottinghamshire 1981). There was a general feeling that some aspects of parenthood education should be included somewhere in the curriculum, but where and how was left to individual schools.

A second point which emerges from this reply is the remarkable variety of courses and elements of courses under this general umbrella of family life education. The Aston project found that in 217 schools in five local authorities, 930 timetabled subjects (4.3 per school) had parent education as a primary or a secondary aim, and in their more detailed study of five schools, over 90 timetabled subjects included some aspects of preparation for parenthood, with over 100 teachers involved (Grafton *et al.*, 1982a). As they point out, there was virtually no part of the curriculum where at least one teacher was not involved. Figure 3.1 indicates the main spread of subjects of which preparation for parenthood was a part. Some subjects have parent or family life education as their main aim – courses in child care, child development, parentcraft education, preparation for family life, child and family studies. But many more have a broader aim of which family life education is a part – courses in health education, personal and social education, education for personal relationships, moral education, religious education, biology, English, group and tutorial work and so on. There is also some evidence of a lack of co-ordination between different departments within the same school, so that children may find themselves studying 'the family' simultaneously in English and humanities; contraception and reproduction in biology; personal relationships in social education; whilst perhaps teachers of less formal subjects, such as art and craft, who feel that they may be doing nothing of relevance to family life education, are providing opportunities for discussion in a relaxed atmosphere, and a good model for adult relationships.

A third – and crucial – point is the importance of the *ethos* and organisation of the school, for a caring environment which can be 'caught' rather than 'taught' is as important as any course which tries to put across the concepts intellectually. The way in which the school is organised, the way in which the head relates to his or her staff, the extent to which pupils are valued as individuals with different needs, abilities and aspirations, the opportunities given for pupils to discuss issues and take responsibility for their decisions – all these are an important part of the school's role in educating tomorrow's parents.

Whilst it is difficult to detect very strong patterns from the information gathered, the contribution that schools are making to family life education appears to be evolving in a number of ways.

Primary schools

In primary schools the topic-based approach has provided many opportunities for work on the family, and the development of 'me' as a person. Although the questionnaire was principally concerned with secondary education, some local authorities sent details of guidelines which include primary schools as well. Hampshire, for

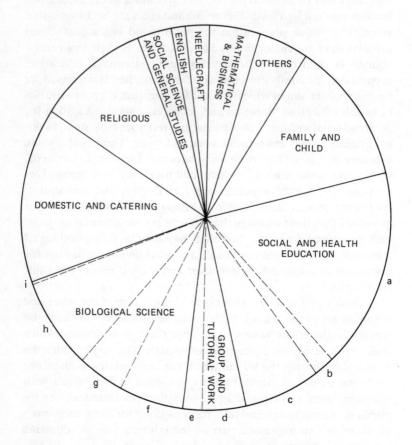

FIGURE 3.1 *Host subject groups for preparation for parenthood in the optional and compulsory curriculum for five LEAs (930 subjects)*

a Social Education
b Careers
c Health and Sex Education
d Education for personal relationships and related courses
e Active tutorial and pastoral
   work

f Combined science
g Human biology
h Biology
i Other sciences e.g. applied
   science

SOURCE   Grafton *et al.* (1983b)

example, has a detailed programme of work for parenthood education in infant and junior schools; but a policy document on health and social education in Somerset, produced as a result of a survey of all primary schools, showed that despite much incidental work, few schools had a co-ordinated scheme (Somerset, 1980).

The major curriculum contributions to this area have been the Schools Council middle school home economics project, published as *Home and Family 8-13*, and the Schools Council *Health Education Project 5-13*. The Home and Family project has provided a theoretical framework for home and family education, identifying cognitive, physical and social skills which pupils at different stages of development can be helped to acquire through working with the course. It is based on five key concepts – development, interdependence, management, nutrition and protection – which include such topics as the development of young children, growing towards adolescence, conflict, responsibility, family roles and factors affecting relationships. As with many Schools Council projects, it was funded in such a way that a dissemination officer was available to run training courses once materials were published, and some sixty LEAs have been involved in these courses.

The Health Education project took as its theme the need for individuals to consider their own values and relationships before making decisions affecting health, and the emphasis was on why people behave as they do rather than on basic health information. Published as *All About Me* (for 5-8 year olds) and *Think Well* (for 9-13 year olds), (Schools Council, 1977), the project is reported as being the 'dominant theme in primary school health education, with at least 600 000 children spending an average of twenty-two hours per year on this broadly based subject' (Reid, 1981). A recent estimate of the number of primary and middle schools with a designated person to co-ordinate health education put the number at between twenty and thirty per cent (Brierley, 1982).

Secondary schools

Child care and development. In 42 of the 62 replies to our questionnaire which provided relevant information, LEAs said that the majority of their parent education work in secondary schools took the form of child-care and development courses. Courses in parentcraft were pioneered by the National Association for Maternal and Child Welfare fifty years ago, but it was not until the 1960s that interest increased and today more than ten thousand pupils a year are taking their examinations. The syllabus for these courses has just been revised and 'Family Concern', a course in Human Development and Family Life, is available at Basic and General levels.

Neither the Schools Council nor the Health Education Council has funded any curriculum development work in child development and teachers do not therefore have the guidance of a project such as the ambitious *Exploring Childhood* project in the United States. Never the less since the introduction of the first CSE examination in child care in 1971, the subject has grown rapidly in popularity, increasing from 1000 exam entries in 1973 to 10 000 in 1976 and 34 000 in 1982. The number of entries for each examination board, comparing 1978 and 1982, is given in Appendix 2. In 1980 the first O-level in child development was introduced, and 1983 saw an O-level in Psychology; Child Development. Even within this group of subjects there are variations which are reflected within the title, the syllabus and the method of assessment. A booklet produced by teachers in Birmingham (1981) makes three main distinctions: courses with 'child care' in the title, which attempt to waken in the teenager an awareness of the needs of young children and which rely on the caring interest of teenage girls for young babies and toddlers; courses entitled 'Child Development and the Family' or 'Education for Parenthood' which have wider aims and attempt to develop in young people a responsible attitude towards parenthood and relationships; and 'Education for Family Life' which is a much broader course 'usually concerned with equipping youngsters with the knowledge, skills and motivation necessary for the efficient functioning of the whole family unit . . . such courses have greater appeal to boys for the emphasis is on personal and social development of the individual'.

Child care and development courses have been under attack from some quarters in recent months, mainly for their divisive nature. Reports from local authorities, examination boards, and the more detailed Aston study (Grafton *et al.*, 1983b) show that the vast majority of pupils taking these courses are girls. It is often seen as a vocational course for less able girls who may want to look after children, and who may well be mothers in the fairly near future. As an optional examination course it is seldom selected by boys. Perhaps this is not altogether surprising in view of the examination questions which ask candidates to 'imagine that you have just given birth to a premature baby'. Almost all the teachers are women, mostly married with children, the majority are trained in home economics and few feel their training is relevant to the child and family aspect of their work (Grafton *et al.*, 1982a). The subject is often of a fairly low status within the school and even when senior staff are involved tends to take second place when there are staff shortages in other departments (Macaskill, 1982).

There is also criticism of the content of some courses, for although many have moved away from bathing babies and making layettes and fluffy animals, towards a fuller consideration of the emotional and psychological needs of young children, there is some evidence from young parents that the courses they did in school were largely irrelevant to their needs as parents. A study of the content of CSE child-care syllabi, and a comparison of these syllabi with the anxieties and needs of 150 parents showed that attitudes and feelings caused far more problems than did bottles and nappies. Young mothers felt they needed more information about relationships between the sexes, marriage, reproduction, conception, contraception and birth, and parental – particularly fathers' – roles. The author – a headteacher – concluded that the least important aspects are the most thoroughly taught at the expense of the more important ones (Clark, 1981).

This dichotomy is further reflected in the current debate about assessment, as national criteria are drawn up for the new combined O-level and CSE exam. For not only is the balance between written work and practical work very different between the two exams, but the syllabus of a subject whose objectives include affective and behavioural change, is inevitably being limited and narrowed to what can be examined by tests of factual recall. As one teacher has pointed out, the most valuable elements of her course – such as spontaneous discussion and organising activities for young children – cannot be examined (Barnett, 1981). The arguments for the use of examinations can be summarised thus: examinations help to achieve status as an academic discipline for what is a relatively new and unestablished subject; teachers also gain status; pupils who achieve success find increased self-confidence; employers use examination passes as indicators of capability; examinations and syllabi need not restrict what is taught (Pugh, 1980; Open University, 1981). The arguments against are as follows: effective family life education is about such inherently unexaminable things as developing pupils' attitudes, self-confidence and awareness of life and increasing maturity; the implications of failing parenthood may severely affect a fifteen-year-old; the syllabus *does* in fact constrain the teacher's freedom to develop new topics with their pupils; despite examinations the status remains low. The discussion is complex, and although it might be eased by use of personal pupil-profiles and records of achievement, the current situation leaves many teachers uneasy but uncertain as to what the alternatives might be.

On a more positive note, these courses have provided for many girls a motivation, an interest and self-confidence which other subjects have often failed to do. They also offer young adolescents practical experience with young children and perhaps their first opportunities for taking on adult responsibilities, in their placements in playgroups, nurseries and with childminders. The importance of planning these placements carefully cannot be over-stressed (Dykins, 1981; Montague, 1979). The facilities are, after all, principally intended for the under-fives in their care, and both the nursery staff and the adolescents themselves need to be well-prepared for the visits. This point is brought out in several booklets produced by the Pre-school Playgroups Association (PPA) (for example, Monson, 1983; Scottish PPA, 1976) and by guidelines such as those produced by the ILEA (1979) and Birmingham (1981) and the resource pack *Teenagers in Playgroups* (CSV, 1978). As these courses continue to increase in popularity, finding sufficient nurseries and playgroups may well become a problem and some schools are considering attachment to families. Nearly 16 000 pupils spent some time in playgroups in 1982 (PPA, 1983) and a survey in Hampshire found that 3200 fourth- and fifth-formers (10 per cent of the age group) and 350 sixth-formers spent some time in nursery classes, playgroups etc. Some schools have their own playgroups (see, for example, Orton, 1979) and one school in Kent arranges a week in a residential centre where each fifth-year girl is in charge of an infant-school child for five days (Thomas, 1982). The positive spin-offs of these placements in terms of increased understanding and maturity are considerable; as one deputy head said of her pupils' placement in a nursery where over the year they ran a party, a puppet show and a sports day:

> The main success of all these ventures is that the consumers of the girls' efforts, the little children, are not critical but spontaneously and delightfully appreciative. This is much more effective than any praise teachers can give them. Particularly valuable is their experience of the joy and fulfilment as well as the responsibility and hard work involved in parenting. (Barnett, 1981)

As one pupil in the Aston study remarked, 'I think it's something everybody ought to know – how to look after children before you have them'.

It is also worth noting that not all child-care courses are examined, and some are attracting boys. A survey by the British Federation of University Women of the extent of preparation for parenthood available in secondary schools, found that 68 per cent of the 151 schools in their sample offered courses and that these were taken by 39 per cent of all girls and 9.6 per cent of all boys. Just under half of these pupils were taking child-development courses, 19 per cent of which were *not* examined (Rubinstein, 1979). The involvement of boys in child-development courses seems more likely when the subject is offered as a non-examinable part of the core curriculum rather than as an option, and when male teachers as well as female teach it. The *Understanding Children* course devised by the Renfrew Child Guidance Service for use in schools is a case in point (Strathclyde, 1978). Teachers of child-care and development courses have pioneered a lonely and sometimes difficult trail in introducing such courses into their schools. But, as one of the few male teachers in the field has recently said, the fact that these courses have been accorded the status of fringe medicine is due:

> in no small part to home-economics teachers who may be guilty of perpetuating this down-market image by default . . . They need to emerge from their specialist rooms to get a picture of the whole school policy . . . to come out from behind the governors' teas and to take their rightful place as decision-makers and innovators in the forefront of developments in parentcraft education in the 1980s. (Troth, 1982)

Personal and social education. The complexities of attempting to unravel on a national basis how schools plan their curriculum are well-illustrated by this second group of subjects. Of the 62 authorities providing information on which subject areas they saw as relevant, 21 stated that preparation for parenthood formed part of their health education programme for all pupils, while links between preparation for parenthood and personal and social education such as education for personal relationships and timetabled tutorial periods were reported by 27 authorities. Whereas child care and development has parent education as a primary aim and reaches a small number of pupils, these broader subject areas have it as a secondary aim, are usually compulsory and therefore reach all pupils. They are almost never examined. Although there is considerable overlapping of these subject areas, our impression is that individual schools tend to place most emphasis on one or other approach, perhaps because they were initially involved in a national curriculum project. The Aston project, for example, found in their five local authorities specific patterns emerging across whole authorities, such as tutorial work in Lancashire, which has always had a tradition for such work. Thus, while recognising the intricate interrelationship of these subject areas, an attempt will be made to determine what each might contribute to family life education.

During the early 1960s it was becoming evident that the needs of many young people were not being adequately met by traditional school subjects. This problem became even more acute when the school-leaving age was raised to sixteen in 1972–3, and a number of curriculum development projects were initiated to try to meet this need. Amongst the most notable were the Schools Council's Humanities Curriculum Project which took as its starting point some ambitious ideas in the mid-1960s. It defined the humanities as the study of human issues which were of universal concern within society to pupils, teachers and parents alike, but which were inherently controversial – for example, the roles of men and women, divorce, abortion, war and pacifism, the right to work etc. These are all areas of experience which encourage disagreement and individual judgement and as such the mode of enquiry was to be discussion rather than instruction, with the teacher taking responsibility for not promoting his own view (Schools Council, 1970).

This concern with the social role of schools, and their contribution to children's personal development and relationships, was reflected in other parallel developments, such as the Schools Council projects in Moral Education, Social Education and Careers Education, the growth of education for personal relationships work in Gloucestershire, the establishment in 1968 of the Health Education Council and work in health education (discussed later). The growth of pastoral care and counselling systems in schools has also helped to foster the personal development of pupils, and the survey of secondary education by HM Inspectorate (DES, 1979) found that the best programmes closely linked personal and social education with the pastoral system of the school. Personal and social education has many facets, and a detailed examination of any of them are beyond our remit here, but the report of a recent Schools Council working party usefully pulls together some of the main threads (David, K. 1982). They define their terms broadly:

> Personal and social education includes the teaching and informal activities which are planned to enhance the development of knowledge, understanding, attitudes and behaviour concerned with oneself and others; social institutions, structures and organisations; and social and moral issues.

This umbrella definition will involve a number of subject areas – for example, careers, moral, religious, health, political and social education – and a range of skills. As the report points out, the choice of skills and attitudes requires value judgements, and this puts teachers in a difficult position. For the teacher's responsibility must be to help pupils to acknowledge, test and qualify their own value position and to relate it to the values of society, and for the teacher this often means facing a contradiction between his or her own values, those of the school and those of the pupils and their parents.

The organisation of personal and social education and those components of it particularly relevant to family life education vary from school to school. Some examples are given in the Schools Council report; a few schools have a faculty for personal and social education incorporating health, personal relationships, the family, the community, the world of work and academic and career choices; a few local authorities have produced guidelines or schemes of work for their schools (Wiltshire, 1978; Somerset, 1980); some focus on tutorial work within the pastoral system (discussed later). In a detailed study of five schools the Aston project distinguished between child-care courses and health and social education courses in that the latter focus on the feelings and behaviour of the individual pupil rather than on those of babies and young children. (Grafton *et al.*, 1982a)

Education for personal relationships, pastoral and tutorial work. The approaches used here are again as various as the schools using them, and in many schools will be subsumed within personal and social education. There have however, been a number of interesting developments in recent years. One of these is work on education for personal relationships, the first schemes being pioneered in Gloucestershire and Wiltshire in the early 1960s. This approach was developed further in Lancashire and a scheme was devised whereby the preparation of pupils for family life was seen as a co-ordinated approach involving the tutorial and counselling staff of the school as well as class teachers (David and Cowley, 1980). The nature of this work and its focus on small-group discussion necessitated in Lancashire, as it had in Gloucestershire and Wiltshire, a parallel in-service training programme. Elsewhere, the pastoral care of pupils, particularly as schools have become larger, has begun to assume greater importance. Indeed the HMI secondary education survey concluded that schools now place considerable emphasis on pastoral care and 'much would be gained if equal emphasis was placed on learning in the classroom and the teaching of an appropriate curriculum' (DES, 1979).

Recent developments owe much to the structured and developmental models of group work with adolescents evolved by Douglas Hamlin and Leslie Button at Swansea University in association with teachers, youth workers and social workers (Button, 1974). The main strategy has been to help local education authorities create their own training teams, and to support this work Button has published a programme for form-tutors to use in pastoral time with groups where 'young people can learn how to help one another in their personal development and in their ability to cope with present day society' (Button, 1981, 82).

Active tutorial work, a structured approach to helping young people in their personal growth and development, marries the techniques of developmental group work to the content of pastoral work. A five-year programme of tutorial work is now published in a series of teachers' guides (Baldwin and Wells, 1981). The content of this programme is of course very much broader than that of family life education and discussion of related topics could be omitted from the course. The Aston project for example, found that although the fifth-year book includes as a formal objective 'to anticipate and examine the role and responsibilities of family life; and to develop a concept of sexual relationships as a caring, responsible human relationship, rather than a purely physical act', none of the tutors said that this was an aspect of their work because they preferred to focus on such practicalities as leaving home, getting a job, joining a trade union etc. (Grafton *et al.*, 1982a). An extensive programme of training and support for teachers wanting to use this approach has been an integral part of the project's work.

A final approach which is being used in an increasing number of schools and colleges of further education is Life Skills Teaching, based on the Counselling and Careers Development Unit of Leeds University. Life Skills is based on the belief that teachers can help the personal development of their students by teaching specific personal and interpersonal skills which will promote self-management and individual competence and equip students to cope with their life roles and tasks (Hopson and Scally, 1980, 1981). Included in their courses are such skills as communicating effectively; making, maintaining and ending relationships; coping with stress; and being positive about oneself. Scally is currently developing these programmes for use in health education, and for use in the youth service. This project too is providing courses for teachers working with groups in the classroom, an important service for teachers who have little experience of discussing sensitive and often controversial issues with small groups of pupils.

Health education. The current upsurge of interest in health education began in the early 1970s when the newly-formed Health Education Council joined with the Schools Council in setting up a working party to look at health education in secondary schools. *Health Education in Secondary Schools* (Schools Council, 1976) defines health education as 'the totality of experience from which individuals learn behaviours related to their health'. It has had far-reaching effects, recommending as it did that each school should draw up an overall policy for health and social education, co-ordinated by a senior member of staff. A broadly defined core course was seen as central to the policy, but major contributions would be required from the specialist subjects. Further spin-offs were the establishment of the Schools Council Health Education Project (SCHEP) 5–13 (already discussed) and a subsequent project for the years 13–18. SCHEP 13–18 aimed to give young people a basic health knowledge and an understanding of human development; help them to adapt to change in themselves and their environment; help them to explore and understand the feelings, values and attitudes of themselves and others, and help them determine where they have control over their health and where by conscious choices they can determine their future life styles. It has been concerned to do two main things – to identify and clarify ways in which health education can be organised and developed in the curriculum; and to develop support material for use in dissemination and in-service education. These materials were published last year (Schools Council, 1982).

This emphasis on clarification and co-ordination was clearly seen in replies to our questionnaire. Several authorities had compiled guidelines on health education (for example, Cumbria, Devon, Nottingham, Somerset) and Calderdale had had a health education policy in operation since 1977. A recent estimate suggests that between 25 and 50 per cent of all secondary schools now have a member of staff responsible for health education, often a deputy head or head of department (Brierley, 1982). One report of attempts to co-ordinate health education work in Nottinghamshire following the SCHEP 13–18 project, points to the need for these co-ordinators to be senior members of staff within the school, as their status and influence on curriculum and timetabling decisions is crucial (McCafferty, 1982). This same report also points to the lack of any real training and support for teachers – simply providing new materials does not result in adequate discussion-based teaching, a point supported by the Aston project which found that none of the health education teachers believed their professional training has been specifically relevant to this aspect of their teaching (Grafton *et al.*, 1982a).

Other subjects. Some 25 authorities in reply to our questionnaire said that *home economics* was an important site for preparation for parenthood. On the whole, subjects were fairly practical, and based on skills related to running a home and preparing food. In some authorities all the teachers on child-care courses were from home economics departments, although most teachers who taught both were careful to distinguish their approach and intentions (Grafton *et al.*, 1982a). Subjects within this area were mostly optional and were taken almost exclusively by girls. Some 20 authorities mentioned *social studies* as having relevance to parent education, eleven mentioned *religious education* and ten *biology*. The more detailed study of five schools undertaken by the Aston project showed an 'unexpected amount of parenthood-focussed teaching appeared to be in progress' in English, where in one school it was described as 'permeating the syllabus' (Grafton *et al.*, 1982a). Most teachers found parenthood, family life and personal relationships a rich source of material, and one who taught English and child development found she had more freedom in English to develop discussion from the current interests of her pupils rather than ticking off topics on a syllabus. A male colleague hoped to combat negative media pressures concerning marriage, parenthood and sexuality: 'Try to get them to realise that there is more to life than getting a fellow – that work is more important than the magazine would suggest – and that the family isn't tangential' (Grafton *et al.*, 1982a). Drama sessions and the use of role-play can also make a useful contribution to the development of decision-making and problem-solving skills.

People and resources

Despite the fact that school forms only a small part of the social and physical environment in which young people are growing up, there is little evidence that teachers have consulted parents about courses in family life education. No respondents to our questionnaire replied very positively about their work with parents, although it is the practice of many schools at least to inform parents that such courses are about to start. It is particularly important to involve parents in multi-cultural areas and areas where child-rearing and family patterns may be different from those of the majority of teachers. It is not always easy, but there have been a few imaginative projects such as those run in association with the National Marriage Guidance Council in Luton and in Dudley, where parents and teachers have worked together on courses on personal and sexual relationships.

Accurate information on the extent to which young people talk to their parents about sexual matters, contraception, family life and so on, or how parents view their own role *vis-à-vis* the school is hard to find. One recent study of how young people learn about sex and birth control found that although friends were the most common source of information, parents and teachers were consulted more than they had been in a study twelve years earlier (Farrell, 1978). More than half the parents and the youngsters said that school was the best place to learn, although as many as 72 per cent of parents had no idea whether or not their children had received sex education. The Bureau's National Child Development Study asked their 14 000 youngsters what were their main sources of information outside the school and, in line with other research, it was found that girls cited their parents for all topics apart from information on VD, and boys cited their parents only on the care of babies and family problems (Lambert, 1977). The peer group and the media continue to be major influences and primary sources of information, even if they are somewhat garbled and inaccurate in the first instance and over-glamorous and unrealistic in the second.

The teaching background of those involved in family life education varies considerably. Those coming from a home economics–child care background are very largely women, whilst those in other subject areas are fairly evenly divided between men and women. The personal qualities of the teacher involved may be of more importance than either their subject background or their sex, and it is certainly important that the teachers who do undertake work in this area should do so willingly, and be able to opt out if they so wish. Whitfield (1980) has suggested that it is an advantage to have first-hand experience of young children.

As with much else in the school curriculum, if these approaches to parent education are to succeed they must have the support of the head teacher (see McCafferty, 1982; Open University, 1981b). Many of the approaches identified, particularly those in social, personal and health education, require the careful orchestration of members of several different departments into one team. They will require the appointment of a member of staff to co-ordinate the course; flexibility in timetabling, time for planning and support and policy decisions which may cut across all the subject departments in the school. It may also be necessary to rework the timetable so that a period of time is available to all youngsters in any one year (see Baxter, 1981) or so that those doing a child-care option can spend the appropriate length of time on their study of young children.

Family-based courses seem to be particularly appropriate as a means of linking with other agencies and individuals in the community, and 57 of the LEAs which responded to our questionnaire reported such links, some bringing people into the school, others taking pupils out into community. Health authorities were frequently cited in this respect, both for the support given to schools by health education officers and for the involvement of health visitors and school nurses in schools. Letters received from the Health Visitors Association and Scottish Health Visitors Association in response to an earlier survey (Pugh, 1980) show that many health visitors see work in secondary schools as an integral part of their brief and several have been closely involved in developing and teaching courses in schools (Hiskins, 1976).

Schools placing pupils in playgroups and nurseries reported links with a number of voluntary organisations such as the Pre-school Playgroups Association. Some family groups, such as Scope in Hampshire, have linked up with child-development sources in local schools (Poulton, 1982). Community education projects in Coventry and Liverpool provide opportunities for mothers to join school pupils doing the CSE child-development courses. The National Childbirth Trust has extended its work in relation to school and members in a number of branches now offer to go into school with their babies and share with the pupils some of their experience of childbirth and life with young children. Many marriage guidance counsellors are also involved in their local schools, and a number of experimental projects have been established within a rather more structured framework. These and many others – the Family Planning Association, NSPCC, Spastics Society, police and probation service, youth and community workers, TACADE, Royal Society for the Prevention of Accidents, among them – are involved in family life education programmes in schools. Whilst these organisations are clearly playing a useful role, care needs to be taken with the use of outside speakers. They should be carefully chosen and well-briefed, and their talks should be part of a well-thought-out course, with opportunities for preparation beforehand and feedback and discussion afterwards.

Limited space prevents a listing of the many teaching resources available. Details of some of the bibliographies and major sources of information are given in Appendix 3.

Training and support for teachers

Initial and in-service training for teachers involved in family life education is particularly important, and yet the evidence suggests that this is far from adequate. As a new area of the curriculum without the advantages of academic tradition stretching back into the annals of teacher training history, no teacher embarking on work in this field will come to the classroom with the security of a body of knowledge that, for example, a mathematician or an historian will have. One has only to look at the range of disciplines which have a part to play to realise the breadth of the problem. For those who are teaching child development rather than contributing to a broad course from their own subject background, the need for this missing body of knowledge is particularly acute. None of the child development teachers in the Aston study of five secondary schools felt that their initial training had been relevant to the child and family aspect of their work, although few felt that they needed any, seeing their experience as parents being more relevant than academic knowledge or specialist training (Grafton *et al.*, 1982a). Two-thirds of the teachers in a further study had had no relevant training, and most said they did not feel equipped to teach the subject in all its aspects (Orton, 1982).

Two things make this problem particularly intractable. One is the sensitive and controversial nature of the subject area itself which, as the Aston researchers remark:

> raises for teachers dilemmas not found elsewhere in the curriculum. Involved are issues about which there appears to be little consensus in contemporary society, with the attendant problem for teachers of the legitimacy of alternative value positions. (Grafton *et al.*, 1982b)

The second is the fact that family life education involves considerably more than acquiring and attempting to put across to young people a body of knowledge. It requires teachers to assume skills and techniques in working with groups that are perhaps more commonly associated with youth work or counselling than with teaching of a more traditional nature. It may well involve teachers in working with a team of colleagues drawn from very different backgrounds and will often necessitate a fundamental rethinking of the nature of authority within a school and of the relationship between staff and pupils. After close involvement over several years in the very thorough programmes of SCHEP and active tutorial work (ATW), McCafferty writes:

I have become aware of just how little real training and support is given to teachers who embark on this type of work. Most of the training concerned with methods stops short of giving teachers firsthand experience of working in what, to many, is quite an alien way. In ATW teachers only seem really at ease when trying ideas that they themselves have experienced. (McCafferty, 1982)

If these are the issues, how much training is available? In response to our questionnaire, 46 local authorities described a variety of training schemes or regional support groups. The majority of these were in specific subjects, particularly child care, health education and social and personal education. They varied considerably in length and in depth, from one-day events to longer courses mounted by local colleges, sometimes as part of a DES regional in-service training programme. Many of these inevitably concentrated on their own particular subject specialism, rather than looking more broadly at family life education across the curriculum. The DES has been running a national one-week training course on education for family life since the mid-1970s, and a number of curriculum development projects offer local authorities training programmes. Some authorities joined with health authorities to run such courses. Others have worked with bodies such as TACADE (Teachers Advisory Council on Alcohol and Drugs Education), which has devised a three-part strategy of in-service work to help teachers look at the organisation of health, social and personal education in the curriculum. Other authorities, such as Lancashire, Gloucestershire and Wiltshire, have a tradition of in-service training in counselling and education for personal relationships.

Since the circulation of our questionnaire, the Open University has published its course *Education for Family Life* (1981b). The preliminary feasibility study for the course showed the high incidence of didactic teaching in this area, the need for activity-based materials and more information, and teachers' unhappiness about informal teaching methods (Cowley and Daniels, 1981). These points have been taken into account in the course, although the materials development phase has only recently started (1983). *Education for Family Life* is concerned to do two main things: it aims to help teachers assess the need for family life education in their own schools, by co-ordinating and capitalising on what is being done already. Curriculum planning is based on observation of classroom practice, the needs of pupils and the expressed wishes of parents, and there are some interesting case studies of how different schools have worked towards this co-ordinated approach in different ways. Second, it aims to provide support for teachers working in this area, an aim that will be more fully realised with the publication of some teaching materials. Two teaching packs are in preparation, due for publication in 1985, one looking at roles and life-styles, the other at childhood. Despite this useful additional resource, training in the field of family life education is very far from adequate and is in no way keeping pace with the growth in courses for pupils.

Summary

This chapter has traced the gradual emergence of family life education from the early days of mothercraft teaching to a point where some schools are beginning to take a more coherent approach to the social and emotional development of their pupils. Young people clearly want and can enjoy such courses, but the extent of provision is still patchy. Whilst there are pockets of development in some parts of the country, and there is certainly a considerable increase in the amount of activity as compared with that even ten years ago, there is little sign of a policy on family life education at either national government or local authority level. Such family life education as does exist tends to be implicit in much of what a school is doing and in a quiet way pervades the whole curriculum.

Where family life education is the main aim of a course this tends to be an optional child-care and development course, often with rather low status within the school. It is taken almost entirely by girls, usually less able girls, and most of the teachers are women. Thus a subject intended to improve family relations is actually tending to reinforce traditional gender stereotypes. The subject is also usually examined, an issue which has raised considerable controversy. It may well give it status, but it has presented problems to those who feel that effective family life education is about such inherently unexaminable things as developing pupils' attitudes, self-confidence and awareness of life. One of the main advantages of the course is seen to be the opportunities it provides for pupils to work with and observe young children in playgroups and nurseries.

It is also often seen to be a secondary aim of broad-based programmes in personal, social or health education, which are likely to be available to all pupils as part of the core curriculum and as such are seldom examined. Subjects in these areas are concerned principally with pupils' personal development and their relationships and as such teachers tend to use a variety of teaching methods, including small-group discussion and role play.

A major problem in family life education is the lack of adequate initial or in-service training opportunities. Not only do few teachers have the benefit of relevant knowledge acquired during initial training; but there are few courses available to help them develop skills in using different teaching methods, or to encourage the examination of attitudes, values and feelings in respect of family life. This is particularly important in a subject area which is inherently controversial and where the personal views of the teacher may conflict with those of the school, the children and their parents.

4
Young People out of School

Introduction

The previous chapter has documented the rapid development in schools of materials and curricula related to family life education, health education and personal relationships. Some young people may have been lucky enough to take part in such tutorial groups or social education courses but not all schools provide these opportunities and not all children take advantage of them.

The peer group is a powerful influence during the teenage years as young people seek to define their own identity as separate from their family. Relationships or friendships formed both in and out of school may lead to marriage or parenthood, or may introduce youngsters to a set of values and attitudes different from parents and family. Economic, legal and social changes have eroded many of the past sanctions related to sexual experimentation, as well as many of the opportunities and expectations for future careers or life plans. Yet the pursuit of personal and sexual fulfilment is still promulgated by the media. The current generation of young people – the baby boom from the sixties – is faced with a significantly different situation to that experienced by their parents and teachers during their adolescence. Two out of three young people currently face a future without any real prospect of paid employment. One out of every two will receive little or no further education or training after leaving school beyond the Youth Training Scheme. In the light of such facts, it is understandable that there has been a pre-occupation with job creation, training schemes, employment and community initiatives. Yet the government departments, the youth service, adult and further education and the new youth training schemes, seem to have virtually ignored the one 'full-time job' which the majority of young people will undertake – parenthood.

There are no separate statutory services for young people and there is no co-ordination of services or comprehensive provision for youth. The period of young adulthood is often seen merely as a short transitory phase from one family to another. The young person moves from being a child in his family of origin to being an adult in his marriage and family of procreation, and the point at which he officially ceases to be a child and becomes an adult is complex and ambiguous.

The youth service and social education

Provision in the youth service over the last three decades has been described as a 'preoccupation with "the club" in the 1950s and with the "unclubbables" in the early 1960s, spreading to a wider concern with the "unattached" in the late 1960s and with community action and the "disadvantaged" in the 1970s' (Eggleston, 1976). To this may be added the 'unemployed' in the 1980s. Throughout this period the provision for young people has been the subject of numerous government reviews, reports, and working parties which are beyond the scope of this chapter. These reports chart the reactive development: the Crowther Report with a consideration of the needs of young people (15–19 years old) in the light of changing social and industrial needs (CACE, 1959); anxiety as to how best to cope with the youth 'bulge' of 14–20-year-olds (Ministry of Health, 1960); concern over the lack of multi-racial integration in the Hunt Report (YSDC, 1969); the Latey Committee made a recommendation for the lowering of the age of marriage to 16 and a complementary need for education for personal relationships and family life (Lord Chancellor's Office, 1967). The Milson-Fairbairn Report (YSDC, 1969) formally stated that the primary goal of youth work was social education; the Skeet Youth and Community Bill (House of Commons, 1979) also listed social education as a main aim (this Bill failed to win the support of the government); and more recently, the Thompson Report (DES, 1982) recommended that social education be available to all young people up to the age of 21 years.

There are few explicit social education programmes within the youth service but it is possible to offer opportunities which both inform and provide a range of appropriate experiences including discussion groups. Social education can enable young people to develop the necessary skills, awareness and understanding to help them make balanced and responsible decisions about their own lives, including parenthood. Social education is about key areas of adolescent development: adjusting to puberty and sexuality, including responsibilities connected with sexual activity; developing a widening range of social skills and competence; relating to peer group and parents; developing emotional maturity and independence, self-knowledge and self-esteem and examining values and norms of behaviour; achieving intellectual potential; increasing awareness of adolescent and adult needs and development, particularly in relation to their own parents and family; considering the relationships between work, home and family; being with young children and discovering what is involved in being a parent; using leisure time, unemployment and enforced leisure constructively and competently.

Informal youth service provision

The lack of a national youth policy makes it difficult both to determine the actual aims and approaches of social education and the potential for further development. In some parts of the country attempts have been made to bring together the many initiatives in social education to provide a 'family' service, in which the needs and services for young people could be seen in the fullest possible context – preparing for adult life and for family life – and not in isolation. In Oxfordshire for example, co-ordination with the different departments of community education, health education and adult education, was achieved with enormous difficulty and, like so many other initiatives depends for its continuation on the key personnel remaining in post (Collins, 1982).

The youth service is commonly understood to embrace the many and varied systems of clubs, centres, recreational facilities and other services provided for young people by local authorities, voluntary and religious organisations. Youth clubs and youth centres in practice are often a partnership between voluntary and statutory sectors. Provisions can range from one-night-a-week church clubs, uniformed organisations or single activity groups (like football coaching) to purpose-built premises with full-time leaders, open each day and every evening. The majority are small groups of young people with autonomous voluntary leaders meeting in church halls, community buildings on estates, school halls or family centres. A number of local education authorities use the title 'Youth and Community Service' to indicate their links with other related services.

Whatever its form, the youth service is concerned with creating opportunities in which different programmes, projects and groups can be provided for young people. One of the purposes of such groups will be to examine and discuss issues related to being a person – as adult, worker, parent and citizen. Many of the programmes and courses outlined in the previous chapter provide readily available material for youth workers and may be more acceptable to some young people outside the confines of the school curriculum. This context of informal settings and natural groups which young people have chosen to attend is conducive to both individual and group approaches and, in particular, can encourage an emphasis on the importance of self-directed behaviour; a positive and significant role for the peer group; and active participation of young people in the planning and provision of activities.

In the more structured settings and context of uniformed organisations there is an assumption that their general method and approach is designed to encourage reliability and responsibility. There are plenty of opportunities for learning in small groups and experiencing the 'give and take' and care and consideration for others, which is seen as important training for future family life. In addition, individual organisations arrange specific opportunities, for example house-orderly badges for cubs and scouts, badges and certificates in home-making, child care and child nursing for brownies and guides; and Design for Living in the Duke of Edinburgh Award scheme.

Many of the youth workers in youth clubs and centres have had specific training in adolescent work, counselling skills, trust games, role play and self-exploration. Few, however, seem prepared to use these skills and the informality of their relationships with young people explicitly to provide family life education or education about parenthood, despite the fact that many young people express interest in learning more about family problems and issues, and child care and child development. Family life with teenagers, married life and young parenthood were found to be the major areas of special value for a group of young people taking part in an out-of-school Family Life project set up by the National Marriage Guidance Council (Proctor, 1983) and a third of the Bureau's NCDS sample when interviewed at 23 years old, said they would have liked some form of preparation for parenthood. Those youth leaders who have found the time to draw up a series of regular group discussions have found not only that it is appropriate and acceptable to many young people, but offers an important opportunity for them to explore previously unexpressed doubts and anxieties. For example, Gillingham Youth Centre has run a series of evening meetings entitled 'Focus on Life' specifically aimed at giving young people enough information to discuss issues that were important to them and enable them to make realistic choices and appropriate decisions about health, sex, personal relationships and parenthood. Similarly the Axe Dale District Youth Office promotes course material on 'Preparing for Adulthood' which can be used in small groups either in schools or youth clubs, to develop an awareness of the responsibilities of marriage, parenthood and family life.

The recent development of girls' groups and a 'girls' night' also lends itself to such opportunities, although one would hope that some discussions would include boys as well. The Gloucester Association for Family Life has recently started a course on child care in which each girl is 'attached' to a family with a young child. This is a practical example of how young people can be given opportunities to become involved in the daily life of a child – visiting the clinic, the playgroup and organising meals. The Fulham Girls Project found that while the girls were not very interested in preparing a leaflet on contraception, topics such as self-image, sexuality, health and 'problem page' questions could be discussed openly and sensitively. The Southdown Project in Bath has also initiated a girls' weekly discussion group with the programme planned by the girls, mainly aged 14 to 16 years. Boys and personal relationships are always favourites, but as confidence grows within the group they are able to express fears and anxieties related to adult and family life, child care and child development and particularly of being the parent of a handicapped child.

Social education for the young is not limited to the youth service. There are many other organisations which can contribute training, resources, ideas and speakers, particularly in the areas of family life education. The Family Planning Association, for example, does not offer a direct provision for young people but over the last eight years over 1200 youth workers have taken part in its sex education and personal relationship courses. An introductory leaflet which some group leaders have found helpful is published by the London Voluntary Service Council – *Young and Healthy*. This outlines a programme for discussions, role play, questionnaires and group counselling, ranging from the problems of adolescence, through marriage and parenthood, to relationships within the family, at work and with other people in the community. Life-skills teaching, which began in schools and colleges of further education, is now being adapted for use in the youth service, and the Open University are developing packs derived from the *Parents and Teenagers* course for use in groups which will be particularly valuable for youth workers.

Young people often go to youth clubs and projects to get away from adults and their own family. Home life and family relationships are particularly susceptible to external pressures such as unemployment and redundancy, and to changes in routine when mothers start going out to work or elderly relatives come to stay. Rising divorce and remarriage rates mean that increasingly young people are being brought up by someone who is not their natural parent and tensions and disagreements over day-to-day incidents may be exacerbated. Some young people may find it easier to talk in a group with their peers than to discuss problems with their family. The opportunity to share doubts, anxieties and experiences, and particularly to consider what it must be like living with and disciplining someone else's teenager, provides a useful exercise in self-awareness and may lead to a greater understanding of what it is like to be a parent.

This whole area of mutual aid is crying out for youth workers' attention. The tendency has been to concentrate on direct intervention with the person who has the 'problem' rather than to work with intermediaries (Smith, M., 1980).

In addition to the opportunities already mentioned there are also approximately sixty *youth counselling and advisory services* offering support, befriending, advice and information. Many describe their work as falling into two parts: centre-based and outreach work. Detached youth workers, such as the Kendal Area Detached Youth

Worker Project, aim to work with young persons 'at risk' on the street, in coffee bars or pubs – the 'non-joiners' – to find out the problems they face and to help overcome them before they drift into trouble. The centre-based work is greatly influenced by the facilities. This may combine a drop-in approach, with a specialist counselling service, over the telephone or by appointment, as well as general information and discussion sessions in youth clubs and centres as in New Grapevine in Islington and Camden. Where there are drop-in facilities with a coffe bar, or lunch clubs for unemployed teenagers, there is a greater potential for informal discussion groups and the development of particular groups and supportive networks.

Teenage Information Network in Southwark puts particular emphasis on the local network by providing an accessible drop-in centre which is creating its own 'usable information bank'. Off-Centre in Hackney, situated in a large house is able to offer a warm informal atmosphere in its big kitchen basement as well as support through its drop-in and appointment service. Specific issues related to employment, young people coming out of care, solvency abuse, pregnancy and single parenthood, and the particular problems facing West Indian and Asian young people, can be discussed both in individual sessions and as a group. Many of the agencies develop particular expertise and interests because of links with other services, for example, the London Youth Advisory Centre works closely with the University College Hospital Drug Clinic. Others aim to fill gaps in current provisions, for example, the Brook Advisory Centre offers an additional service on birth control and sexual help to disabled people.

The youth service is in an ideal postion to extend the notion of social education. Young people have *chosen* to gather as a group and attendance is not compulsory as it is in schools. Youth workers *do have* the necessary training and experience in group work, and *there are* materials and resources to draw upon. Very few schemes and services however actually provide any form of family life education or education about parenthood. The responses of many people working in such settings indicate that they would not feel it appropriate to provide structured 'labelled' discussion groups since these are often perceived as a prescriptive exercise rather than as offering young people an opportunity to explore the choices available to them. This is ironic, since parenthood is probably one of the few areas in which young people do have an opportunity to exercise choice: on whether or not to become a parent and on how to use their time, skills and abilities in creating a positive environment for any children they choose to have.

Many of the skills of parenting, as we have seen, are based on social skills which relate to seeking advice, making decisions, using community resources, negotiating, setting boundaries and communicating clearly. Young people are at a crucial stage where the development of such skills may determine their successful transition to adult life and for many it will come all too soon. 20 per cent of men and well over 33 per cent of women marry at 21 or younger, and yet the youth service which aims to cater for all 14–21-year-olds provides very few opportunities for them to prepare for marriage or for their role as parent, which may be the only permanent job they ever get.

Preparation for working and adult life : the Youth Training Scheme

The Youth Opportunities Programme (YOP) officially ended in 1983 and the replacement Youth Training Scheme (YTS) started nationally in the same year. One million jobless young people took part in YOP during its five years and one of its aims was to increase their self-development and personal growth through health education and social and life skills (SLS). YTS was planned to be available to all 16-year-olds who had neither a job nor an educational place. Clearly with such large numbers taking part annually in such a scheme it is appropriate to ask whether some form of family life education should be offered as part of the general studies or social education of these young people.

First, are there lessons to be learned from the YOP schemes? There seem to be three important areas to look at: (i) who comes on the scheme, (ii) what form of social education is provided and (iii) who provides it? The YTS is designed to be available for all those not already engaged in further education or work. A report from the Further Education Unit (Miller *et al.*, 1983) states that many of these young people lack stable family support and suffer social problems which might affect their behaviour and motivation. It recommends offering help on a wide range of issues, from education and training to family and personal problems. In terms of the social education offered, this was commonly described as social and life skills and covered an average of twelve topics per course. One study which looked at these topics discovered that all the courses they observed offered 'job-getting' skills, like writing letters and claiming unemployment benefit, but topics such as coping with adult life seemed to centre on relations with the police, housing and the use of public transport. Few of the areas that might be relevant to family life were offered at all and both sex education and leisure activities played a minor role and were offered very infrequently (Greaves *et al.*, 1982). Few colleges of further education have had any experience in catering for less-able 16-year-olds, few appear to have any knowledge of the new curricula, materials or style of the SLS approach and little attempt has been made to involve youth and community workers, many of whom do have some experience of the life skills techniques and certainly have training in group work (Coombe Lodge, 1983).

Is there a place then for parent education or for family life education in the social education provision? To provide a social education programme relevant to the different needs of individuals within this age group is fraught with problems, but given the number of young people involved it is a good opportunity and an important one. Many young people are sexually active, and for some parenthood and family life may soon become a reality: each year there are approximately 60 000 births to girls between 16 and 19 years and over 33 000 legal abortions (OPCS, 1982).

One area in which interesting developments are taking place is where YOP placements were provided within community projects or centres, and there was a natural development of courses on parent education and child care, linking the on-the-job and off-the-job training. In Skelton for example, a course on Education for Living is offered in the Health Centre where the boys and girls help out in the baby clinic as well as learning about family planning, baby care and personal relationships. At the National Children's Centre in Huddersfield over 100 boys and girls annually attended courses on child care through YOP. The world of future parenthood was incorporated into the life and social skills element of their training and complemented the day-to-day child-care and child-development aspects relevant to their placements in the infant or nursery schools, or within the centre itself. Many family centres, health centres and playgroups have also provided opportunities for boys and girls to experience being with and being responsible for young children, and for meeting, observing and talking to parents, many of whom may be only a few years older than the YOP trainees.

A survey in Cleveland (Lilley, 1982) attempted to discover whether girls not working with children as part of their YOP scheme had been offered any child-care or parentcraft teaching as part of the life and social skills training component. Out of 104 of the girls, 25 had received some teaching, varying from three who had a single one-hour session to one girl who had three hours per week for three months. Health education officers in Northumberland have offered informal discussion sessions, entitled 'Chance or Choice', to small groups of girls working as school assistants on YOP, looking at individual choices in marriage and parenting. This has been followed by a parentcraft course with a more structured format in six whole-day sessions, in which thoughtful planning combined the personal and vocational elements.

Clearly there are committed individuals who believe it is important to offer young people opportunities for discussion, to develop the knowledge and skills to make their own decisions and choice about marriage and parenthood. The additional knowledge they acquire on child care and child development will stand them in good stead when they do become parents.

Formal educational settings

There are approximately 600 colleges of further education in the United Kingdom offering a variety of full-time, part-time and day release courses. Many of the day release courses have provided opportunities for off-the-job training in life and social skills for YOP trainees and this development will increase with the new YTS. Opportunities for studying courses more specifically related to family life and parenting are also available to students who may choose to study part-time while they work or who enrol for full-time vocational, preparation or foundation courses.

The concern here is with the many young people who are attending further education colleges and the opportunity that this presents for providing a core curriculum on family life education as part of the social education of both young men and women. Although some young men do enrol for the courses mentioned later, they are few and far between and often transfer to other courses or drop out when they find being the only one in a group of twenty-eight females too much!

Just as many community schools are beginning to open their fifth- and sixth-form classes to adults, it may be appropriate for further education colleges to create mixed sessions. Courses in family life education, child care, community care and home management are particularly appropriate for shared discussion between young and older students. Bringing young people into contact with 'practitioners' of family life and parenthood provides an excellent grounding in parenting skills for prospective mothers and fathers, as well as training young people for jobs in day and residential nurseries and preparing them for careers in a wide variety of social, community and health agencies.

TABLE 4.1 *Courses provided in colleges of further education relevant to parent education*

Departments	Subject Areas	Students
Child study and community services	Psychology	Nursery nurses
Home economics and community welfare	Sociology	Childminders
	Education	Foster parents
Home economics and health	Social welfare	Home-helps
Nursing and social welfare studies	Nursing	Playgroup
Child study and community care	SLS (Social and	leaders
Social studies	Life Skills)	Health visitors
Creative and domestic education		Voluntary workers
		Day care workers
		Residential care workers

Table 4.1 shows the number of courses in colleges of further education relevant to parent education. There is a profusion of validating bodies and a lack of comparability of the various certificates and diplomas, some awarded by national bodies, some regional and some by the individual colleges. The numbers enrolled on any one of these courses are often small, with an average of twenty students in a group on any one course. However, certain colleges

tend to concentrate their resources on particular areas of training and this encourages a greater application and provision of places. This is particularly true of the NNEB Nursery Nursing courses which may have anywhere from 50 to 250 students attending any one college at a time.

Other education opportunities

There are obviously many informal settings where workers other than youth and community workers and further education lecturers create opportunities for individual counselling and advice or informal discussion groups. Two examples have been highlighted because the 'captive' nature of the audience, and the fact that they represent groups of young people who tend to marry young and have children early, make the introduction of family life education particularly relevant. Community homes, mother and baby homes, long-stay youth hostels, young people in the armed forces and other similar settings where young people are living away from home, also offer opportunities for informal discussion groups and the development of personal skills.

Intermediate treatment (IT)

The majority of IT groups appear to have been mainly male activity-based programmes combined with intensive work designed to change the behaviour of young people which has led them into criminal activities. In the past girls seem to have been excluded, mainly because there were so few that they did not even warrant mixed groups. All-girl groups have now been introduced into a number of different youth settings and IT groups over the last few years and provide a good opportunity for family life education. A group in Doncaster described the girls as having low self-esteem, many had experienced bad parenting and had had poor relationships with parents and teachers, and nearly all were sexually active and not using contraception (Flynn, 1983). Group discussion provided an important learning experience and encouraged the girls to explore issues such as the woman's role in society, the role of wife and mother, parenting, child-rearing practices in general, and non-accidental injury.

Prison

Each year numbers of young men and women spend part of their early adult years in prison, with over half of detected crimes being committed by people under 21 years. In 1981 75 000 young men between 17 and 21 years were sentenced to immediate imprisonment (Home Office, 1982). Most prisons provide some form of personal development courses or life and social skills programmes, as well as the pre-release course, which includes a session on family planning and sexually-transmitted diseases. Some of these young people may already be parents and many are likely to become parents within a few years of their release. A Home Office study in the mid-1970s illustrated that many prison trainees welcomed the opportunity of developing social skills and learning problem-solving techniques to help cope with a wide range of everyday problems. A similar group experience could provide discussion sessions on issues related to 'Why be a parent?', the different parental roles, the stresses of family life and an understanding of early child development. Such a course has already been introduced in HM prison in Castington where education about parenthood has been included in the life and social skills programme. One of the young men remarked at the end of a session 'It's the first time I've ever really thought about it. I have a kid somewhere but I never thought about it or its mother again till now – the next time I'll plan it'.

Those working in the youth field, in further education and the new YTS have a responsibility to help young people to cope with the choices and responsibilities of adult life, including the parental role. As Davies has argued, there is a need to look more explicitly at the content of courses being offered and to ask whether the education and training objectives are designed to meet personal needs or societal goals (Davies, 1979). It is the balance of goals that needs to be clarified. Parent education, as part of a general social education already recommended for all young people up to the age of 21, can encourage confidence and competence, can provide opportunities for exploring changes in self-image and give practical experience with young children and a realistic idea of the parental role. Many school-leavers have remarked that while decision-making skills and self-confidence are important aspects of life, schools do not provide adequate help in developing these skills (Porteous and Fisher, 1980).

The goals and content of social education and the provision for young people are being interpreted as a form of social control in response to massive youth unemployment, increased criminal behaviour and social unrest. Despite much criticism and frequent public debates, both at the academic and popular level, the emphasis is still on keeping young people off the streets (and, it is hoped, out of trouble), off the dole (and off the streets and out of the statistics) and educating them for non-existing jobs rather than using the opportunity creatively and educating them for life as an adult, citizen and potential parent. As one headmaster put it 'My great fear is that everybody is putting such great emphasis on the work ethic and on producing fodder for industry that they may leave out the broader elements of education which are so important to this age group'. Even though the Manpower Services Guide to Social and Life Skills states that the importance of such skills is not least because 'a satisfactory private life can contribute to a person's work motivation' (MSC, 1973) the emphasis within the SLS courses is almost entirely limited to job-related skills.

Teenage parents

'Teenage parents' is a term widely used as a shorthand description without adequate awareness of the different needs of the different groups, for example, schoolgirl mothers, single mothers and teenage couples who are parents. Despite sex education in schools, greater availability of contraception and access to legal abortions, the number of teenage pregnancies and births has been increasing. Although there has been a rise in the number of terminations, young people are now more likely to keep their babies than would have been the case twenty years ago. There is evidence that these teenage parents, many of whom subsequently marry, are particularly vulnerable because of a lack of stable relationships, inadequate accommodation, poverty and unemployment, as well as their youth. A recent survey of 533 teenage mothers also found that one third were themselves daughters of teenage mothers (Simms and Smith, 1983).

These young parents often need many of the schemes and services described in this book all at the same time. Because of their age, they need the type of education and preparation for parenthood provided in schools and the youth service. Because of their status, they also need the various opportunities described in the following chapters in the antenatal and post-natal periods and the supportive services available for young families. Unfortunately, because they straddle the different services and stages they are in danger of being forgotten or ignored. Their needs as young people may be separate from their needs as parents and it may be difficult to strike a balance, especially when they feel excluded from their natural 'teen' peer group and uncomfortable in the groups of mothers and toddlers.

There is also concern from many social workers, youth workers and teachers that some young girls are choosing to become pregnant, and see early parenthood as an alternative to unemployment. Comments like: 'there are no jobs so I might as well have a baby' are becoming alarmingly frequent. Few young parents realise how isolated and lonely their lives may become when they can no longer go out in the evenings with their friends, especially if they have no job, little money, and live alone away from family and friends. At a conference on the consequences of teenage sexual activity, sponsored by the Brook Advisory Council, an 'agony aunt' said: 'It is clear to me that the majority of teenagers who have sex relations before they are ready for it do so because they are ill-informed, because they lack self-esteem, status or sexual identity, and believe sex will repair this lack' (Tyerman, 1982). The studies of young pregnant girls indicate that many do not receive sex education at school, few of them were using any form of birth control and there was little awareness of the impact that pregnancy and parenthood might have on their lives.

The brief account in this chapter illustrates the size and nature of this problem and what action can and is being taken to offer support and encouragement to these young people to enable them to feel confident and to be competent in their new role as parent.

Schoolgirl mothers

The term 'schoolgirl mother' strictly refers only to girls under 16 at the time the child is conceived. It is not known how many girls of 16 who give birth or have a termination became pregnant while still at school. Whilst young people are more sexually active, the increasing use of contraception and the rising numbers of legal abortions means that the actual birth rate to girls under the age of 16 remains fairly steady. Table 4.2 gives the statistics of legal abortions and live births to girls in this age group, in selected years from 1969–82.

TABLE 4.2 *Legal abortions and live births to girls under 16 resident in England and Wales*

	Legal abortions	Live births
1969	1200	1465
1975	3570	1414
1980	3650	1274
1981	4202	1217
1982 (Jan – Sept)	2850 (provisional)	1161

SOURCE OPCS and DHSS, Social Trends (1983)
NCOPF, Key Statistics (1982)

This means that pregnancy is still a relatively rare occurrence for each individual school. A study in Sheffield showed that with approximately forty to fifty pregnant schoolgirls annually this meant on average one girl per school per year. This makes it difficult to provide a flexible range of provisions to cater for all the physical, medical, social, emotional, residential and educational needs of the schoolgirl mother-to-be and her baby (Cox, 1982).

One of the most immediate and serious consequences of a pregnancy whilst at school is the disruption and often total cessation of the pupil's education. In theory home tuition is available, varying from two to ten hours per week, both during and after pregnancy, but many girls do not receive it and the majority do not return to school. Some schools refuse to have either pregnant girls or schoogirl mothers because it would be an 'unsuitable influence'. Out of over a hundred educational authorities only a handful provide special units and there are some who argue that isolating schoolgirls in this way adds to their problems, by separating them from their school friends and disrupting their educational routine.

The benefit of special units (such as the one in Bristol funded jointly by the education and social services departments, or the Arbour Schoolgirl project in Liverpool, financed by the statutory bodies of education, social services and health and run by a voluntary body) lies in co-ordinating the transition from schoolgirl to motherhood. The girls are able to continue their education as a group, with three quarters of their time spent on normal education (CSE and GCE courses) and the rest spent on learning about health during pregnancy and childbirth, attending antenatal clinics and acquiring knowledge and experience in child care from observing and helping with those babies in the nursery. For those living in Huddersfield another option is available. Some pregnant schoolgirls have been given places at the National Children's Centre where they can combine their formal education with practical activities, alongside the teenagers on child care schemes sponsored by the MSC Youth Opportunities Programme.

There are very few of these units in the country as a whole and they are all small, taking eight to fifteen girls at any one time. Some are able to offer a few additional places to mothers and their babies on a part-time basis.

Schoolgirl mothers are not eligible for most state benefits. As the Joint Working Party on Pregnant Schoolgirls and Schoolgirl Mothers (NCOPF/CDT, 1979) noted, this intensifies problems and causes hardships for many of the girls and their families.

Single mothers (16–19 years old)

As might be expected, the number of pregnancies within this age range is significantly greater. In a year there are over 92 000 known conceptions, of which one in three is terminated. A third of the babies born to girls under 20 are illegitimate, one third are conceived within marriage and one third are premaritally conceived. The character of illegitimacy is however changing with some births registered jointly by the parents at the time and a number who subsequently marry.

Many of these births are, as one community worker put it, 'unplanned pregnancies in unplanned lives'. High youth unemployment and lack of job opportunities have undoubtedly played some part in the increased number of births. A study of disaffected school pupils, however, found that several of the girls were pregnant a year after leaving school and admitted that they were not accidents but planned ways of getting out of tedious unskilled jobs (Johnson, 1980). Others who have been unable to find a job want to have more independence and leave home, see pregnancy as a way of obtaining an income and a flat.

There are also cultural differences. The proportion of births to both West Indian born and UK born women has been increasing, while births outside marriage are less likely for Asian women. A study in Bristol indicated that 20 per cent of pregnant teenagers were black girls, mostly living alone and none of them married (Wells, 1983). The Family Support Service in Lambeth was set up by the Council for Community Relations when they realised that a high proportion of West Indian single mothers were isolated and depressed at home. Off-Centre in Hackney also works primarily with West Indian teenage mothers and their children, many of whom are isolated and withdrawn, living in poor housing conditions with very few supportive links in the neighbourhood and little guidance on parenting.

The workers felt that the most important element of their group work with these single mothers and their children was 'reparenting' the mother. Many of them seemed to have lacked adequate parenting themselves and the group acted as a 'good parent' providing caring, emotional nurturing, consistency and safety. In Rugby, the NMGC and social services department run a 'Teenage Mothers Group' which not only reduces isolation and acts in a preventive way by identifying and tackling problems early but also aims to increase the self-confidence of the women and help them improve their parenting skills by increasing their understanding, self-esteem and self-awareness.

The voluntary organisations and the churches have traditionally provided 'mother and baby' homes. In the past these often concentrated on providing a refuge during pregnancy and a home for the first few months of parenthood. Some still provide a short-term home for young, vulnerable and unsupported mothers who need space away from the pressures of parents and boyfriends to make realistic decisions about their future, but increasingly these are widening their educative role. For example, St Michael's Fellowship in Notting Hill runs both a Family Unit short-term hostel and a longer-term supportive unit.

For those girls who plan to keep their babies, a balance has to be achieved between 'personal education', encouraging any interest or ambitions they may have, bringing to their attention opportunities that exist in the community and helping them to take advantage of these; and 'parent education', helping them to develop an understanding of the physical, emotional and developmental needs of their children and the demands their babies will make upon them. In some of the long-term hostels, girls may stay for up to two years, living in their own bed-sitting rooms, handling their money and learning to cope on a tight budget, helping to run the playgroup and, for many, catching up on 'missed schooling' through literacy classes or developing new skills on YOP courses. Many of these homes do not provide substitute day-care, so the mothers are introduced to the real problems of finding a nursery place or childminder from the start. A new venture in Southwark run by Wel-care is designed to provide accommodation and an educational course which it is hoped will give young mothers sufficient training and practical experience of working with their own and others' children to enable them to find jobs as childminders or in nursery or day-care centres. Like the schoolgirl units, these initiatives are few and, as small residential units, are often limited to eight to fifteen girls at a time. A great number of single mothers find themselves placed in bed and breakfast accommodation, which is particularly unsuitable for life with a young baby.

Parents in higher education receive very little support. For them pregnancy can mean giving up a training or education which could have provided a sound basis for future employment. Student grants only provide allowance for children if the mother is married. In this situation, especially if the father is also pursuing an educational qualification, young people are often forced into making choices about marriage, parenthood and their long-term education without adequate guidance or counselling. Even if the mother has financial help from parents or from the father, there is a severe shortage of crèche and day-care facilities in colleges and universities (EOC/NUS, 1980).

Poverty and poor health care are often distressing features of single parenthood, whether the mother is working or unemployed. A survey carried out by the National Council for One Parent Families (1979) concluded that 25 per cent of the most vulnerable mothers-to-be received no help whatsoever at a time of severe financial difficulty. A study of antenatal classes, which showed that many young single women do not attend, found that they had not been told about the classes because it was assumed they would not want to attend (Perkins, 1978). The health and social services are failing to meet the needs of these young mothers and their children. Education, preparation and support during pregnancy need to be made more accessible to enable them to make the transition to parenthood with more competence and less stress.

Teenage marriages and parenthood

Teenage marriages are particularly at risk of breakdown. A bride in her teens is twice as likely to become divorced as a bride of 20–24 years and four times as likely as a bride of 25–29 years. A study of teenage marriages which had ended in divorce found that pre-marital pregnancy, short courtships, lack of kinship support and low income were common factors. These teenage couples were already experiencing personal and environmental stress (Thornes and Collard, 1979). Early parenthood means that young couples have had very little time to adjust to the new relationships and responsibilities of marriage when the arrival of a baby is added to problems of housing and income. A DHSS study on teenage mothers and their partners points out that it may be unrealistic to expect such marriages to survive if immaturity is combined with adverse social and economic conditions (Simms and Smith, 1983).

Making provision for young married couples who are also parents seems to be a neglected area. A youth worker who became aware of this lack of provision found that clubs and centres varied enormously. The Young Farmers Clubs, 18 Plus groups and youth branches of political parties acknowledge couples rather than parents. Some teenage couples use the youth service facilities as an inexpensive source of leisure in the company of others of the same age, whilst other couples were almost apologetic for being there (Fabes, 1980). On the whole, where couples did still go to the youth club it tended to be the fathers using the facilities and the mothers turning to the youth workers for advice. Youth workers have often found themselves working with individual unmarried mothers but traditionally the youth service has not catered for toddlers and babies. If young parents are to be encouraged to join in the activities, some form of provision for children has to be arranged. Equally, evening activities may not be suitable because of baby-sitting problems. Many centres and clubs are now offering more activities and facilities during the daytime to meet the needs of the unemployed school-leavers and a few of these have been usefully extended to include young parents.

Some initiatives centre on the couple and others on the mothers. The Caxton House Settlement in London runs a 'Young Parents' group which meets once a week and brings together a number of previously isolated couples. They are offered a wide range of events: health films, discussion groups, video films, museum trips, crafts and fruit-picking. In Birmingham a weekly 'Young Couples Group' was set up by the probation service to provide an opportunity for young couples to discuss some of the problems they were experiencing and see how they themselves and the workers could offer more support and help. The Fulham Girls Project in London has a weekly 'Young Mums Group', providing an informal setting for young mothers to meet and develop mutual support as well as offering opportunities for the children to meet and mix with those of similar age.

Providing specific support for these young couples is difficult. Many suffer from the stress of caring for young children in isolated and inadequate surroundings, with husbands in unskilled low-paid jobs. Youthfulness, inexperience and immaturity are significant features in many of the teenage marital breakdowns (Simms and Smith, 1980; 1981). Opportunities which could offer both personal education and parent education seem to be one way of trying to increase their self-confidence. Family centres and community and adult education workers are beginning to realise the enormous potential for helping these young couples to develop both as people and as parents. 'Well-health' groups, woodwork clubs, keep-fit, do-it-yourself, are all ways of bringing couples into the centres to develop and exchange skills. During these activities many worries may be expressed, often concerning health or behaviour problems with their children, and out of this have grown weekly discussion groups using materials from the Open University parenthood courses. As unemployment hits more and more young couples, such community opportunities to share hobbies and interests, to develop new skills and to understand more about bringing up their children will become important life-lines in balancing their needs as young people with their responsibilities as parents.

Summary

During adolescence and late teens, young people are beginning to make friendships and develop relationships which may lead to marriage and parenthood. Outside the school classroom, and particularly after leaving school, there are few opportunities for young people to discuss issues, choices or fantasies related to adult life, marriage, parenthood and families. 20 per cent of men and over 33 per cent of women marry at 21 or younger. Despite sex education and the greater availability of contraception, there is an increase in teenage pregnancies: one third are illegitimate, one third are pre-maritally conceived and one third are conceived within marriage.

In the youth service, the wide range of schemes and activities together with the fragmentation of responsibility, provision and funding has resulted in a lack of unity about purposes, boundaries and co-ordination. Social education is a primary goal of the youth service but there is no clear policy on the context or form of such provision. For example, although the youth service officially caters for those aged 14–21, little provision is made for married couples or teenage parents. Youth workers have the necessary training in group work skills and there are discussion materials available but few youth leaders offer courses or opportunities for family life education. Within the youth service the emphasis tends to be on leisure activities and individual counselling rather than mutual support and group learning.

Social education, particularly social and life skills, is also an important aspect of further education provision particularly in relation to the anticipated 460 000 young people taking part in the YTS. In response to the high youth unemployment, however, there has been an emphasis on work-related skills rather than on overall personal development with opportunities for health education, family life education and courses on social and personal relationships. Many further education colleges offer a range of courses for young and mature students which could provide the basis for mixed discussion groups, particularly in relation to family life education. There are also opportunities to integrate family life education into other forms of existing social education provision, for example, those in intermediate treatment and prison. This is especially important with groups of young people who are likely to marry and have children early.

For schoolgirl mothers, single teenage mothers and teenage couples who are parents, there is very little evidence of education and support for them as young people, for preparation and support during transition to parenthood or for continuing education and support in their new role as parents. Although teenage pregnancies overall have increased, the number of schoolgirl mothers has remained fairly steady (in Sheffield for example, an average of one per school per year). Few of these girls receive adequate provision of formal education, personal and social education or parent education. Single teenage mothers are often isolated and lonely, suffering from depression and living on low incomes, many in bed and breakfast accommodation, and they tend not to use the antenatal and post-natal services provided. Their babies have a higher perinatal mortality rate and are smaller than average. Many teenage couples also suffer from adverse conditions of poverty, poor housing, immaturity and poor relationships with their own parents. These are often couples who have married because of a pre-marital pregnancy and are considered to be a 'high risk' for divorce.

5
Antenatal Education and the Transition to Parenthood

Introduction

The Court report suggested that our chief concern during the transition to parenthood should be to improve an individual's ability to cope with life. Subsequent research studies have indicated that in coping with birth and the transition to parenthood it is not so much what you know that is important but how the experience is managed (Clulow *et al.*, 1982; Draper *et al.*, 1981). A supportive network of friends, family and professionals which will provide continuity of care and advice from early pregnancy to the early months of parenthood may well be of more value in coping with a major life-change than a series of informative classes.

This chapter will explore the facilities and opportunities that currently exist to help young people plan their parenthood; the support that is available during pregnancy in antenatal clinics and classes; the various options and choices in childbirth; the need for care and support and the attempts to meet them in the post-natal period.

Planning parenthood

The idea of being able to plan parenthood assumes certain conditions – choice, rationality and means. Family planning is now generally socially acceptable and there are a variety of contraceptive methods available, but for many, whether for legal, social, religious or medical reasons, the choice is theoretical rather than real. Although the present trend in cohabitation suggests that it is a period of living together before marriage rather than two mutually exclusive states (Rimmer, 1981) it is important to encourage young people to question and prepare themselves for future personal relationships. Much of the material used in family life education courses at school and with young people seems to assume that couples will marry and have children (Torkington, 1981). Once married, newly-weds seem to see children as inevitable and as a (mostly) desirable consequence of marriage (Mansfield, 1982). Indeed, it has been argued that this relationship between marriage and children can become self-reinforcing 'it makes those who want to have children marry and those who marry feel they should have children' (Busfield and Paddon, 1977).

Many of the studies on parenthood suggest there is a reluctance among couples to sit down and discuss contraception and parenthood and that a very high proportion of first pregnancies are unplanned. Graham and McKee (1980) noted a certain ambivalence about pregnancy, with the method of contraception sometimes being changed as a half-conscious preparation for conception. There is a tendency to avoid deliberate planning 'a decision some couples would rather not have to take; the contraceptive pill feels "too safe" – too safe to let chance tilt the balance and make the decision for them' (Breen, 1981). As Oakley (1979) points out, people rarely have clear motives as far as having children are concerned and conceiving a child is not like buying an item of furniture – demand and supply may not be easily equated.

'Planning' often seems to be used as a euphemism for 'being open to the possibility'. It may mask an ambiguity and uncertainty about ever having children, or a superstitious belief that to talk about it and consciously 'try for a baby' may jeopardise the chances (Mansfield, 1982). Although fathers are taking a more active role during pregnancy and childbirth, it seems that the decision to become pregnant still lies primarily with the woman. Many couples do not anticipate the impact of parenthood, planned or unplanned, on their lives and too little of the sheer hard work and inconvenience of parenting is conveyed to young people before they commit themselves.

Pre-conceptual care

The importance of preparation for both pregnancy and childbirth in terms of the mother's general state of health has long been recognised (Ministry of Health, 1932). Despite the numerous studies and reports which have documented the links between poor health care and nutrition and the increased risks to both mother and baby, the National Health Service does not actively provide clinics or centres to give nutritional counselling before pregnancy. In 1980 the DHSS (1980b) reply to the Short Committee justified *not* putting additional resources into the existing health service because it accepted that social factors may have a greater influence on perinatal health than medical factors. This was despite a report from the Royal College of Obstetricians and Gynaecologists which reaffirmed that 'too little attention has been paid to the health of a woman to undertake pregnancy' (RCOG, 1982).

Some groups however have been providing information, advice and services to parents and the professionals who are interested in developing better pre-conceptual care. In 1971, the Foundation for Education and Research in Child-bearing was established. They have consistently promoted the need to recognise that low birth-weight and handicap are associated with maternal nutrition (Wynn and Wynn, 1981). In 1978 the organisation Foresight was formed to help prospective parents achieve optimal health by providing relevant education, physical screening and necessary treatment prior to the conception of a child. There are now twenty-two private clinics and one planned at the West London Hospital as part of the NHS. Some health visitors have seen the advantage of running informal weekly pre-conceptual counselling clinics in well-women centres and family planning clinics. Referrals can then easily be made when someone happens to mention 'I'm thinking of coming off the pill soon' and opportunities for promoting healthy life-styles and nutritional counselling become part of a positive approach to health.

Genetic counselling is available to those couples who have reason to suspect that a child might be handicapped but pre-pregnancy advice has not been more generally available. The Maternity Alliance (1982) have produced a leaflet *Getting Fit for Pregnancy* covering eating, social habits, work hazards and relevant medical checks. The Health Education Council is in the process of revising its advice to couples contemplating pregnancy, recommending them to visit their GP at least three to six months beforehand for a physical overhaul and advice during the 'getting ready' stage.

Concern for the health of the baby is often an underlying fear and anxiety during pregnancy and a primary concern at the time of the birth (Cartwright, 1979; Oakley, 1980; Elbourne, 1981). As one mother put it 'I tended not to believe in my pregnancy (only so that there would be less explaining if anything were to go wrong) ...' (Clulow, 1982). It is important in the desire to achieve better health for mother, father and baby that mothers are not blamed for babies which are not deemed 'perfect'. As Dally (1982) warns us 'Motherhood has become full of uncertainty and paradox ... the prospect of becoming a mother seems a tremendous step, a total change in life-style, a fearful responsibility, an impossible expense, a frightening emotional commitment'. Nowadays it is assumed that babies will be healthy and survive. If parents genuinely find it difficult to change particular habits then other ways need to be explored to help them prepare for their baby. Improved teaching may be required in an attempt to convince prospective parents of the importance, for example, of giving up smoking.

The new Open University course *Getting Ready for Pregnancy* appears to meet some of these conflicts and dilemmas head-on, starting with 'Do you really want a baby and do you really want it now?' An important new element is the idea of promoting assertiveness, how to develop confidence in talking with professionals and communicating effectively to get what you want. However, exploring the social, psychological, physical and economic aspects of the decision to have a baby rarely happens before conception. For the majority of couples prospective parenthood only becomes a subject of interest when pregnancy has been confirmed.

Becoming a parent

Becoming a parent is a critical and transitional point in any one's life, particularly with the first pregnancy if the mother is working, but also with subsequent ones. Parenthood often has a greater impact upon mothers than on fathers and this transition has been variously described as:

Crisis – Satir (1972) outlines the process of conception, pregnancy and birth of a child as 'major, natural, common steps. All (of which) mean crisis and temporary anxiety and require an adjustment period and new integration'.

Loss – 'What is characteristic of childbirth and becoming a mother today is the tendency for women to feel they have lost something, rather than simply gained a child. What is lost may be one's job, one's life-style, an intact 'couple' relationship, control over one's body or sense of self, but the feeling of bereavement cannot be cured or immediately balanced by the rewards of motherhood' (Oakley, 1980).

A developmental stage – this view holds that the birth of a child is a normal stage in adult development, complementary to two other major adult roles – work and marriage. Women respond to this biological and psychological event either through 'adaptive or maladaptive' processes (Breen, 1975).

Motherhood has been described as a 'multiple status passage' as the woman moves from non-mother to mother, from worker to housewife. For teenage mothers it may also be a shift from childhood to adulthood and for most women the medicalisation of childbirth also brings 'patienthood' (Ong, 1983). The changes may not seem so explicit for fathers but if they become the sole provider the increased financial responsibilities may lead to more overtime and less leisure-time at home. One attempt to classify fathers' reactions to pregnancy noted a few extreme cases where on the one hand the pregnancy was denied or on the other hand the identification of the father with the foetus excluded the mother (Richman and Goldthorp, 1978). The majority of the men, however considered either that pregnancy was nothing unusual and was the wife's responsibility, or wanted to share the experience and offered increased emotional and practical support. As Richards (1982) points out there is little in current research that provides an adequate conceptualisation of the social institution of fatherhood. Many studies have simply substituted men for women in the traditional 'mothering' role and failed to examine what fathers bring to parenthood or how it links with male life both inside and outside the home.

Antenatal care

What could parent education offer during this transition period? Studies suggest that a network of relationships with other couples and with the health services is more important in the management of the transition to parenthood than the level of knowledge about pregnancy (Clulow, *et al.*, 1982; Draper *et al.*, 1981; van der Eyken, 1982). Parent education can include the provision of opportunities for couples to talk with each other, with other couples and the professionals involved about the experience of pregnancy and parenthood. It would still be important to give realistic information about the process of pregnancy and childbirth and this exchange of information and sharing experiences could continue in informal groups throughout pregnancy and after the birth.

For those couples who have not sought pre-conceptual advice the first point of contact in the confirmation of pregnancy is likely to be the GP or the family planning clinic for a pregnancy test. Although many women like to diagnose themselves (Perfrement, 1982, found that over one third used home or pregnancy testing services) most like to visit their GP. As Oakley (1979) describes it 'pregnancy having become a "medical" condition, requires a specialist diagnosis'. This is an important point for couples to receive early advice on health matters such as diet, smoking, alcohol or drugs. A joint statement from the Royal College of Midwives and the Health Visitors Association suggests that Maternity Advice Centres should be set up in each local 'market place' to provide on-the-spot professional confirmation of pregnancy and really early contact with both midwife and health visitor (HVA/RCM, 1982).

The National Health Service provides two services for pregnant women: antenatal care through clinics, primarily concerned with the physical health of both mother and foetus; and antenatal classes which provide information and advice to the woman and her partner. Voluntary organisations provide more parent-run and parent-centred groups with a greater emphasis on peer education and mutual support after birth, and, in many instances, these innovative and supportive services fill the gaps in existing statutory provision.

Antenatal care is currently provided in three main ways: total GP care, total hospital care or a combination of the two usually known as shared care. The policy advocated in the Peel Committee Report (CHSC, 1970) of moving towards a 100 per cent institutional confinement rate has almost been reached and childbirth at home is now a rare event. Modern antenatal care, with its emphasis on elaborate techniques and expensive equipment such as ultra-sound for diagnosis and treatment of potential problems has been pursuing its primary purpose: to detect and deal with any complications as soon as possible. The trend towards centralising care to incorporate access to high technology monitoring has not only resulted in a geographical distance but also a psychological distance between the patient and hospital staff, who are more inclined to concentrate almost exclusively on the physical aspects of pregnancy. The social and emotional aspects such as reassurance, relief from anxiety and the need for information and discussion tend to have been sacrificed to the sophisticated technology.

Antenatal clinics

Surveys have shown that those who do not seek early confirmation of pregnancy often fail to use either antenatal clinics or classes. Those groups found to attend late in pregnancy and who receive little or no antenatal care include the very young, single women, some ethnic minorities particularly Asian women, mothers with four or more children, women with social or financial problems and those married to men in semi-skilled or unskilled occupations (Parsons and Perkins, 1980; O'Brien and Smith, 1981). Although no direct link has been established between the poor use of antenatal care and the outcome of pregnancy these are groups of women who already have indicators of poor health care and nutrition, inadequate housing and low levels of income.

In a few cases, late attendance occurs through a GP's slowness in referring women to the hospital or through delays in the hospital appointments system. For the majority, however, women either do not have the information or the services are inappropriate, inaccessible or not amenable. The Maternity Services Advisory Committee (1982) has called for local and national campaigns to make sure these groups of women know of their rights to existing services, and to provide alternative access. Such alternatives could include walk-in clinics during the evenings and at weekends, clinics in the workplace, mobile clinics, and care in the woman's home if necessary. In addition, information could be given inside all pregnancy testing kits and at all pharmacists offering such a service. The Short Report (House of Commons, 1980) referring to those who do not attend as 'antenatal defaulters' recommended that the primary health care team should acknowledge and provide for three special groups of high risk women: those with practical difficulties, those with fears of hospital and clinical procedures from negative experiences (for example, stillbirth, miscarriage) and poorly motivated patients with social problems.

During the past few years there has been growing criticism not only of the failure of antenatal clinics to accommodate the 'at risk' groups but also increasing dissatisfaction expressed by those who do use them. Although many women are happy with the actual antenatal care they receive, they are less happy with the way in which they receive it. Two national surveys – *Mother* magazine (1981) with a sample of 2000 and *That's Life* (Boyd and Sellers, 1982) with 6000 – together with reports from leading pressure groups, the National Childbirth Trust (1981), the Maternity Alliance (1981) and the Spastics Society (1981) have produced a clear catalogue of reasons for non-attendance and are highly critical of present practice in hospital antenatal clinics. Enough is now known about the difficulties: the time and cost of travelling to distant clinics; lengthy waiting times; lack of facilities for children; the impersonal nature of visits; lack of privacy and of confidentiality; lack of information and the cultural and social barriers. What is required now is action to improve both practice and facilities.

A government committee has produced a guide (MSAC, 1982) to good practice and a plan for action which leaves no room for excuses: 'many improvements could be made by changes in attitude and reorganisation of procedures which would not involve additional expenditure'. The National Council for Voluntary Organisations report on the contribution of voluntary action in antenatal services (Allen and Purkis, 1983) shows how readily clinics can be made more welcoming and accessible. The extra resources of time, effort and ideas from voluntary groups can create a more educative and sensitive service. More flexibility and adaptation can meet the diversity of needs and circumstances. Involving parents can also encourage changes in personal behaviour and attitudes through self-help and exchanging experiences in groups.

Antenatal *care* is primarily a screening process concerned with monitoring the mother physically for the job of labour and childbirth. Antenatal *classes* have an educational role and are designed to prepare the mother through information, instruction and discussion. Few mothers however make this distinction between receiving clinical care and wanting to discuss the purpose and implications of tests, routine procedures, the processes of labour and delivery, the various forms of pain relief available and so on. In fact, not only are important opportunities for education being lost but this assumption of the mother as a 'passive' patient may undermine self-esteem and reduce self-confidence. A successful example of combining routine clinical care with impromptu education came from a group of mothers shown the image of the foetus at an ultra-sound examination and given explicit information about their unborn child. Significant changes were found in their smoking habits and consumption of alcohol when seen again two to four weeks later. The information and the 'reality' of the foetus seemed to emphasise the personal relevance of the health care advice (Reading, 1982). Explicit information and an opportunity for discussion on diet is also important – 'make sure you have a good diet' is not sufficient. Perfrement (1982) found that many women who were not eating appropriate types of food thought it was a good diet. Others were aware of the importance of fresh fruit and vegetables but could not afford them.

Social factors are important determinants of social habits and additional financial benefits for pregnant women may be necessary to supplement their diet. For the increasing numbers of people living on supplementary benefit who cannot afford to eat the right foods, detailed instructions on diet may be of less value than an increase in maternity benefits to help them to purchase the recommended foods.

Bringing care directly into the community not only increases the likelihood of mothers using the services but may also make the professionals more aware of the particular social and economic problems in the area. A community-based antenatal care programme at Sighthill in Edinburgh, where much of the care and education has been transferred to the general practitioners and community midwives, has resulted in a 95 per cent take-up of services and a dramatic improvement in the perinatal mortality rate. The amount of monitoring in hospital-based clinics for all pregnant women is now seriously under question, especially as it is creating stress and dissatisfaction. It is argued that pregnant women who are at little risk could receive antenatal care at small local centres which would be more accessible for parents and regular visits could be made by specialist obstetricians (Zander *et al.*, 1978). Such centres could provide both clinics and classes and create a continuity of care through the antenatal and post-natal stages. An experimental clinic for community antenatal care has been set up in Cambridge and will act as a prototype for the antenatal services at a new obstetric unit (Draper, 1983).

Antenatal classes

Most hospital and community clinics organise classes in the last two or three months of pregnancy and increasingly men are being encouraged to attend. These may be run by midwives, health visitors and physiotherapists, alone or as part of a team, and most now include parentcraft (92 per cent in the *That's Life* survey) as well as preparation for the actual birth. Their potential lies not so much in the teaching of specific skills or conveying of information but rather in the opportunities available to prospective parents to express and discuss their needs, fears and expectations, to enable peer-group support and to encourage self-help through discussion and questioning. The HVA/RCM joint statement (1982) recommends a basic syllabus which includes pregnancy, labour and delivery; infant feeding; diet; family planning; foetal development; care of the infant; and family relationships. Physical preparation for labour through relaxation and breathing exercises may also be offered at these classes but are usually taught separately.

The task for the antenatal teacher is a difficult one. Many courses are one session a week for eight or ten weeks, often with groups of thirty to forty people in the hospital-based classes and rarely lasting more than two hours. In such circumstances it is impossible to accommodate the particular needs of so many parents when they may be at different stages of pregnancy. As a result, classes are often offered too late, with information being given, for example, on diet, that would have been more appropriate in the very early months of pregnancy, or mothers delivering before they finish the course. Mothers have also criticised the content and form of the classes, for not giving realistic and adequate information on the process of labour and birth and the range of medical interventions or for 'pretending that childbirth is perfectly painless, that it's all easy and straightforward and natural – so it's all rather a shock when it isn't'. Others were disappointed that there were too few opportunities to discuss their feelings and anxieties – 'I think that instead of them sitting talking they ought to let you all talk, because it is then that you spill your fears' (Draper *et al.*, 1981). With the range of different forms of birth, of pain-relief and monitoring, there is a danger of becoming over-technical merely to get across all the information, without leaving adequate time to explore the emotional and psychological impact of pregnancy and parenthood on couples.

Learning about parenthood occupies only a small part of the time available in classes. As one mother remarked 'I thought antenatal classes were a really good preparation for childbirth, but not for parenthood' (Draper *et al.*, 1981). Perkins (1979) also questioned the appropriateness of the content of some classes, many of which are concerned with baby-care skills which might be better dealt with after the birth. She suggests concentration on three main topics: the process, rather than the skill, of feeding; some firsthand experience of young babies; and discussion of some of the choices involved in parenting.

Attempts are being made to develop a more informal and relevant approach both by bringing in parents and creating opportunities for friendships and discussions. This may be by making links with others, for example, where NHS antenatal teachers invite the local National Childbirth Trust (NCT) breastfeeding counsellors or the Association of Breastfeeding Mothers to attend sessions. Or by creating links between mothers, as for example in the Lisson Grove health project and Newpin (New Parent – Infant Network) which both link prospective parents with new parents in their local community. Or by developing a community approach such as the Health in Homerton project in London which aims to offer information, guidance and support throughout pregnancy and early parenthood. The value of this joint venture by community workers and health professionals is expressed by a mother from the project 'I found my local support groups to be an enormous benefit during my pregnancy. There was plenty to share and talk about together. It made me feel less isolated and we all became good friends'. (Health in Homerton Annual Report, 1983).

In order for supportive networks to develop, classes need to be reasonably local and informal enough to encourage the development of friendships. For many NHS classes this is rarely the case. Many are too far away, often based in the hospital, are unwelcoming, with few facilities for other children and are too large to promote the sharing of anxieties. As a result many women do not attend. Surveys of attendance at antenatal classes have shown that there is enormous variation, particularly between relatively poor and more affluent areas. A Community Health Council survey found attendance varied from 15 per cent in South Shields to 75 per cent in the London Borough of Camden (Garcia, 1981). The Family Start project in Oldham found less than a quarter of mothers intended to go to either parentcraft or relaxation classes (Ong, 1983) while another London study found a 74 per cent attendance (Moss, 1981).

The mothers who do attend classes tend to be the older, more educated, white, middle-class women. When almost half of all pregnant women do not attend classes it is important to consider the ways in which they are promoted as well as the content, form and relevance to parents' lives. A study in Waltham Forest found that 40 per cent of women interviewed had got the impression from professionals in the NHS that they were not important (Adams, 1980). A Nottingham survey found that many mothers, particularly the young single women, were never offered classes (Perkins, 1978). Those who speak no English see little point in attending and those who have already had one pregnancy often see no perceived benefits and are also hampered by other young children for whom there are seldom crèche facilities. Many women are working and are unwilling to take further time off work especially if they are already spending up to half a day attending the clinic.

It does appear that attitudes are changing, although the majority of innovative schemes and services seem to be one-off initiatives. In the NHS, for example, South Glamorgan made a thorough evaluation of both content and presentation of classes and renamed them 'Ready for Baby groups'. Redbridge and Waltham Forest offered an alternative to the formal antenatal classes by inviting working-class women to join a small informal group. In South Hammersmith, the senior health education officer ran a course at the Town Hall for pregnant employees. Norfolk and Norwich Hospital recognised the need to provide different types of groups for different types of consumers. Their range includes the standard antenatal classes for prospective mothers, a toddlers' group, couples classes with never more than eight couples and no admission after the start of the course, a more flexible 'solos' group for single mothers, and a reunion which encourages mutual support. St George's Hospital in London has concentrated on the provision of a continuity of care so that women have the same four midwives during both antenatal clinics and classes. This provides a more personal service since they all get to know each other better, a continuity of clinic care from antenatal to post-natal, and consistent advice and information related to their particular needs.

Many of the most interesting developments have been described in the report on voluntary action in the antenatal field (Allen and Purkis, 1983). This outlines numerous voluntary projects providing courses for particular cultural groups, for example Vietnamese refugees and Asian minorities; developing educational and teaching materials in different languages; providing opportunities for the promotion of good health-care and information on all aspects of home and hospital birth; and developing local community projects which encourage continuity of information and mutual aid.

One new development is the expansion of befriending and self-help schemes. Many of these have grown from well-women's centres or neighbourhood health education centres, where concern for the state of local antenatal services or the lack of provision for parents in the early months of parenthood have led to community action. Home-visiting schemes can provide help for mothers on a one-to-one basis. For example, Newpin a voluntary befriending and support project in London; Home-Start, a home visiting scheme to support families with young children; the Maternity Services Liaison Support project in Tower Hamlets for ethnic minority women; the Lisson Grove project for prospective parents, which facilitates social contact and emotional support in North London; and the Barrack House Health Education and Language project in Leeds, mainly for ethnic minority women and unmarried mothers. Groups such as Health in Homerton can offer support and practical sharing of experiences and resources. The Leigh Park NCT group in Portsmouth encourages women's self-help on a large council estate. The Balsall Heath neighbourhood health education project has initiated women's health groups both for English-speaking women and for Asian women. Family Start in Oldham, based on an isolated estate with poor amenities, helps to alleviate some of the stress associated with the transition to parenthood by providing a drop-in group to enable both prospective and new parents to talk about their feelings, problems and parenting experiences. A food scheme helped to supplement poor diets and encourage better dietary habits. The fathers' group has become part of the general activities, creating a supportive network on which parents can draw for both emotional and practical advice.

In 1976 the Court Report stated 'We could find little evidence regarding the value of "parentcraft classes"; or even that their content has been systematically constructed.' (Committee on Child Health Services). A number of initiatives have taken place since that report to examine both the content, the form and the setting of such provision. However, the quality of such classes is often variable because few midwives and health visitors have been trained in group-work skills, and in one study a third of the health visitors expressed a positive dislike of group teaching (Clark, 1973). As one parentcraft co-ordinator states 'No one would expect a teacher to train for three years and then come to a delivery floor and deliver babies, and yet we do expect midwives to train as midwives and then offer themselves as teachers, with no further tuition' (Jamieson, 1982). Large groups of thirty to forty people, in any case, are not generally conducive to informal or intimate discussions and it is difficult to know what benefits have been gained from attendance. Although the majority of attenders in one study could not re-member anything that they had been taught, and no significant behavioural changes were found in the women who attended (Adams, 1980) many others do, however, appear to be satisfied (Moss, 1981; Boyd and Sellers, 1982).

Assessing the actual value of classes is difficult to interpret since the expectations and participation of the parents depends largely on their own knowledge and confidence. Many parents do not attend but there are still considerable numbers who do. Moss (1981) found that parents who attended classes were more likely to find coping as parents difficult, and fathers who attended saw their babies as 'not easy', while Birch and Chambers (1979) found fathers were more likely to be involved in the care of their baby. Whether this reflects a difference in classes, teachers or fathers, or whether being more involved in the care makes you more aware of problems, is hard to say. Class-goers seem to be more confident and self-reliant during labour (Rathbone, 1973) more likely to have a normal delivery (Moss, 1981) and apparently less anxious late in pregnancy and soon after birth (Hibbard, 1979). There is also a close relationship between breast-feeding and class attendance (Moss, 1981). It has been suggested that women who attend may not only be better educated and of a higher socio-economic status but also a certain personality type. Leff (1983), for example, in researching into post-natal depression has described two types of mother: the facilitator, who embraces motherhood as a way of life, is actively involved in the birth and has high expectations of parenthood; and the regulator, who sees birth as a 'career crisis', a medical experience making use of modern technology and defines her role as regulating the baby to a convenient routine.

An organisation which has traditionally been seen as catering for 'facilitators' is the National Childbirth Trust (NCT) with its emphasis on the feelings and attitudes of prospective parents and a concern to make birth a more enjoyable event. It is the only self-help pregnancy group with a nationwide network of antenatal classes and post-natal schemes. In 1982 approximately 18 000 expectant mothers and fathers chose to attend classes for which they had to pay, rather than take up the free service available in their local hospital or community clinic. NCT, which celebrated its silver jubilee in 1981, has become an important 'consumer' organisation, campaigning for choices in childbirth, for the presence and involvement of fathers in the labour and delivery room, and against the routine use of drugs, episiotomies and technological monitoring. Through its volunteer and self-help network it is able to link the educational, social and supportive role by bringing new parents together with prospective parents to share experiences of labour, birth and parenting. The post-natal support groups and breast-feeding counsellors are an example of mutual aid at a crucial time in the lives of many new young families. Although often criticised for its middle-class image, NCT is attempting to develop an outreach approach as part of its continuing training and educational role, not only developing links with schools and youth clubs, hospital and community clinics but also trying to work with others on projects for the more vulnerable 'non-attenders'.

Choices and options in childbirth

Numerous surveys and reports have documented the disparity between the services which the NHS offers and the actual needs and wants of women. What is more disturbing is that so many women describe their labours as a bad experience. This dissatisfaction, aroused by the increasing 'medicalisation' of pregnancy and childbirth, has become an important issue over the last few years and has often been portrayed as a conflict of power and goals. The health professionals in pursuing greater safety for mother and baby have centralised services and introduced a 'high technology' impersonal screening and monitoring system. Women, however, who on average, only have two babies, see childbirth as a unique and extraordinary process, a highly personal process and often the fulfilment of a dream. The resentment at being treated as patients, of no significance as individuals, has been expressed in the past through the only option available – non-attendance at clinics and classes. Over the last decade voluntary and consumer groups have been meeting the practical and social needs of many women. Now there is active campaigning both within and without the NHS service. Groups like the Maternity Alliance, AIMS and the Radical Midwives are questioning the priorities of health-care provision, trying to change attitudes and the nature of the services and their organisation.

Despite the great improvement in the general safety of childbirth, the loss of the option of a home delivery and the frequency of obstetric intervention have become significantly linked with postnatal depression and difficulties in the marital and parenting relationships. Oakley (1979) lists twenty-one procedures which are routinely used without any regard for their iatrogenic (illness-producing) qualities. Others have argued that while such medical procedures may be imposed in the name of safety of mother and child, there is no official intervention on other equally important matters such as smoking, alcohol consumption, poor diet or failure to use antenatal care (Shepperdson, 1980). A report from the Council for Science and Society on *Childbirth Today* (1980) states:

> Most patients want to be partners in a working alliance with the professional staff. The new technologies make possible a more efficient monitoring and control of processes within the patient. That they also have important effects on the partnership has been inadequately recognised.

The recent plan for action from the Maternity Services Advisory Committee questions the excessive demands on the hospital consultants and recommends that frequency of attendance and style of care should depend on each woman's circumstances. Further, it states that a high level of communication will be essential between women and the professionals involved, and that a trusting relationship, a maximum amount of continuity of care and provision of information should be priorities for all pregnant women (MSAC 1982).

Developing parenting skills requires building on the individual's own abilities and skills and providing positive experiences. Parent education aims to enhance the self-esteem and self-confidence of couples at this stage; to encourage a partnership with health professionals; and enable parents to make choices and decisions about the birth of their child. It seeks to encourage those abilities they will later need as parents.

Post-natal care and support

Once the baby is born it is important that there is continuity of care with consistent practical help and guidance whether at home or in the hospital. The shared-care domino scheme (domiciliary-in-out) is one form favoured by many women. Here the community midwife cares for the woman during pregnancy, delivery and in the post-natal period. This form of integrated midwifery service in the community should minimise the chance of antenatal care and delivery by strangers and maximise the knowledge and use of community resources and supportive networks. The complementary roles of the midwife for clinical care and the health visitor for the educative, social and psychological care are beginning to be recognised. Whether such a service operates efficiently, or at all, will depend on factors such as how willing consultants, GPs, community midwives and health visitors are to work as a team.

Another way of developing continuity is through encouraging the health visitor, who has a statutory duty to visit all mothers and new babies ten days after the birth, to join with the midwife in running classes on childbirth and health in pregnancy, forming local groups of prospective parents and creating links with established parents. An attempt to encourage a couples group prior to childbirth, to act as a supportive network afterwards, is described by Clulow *et al.* (1982). This highlighted the possibilities for the health visitor to provide a continuous link bridging the transition from being a couple to being a family, but again identified the need for health visitors to develop group work skills.

Isolation, loneliness and lack of adult company have been thought to increase depression after childbirth and to undermine self-confidence. Typically such depression falls into three types: the transient, common fourth-day baby-blues, post-natal depression and puerperal psychosis. The first affects four out of five of all women with weepiness as the outstanding feature and support, reassurance and the understanding of husband, relatives and friends in the familiar circumstances of home are often seen as the best remedy. Post-natal depression, developing in or after the third week, is also alarmingly frequent with over two-thirds of women still feeling low six months after the birth (Moss, 1982b) and a third after one year (Draper *et al.*, 1981).

Why such depression should be so common is unclear and disputed. Medical involvement and high technology during delivery may provoke certain kinds of responses in mothers (Oakley, 1980; Cartwright, 1979). Psycho-social stress, low social class and unsupportive emotional relationships are also implicated (Martin, 1982). Breen (1981) found that women who expressed considerable anxiety during pregnancy were less likely to become depressed after the birth, but Elliott (1982) found that anxiety and tension in early pregnancy were associated with post-natal depression. Others have assumed that since birth is followed by rapid changes in oestrogen and progesterone, this is likely to be a contributory factor. Whatever the cause, the fact remains that post-natal depression is a very common, debilitating and upsetting situation which clearly has implications for both the bonding of mother and baby and the possible effects on other children and relationships within the family, particularly the marital relationship. A number of groups are beginning to respond to this widespread problem. The Association for Post-Natal Illness, for example, has over three hundred volunteers who offer advice and counselling, whilst other groups will also help with such problems as a crying baby or breast-feeding. The Family Support Service in Lambeth was set up to deal with the high rates of depression and isolation amongst single parents. Both group support and individual counselling is available together with educational and recreational facilities. This scheme is used by both pregnant women and parents of young children.

In 1982, an international society, the Marcé Society, was formed to advance the understanding, prevention and treatment of mental illness in mothers related to childbearing. It is significant that almost all the postulated explanations of post-natal depression relate to behaviour or circumstances during pregnancy which gives further weight to the need for continuity of care, a partnership between mother and health professionals, and the importance of creating a supportive social network.

Special areas and needs

This book assumes that different families will need different forms of advice and support at different times for different reasons. Pregnancy and childbirth is a particularly vulnerable time for any couple and when events do not turn out as expected there is an additional need for support. The fear of losing a planned child is a very real one for many couples. It is thought that one in five or six pregnancies end in a miscarriage. The Miscarriage Association has a newsletter and local support groups to help members survive loss and provide support for future pregnancies. This kind of emotional and practical support is particularly relevant as it is suggested that stress may well be a factor in many miscarriages. The Stillbirth Association fills a similar function, but in this situation there is an actual baby rather than a promise to be mourned, buried and grieved over. In 1982, 4205 stillbirths were recorded. At a time of grief, confusion and often of physical exhaustion of the mother, parents have the added burden of having to make decisions about seeing the dead baby, post-mortems, burial and registration of both a birth and death (Borg and Lasker 1982).

Other organisations have been formed both to educate and support parents who feel they are different from the perceived norm. These are nearly always voluntary groups based on self-help and experience. The Caesarian support group of Cambridge provides a telephone, personal and postal counselling service for parents who have either had, or think they may need, a Caesarian delivery. The Pre-Eclamptic Toxaemia Society produces a newsletter and is working towards evaluating current medical treatment as well as trying to discover the actual cause. The National Association for the Welfare of Children in Hospital has produced *Notes for Parents: Your Baby in Special Care* for the 100 000 newborns who start life each year in special care units. The Twins Club Association runs informal meetings for parents and children at its local clubs with opportunities to bring and buy clothes and equipment. Leaflets, books and a newsletter also give advice on how to manage with twins, triplets or more. There are also, of course, the many specialist groups such as Mencap, the Spastic Society and Down's Children Association, that provide invaluable advice, support and encouragement to all parents whose children are born handicapped. Details of all such groups are given in *Help Starts Here* (VCHC, 1984).

Summary

Becoming a parent involves more than just the arrival of a baby. There are often fundamental changes in the relationship between the parents, for example, as the woman stops paid work, even if only temporarily. There may also be changes in social and economic life-styles. Few parents explicitly plan their pregnancies but the majority of couples who marry do want and expect to have one or two children. The links between poor health care and nutrition of the mother, and increased risks to both mother and baby, have highlighted the need for pre-conceptual counselling. Although little is provided by the NHS, informal sessions run by health visitors and a number of private clinics are now offering pre-conceptual advice.

Antenatal care is provided by the NHS in two ways: clinics primarily concerned with the physical health of the mother and foetus; and classes to provide the necessary information and advice to prepare both parents for the forthcoming labour, birth and parenthood. Antenatal clinics have been consistently criticised for their inability to attract those who need them most: the very young women, single women, some ethnic minorities, women with large families and those with social and financial problems. Those who do attend express dissatisfaction with the lengthy waiting times, lack of privacy and of facilities for other children and their inaccessibility. Health-care personnel have also been criticised for not giving more explicit and realistic information to parents. Only about half of all pregnant women attend antenatal classes. Some of these involve prospective fathers but few provide the opportunities for couples to talk with each other and with other couples to share their feelings and anxieties about pregnancy, childbirth and parenthood.

Research has indicated that the ability to cope with major

changes in life is more important during the transition to parenthood than the level of information. Realistic information, however,
together with the opportunity to question others, sharing knowledge and feelings and creating a supportive network are seen as
potential goals for all antenatal classes and particularly for local and
community based groups. Innovative schemes have begun linking
parents, forming local groups, reviewing the content and presentation of classes, bringing in speakers and parents from voluntary
groups to NHS classes and offering alternative provision.

Recent surveys and reports have recommended a reduction of
monitoring and routine medical intervention in hospitals and the
establishment of peripheral community-based antenatal care services. The frequency of obstetric intervention has also been linked
with the high incidence of post-natal depression which affects
almost all women.

Continuity of care, shared with the midwife and health visitor, is
favoured by the majority of women. Childbirth can be an emotionally, physically and psychologically exhausting time for both parents
and it helps couples to have the same professionals attending them
through the pregnancy and delivery and the early months of parenthood.

For some parents the birth may not be as expected and for them a
number of services, often self-help groups, exist to offer advice and
guidance, and provide support and counselling.

6

Parents with Pre-school Children

Introduction

Despite evidence which suggests that adverse experiences early in life need not be permanently damaging (Clarke and Clarke, 1976), the quality of children's early interactions with adults close to them – usually their parents – clearly has important implications for their development into competent, caring and fully-realised adults. An increasing body of research now supports the view that optimum development is associated with highly interactive parent–child relationships in which the adult is consistently responsive to behaviour initiated by the child, elaborating the child's language and encouraging play and exploration (Schaffer, 1977; McGlaughlin and Empson, 1979). Burton White, for example, who as director of the Harvard Pre-school Project spent many years observing hundreds of young children in their homes, found significant differences between 'competent' children and those who developed less well in terms of the extent of interaction with their mothers and the type and quality of this interaction. He concluded that a mother's ability to respond effectively to a 12 – 18 month old infant, at a stage when she is learning to walk and talk, by providing opportunities for expression and exploration without the use of negative control, is the most important measure of competence in child-rearing. In his book for parents based on his research he claims 'I am totally convinced that the first priority with respect to helping each child to reach his maximum level of competence is to do the best possible job in structuring his experience and opportunities during the first three years of life' (White, 1975).

A key factor in the quality of this interaction and indeed in all aspects of bringing up children, is the emotional state of the parents and particularly the mother, for a mother who is tired, lonely, isolated or depressed, with little self-esteem or feelings of control over her own life is unlikely to respond willingly or positively to her child's needs and demands. The main focus in this chapter will therefore be those sources of information, education and support which work *with* parents and are specifically concerned with parenting skills and the quality of relationships within the family.

For even the most fully prepared new parent the first few weeks – or months – of life with a new baby are seldom easy. Feelings of isolation and of vulnerability in the face of the high expectations that society places on parents, suggests that society 'has a corresponding responsibility to ensure that parents are afforded access to help, advice and support in bringing up their children, not just to combat particular moments of severe and identifiable vulnerability, but also to deal with the common concerns of every day life' (Children's Committee, 1980).

The availability of support for *all* families is an important point, for all too often families are seen as falling into one of two camps. Either they are coping adequately and are felt to need no assistance at all, or they fall below an accepted level of providing 'good enough parenting' and become the focus of immediate state intervention. The vast majority of parents, regardless of their social and economic circumstances, are capable of providing the opportunities for their children to which Burton White refers. But whilst they manage well on their own for much of the time, most would welcome some support some of the time, and there can be few who, at particular points of crisis, do not seek additional help and guidance. The universal relevance of parent education and support is a key to how the immensely complex network of schemes and services is presented in this chapter. In many ways it would be easier to classify schemes according to the main providers – health, education, social services or the voluntary sector. But as one of the fundamental issues is of the need to work co-operatively across these traditional boundaries, looking at the needs of parents and of families as a whole, just two main divisions have been made, between schemes and services which are – or should be – available to all families; and those which work with vulnerable families experiencing particular difficulties, which may include measures to prevent children coming into care and work with families at risk of abusing their children.

Widely available services

Individual approaches

For many new parents the first sources of strength and support are their own families and their friends and neighbours. But changing patterns of family life and of employment mean that families and friends are often widely dispersed, and if the needs of individual families are to be met, a broad spectrum of services will be required in any one area, to complement – or in some cases to supplement – family networks, and to enable parents to be able to 'plug in' at whichever point they feel is relevant. Evidence in the previous chapter pointed to the importance of continuity between the ante-natal and post-natal phases, and the health professionals can play a crucial role here – the midwife, general practitioner, practice nurse, and particularly the health visitor. The Court report emphasised that 'the key community worker in preventive child health services is the health visitor' and whilst this is undoubtedly true, the increasing demands on health visitors that each new report brings, have led the secretary of the Health Visitors Association to speak of the danger of health visitors being seen as a panacea for all the problems within the family (Goodwin, 1982). Nevertheless the health visitor is uniquely placed to be available to individual families in their own home and in child health clinics, with a knowledge not only of child health and development, but of local resources and of other new mothers experiencing similar problems with whom contact might be made. The health visitor is also in a good position, either alone or as part of a team, to undertake regular developmental screening of all mothers and babies in order to identify any problems as early as possible (Hardy *et al.*, 1979; Wolfendale, 1979). Whether or not these approaches are followed depends very much on the time and inclination of individual health visitors.

The availability of an individual and relaxed discussion at home, without the hassle of taking a young baby to a clinic or surgery, can be of considerable value to a new mother. It is a practice recommended to general practitioners by one GP who always does his tenth-day examination of the new baby in the home with the mother watching (Jenkins and Newton, 1981) although evidence would suggest that this type of home visit is the exception rather than the rule.

One of the main problems in promoting a more positive approach to health care is the dual system of preventive facilities provided by health clinics and the school health services, and therapeutic care as provided by GPs and hospitals. Both the Court report (1976) and the Royal College of General Practioners' report *Healthier Children – Thinking Prevention*(RCGP, 1982) recommended their integration. One of the few areas which is experimenting with this integrated approach is Newcastle, where the first priority of the Riverside Child Health Project is that parents should be given the information to enable them to take a greater share of responsibility for the health of their children. The RCGP report also re-emphasised that the main factors affecting the health of children were to be found in the home and the family, and in pressing practitioners to get to know 'their' families better, suggested that as their contribution to preventive care, GPs should undertake six basic examinations of all children: at birth, six weeks, seven months, 2 years, 4½ years and between 12 and 13 years.

Informal post-natal and parent and toddler groups

Whilst the value of the home-based approach speaks for itself, loneliness, depression and isolation are key themes in studies of mothers with very young children and the availability of informal groups which provide an opportunity for meeting with other new parents and exchanging experiences is an important part of the network of services. The White Paper on violence to children (DHSS, 1978) recommended that the community at large should become more aware of its responsibilities towards families with young children and that self-help groups and voluntary organisations should be encouraged. It is therefore encouraging to note a considerable expansion in the number of post-natal groups, drop-in centres, network schemes and parent and toddler groups over the past decade. There is still relatively little provision for mothers of children under a year old, but even here some new schemes are developing. Some simply aim to increase neighbourliness by linking new mothers at home with their babies with others in their immediate area – for example the Highbury Meet a Mum project in Islington, or Network in Watford, two projects using local mothers as volunteers but with a little financial help for a part-time co-ordinator.

Other approaches have extended the antenatal group into the

post-natal period, and health visitors are again key workers here, putting new mothers in touch with each other, assessing the needs of local mothers and running informal weekly groups in health clinics, surgeries, community groups or homes. There are many examples of such groups, some of them run by the mothers themselves, once the health visitor has helped to make the initial arrangements and introduce new mothers to each other. These may be in the homes of group members, as is the case with the thirty or so CHAT groups (Contact Health And Teaching) set up by a health visitor in Pinner, some of them running for ten years or more (Hiskins, 1981); or in clinics and child health centres, as not all mothers wish to invite others back to their homes. A study of parent and toddler groups within the health service in West Glamorgan for example, recommended that every health visitor should run a group for twenty mothers as a highly productive way of working with more families and using premises that were already there and for which no extra charge need be made (Jones, undated).

Whilst many of these post-natal and parent and toddler groups set up by health visitors are very informal and aim mainly to provide opportunities for mothers to share experiences, some have taken a rather more structured approach, offering opportunities to take Open University courses. A study of three different groups set up by a health visitor in Widnes, for example, found that it was possible to involve families, even in 'at risk' categories, in mother and toddler groups and that, provided a crèche was available for the children, the mothers were keen to discuss materials from the Open University courses. The mothers not only learned from each other's experience and supported each other, but also made greater use of health facilities (Palfreeman, 1982).

Health visitors are not alone in attempting to meet the needs of mothers with very young children. Some GPs have set up groups attached to their surgeries or in mothers' homes, with the help of practice nurses and health visitors, making themselves available on a weekly basis to discuss any problems relating to child health. A practitioner in Kent, for example, who had experience of running groups for parents who had abused or neglected their children, found that by setting up a similar scheme which was open to all new mothers, he was able to provide specific and practical help, and that the groups appeared to generate high self-esteem, help the mothers to cope more adequately and change their approach to seeking medical advice (Chapman, 1982). A study in Cambridge of a more structured group in a surgery, which also provided a crèche for the children, recommended that such groups could be developed as a normal adjunct to well-baby clinics by primary health care teams (Ruel and Adams, 1981).

Many nursery schools and classes are working more closely with parents and are taking advantage of falling rolls to use empty classrooms to set up parent and toddler groups, toy libraries, drop-in centres, English classes, parents' rooms and as the basis for home-visiting schemes. These various initiatives are discussed in more detail later.

Whilst health visitors, teachers and community workers have a crucial part to play in the establishment of informal groups of this type, the majority of parent and toddler groups – or mother and toddler groups as some are still called – are run by parents either on their own or in association with voluntary organisations such as the Pre-school Playgroups Association (PPA), the National Childbirth Trust (NCT) or Meet A Mum Association (MAMA). The PPA's interest and involvement grew from the demands of mothers with children, under playgroup age (that is, under three) and although there is no way of knowing exactly how many such groups exist, the 1983 figures from the PPA show that they are continuing to increase in number. Those mother and toddler groups in membership of PPA nearly doubled between 1979 and 1982, when some 6300 groups were reported by PPA branches (PPA, 1983). A survey found that the main aim of mother and toddler groups was to provide a pleasant meeting place for mothers while also providing satisfying play material and a safe place for babies and toddlers, within sight and sound of their mothers, who remain responsible for them (PPA, 1981). Whilst parents could make friends, watch their children play and perhaps find that they were not the only parents whose children wouldn't sleep or had problems with teething, the children had the opportunity of playing alongside other children with toys they might not have at home. The survey concluded that these clubs have arisen 'as a natural answer to many of the most pressing problems of today's young families, as parents struggle, perhaps unconsciously, to find ways of including other known and trusted adults in the lives of the care-taking parent and the young child – a substitute for the old style family' (PPA, 1981).

Most parent and toddler groups provide for mother and children together, and few therefore have opportunities for formal group discussions or films, unless a separate crèche is provided. But learning together can be an important experience. A report from the Stepping Stones project in Glasgow speaks of the challenge, the demands and the exhaustion that toddlers present to their parents, and points to the importance of helping parents to manage this very critical stage as well as possible. The report argues that for a harassed mother to see a professional handle her child better than she does, does little for the mother's self-esteem or self-confidence, and that groups can more usefully support mothers in building up good relationships with their children (Overton, 1982). The various groups under this umbrella of 'informal support' clearly have a role to play in reducing isolation, increasing self-confidence and an understanding of their children in parents with children under three. Many are run by mothers, yet it is important to recognise the difficulties under which most of them operate, in finding premises, buying toys, finding someone to lead the group regularly and building up their links with local parents. It is to their credit that some local authorities are employing a co-ordinator of such groups – usually on a part-time basis – who can provide this type of support and help in the establishment of new groups. It is also unrealistic to expect that mothers using groups and drop-in centres will necessarily be willing or able to set up their own groups. The Moorland Drop-in Centre in Milton Keynes for example found that parents were not willing to establish a self-sufficient group, and once the paid leader was withdrawn the group collapsed. The existence of a regular paid leader has been found by most groups and drop-in centres to give a sense of purpose and stability.

Groups and schemes with a particular emphasis on parenting

Playgroups There is a sense in which any group or scheme or service involving parents is concerned with parenting or parent education but some place a particular emphasis on being a parent and bringing up children. In the twenty-one years since they started as a response to the lack of nursery education, playgroups have provided both education and support for hundreds of thousands of parents and their children. During this time the Pre-school Playgroup Association (PPA) of which some 80 per cent of playgroups are members, has developed from its original concern with providing facilities for young children to its current focus on helping parents to understand and provide for the needs of their young children. Some 14 000 playgroups were members of the PPA in 1982, with a further 1612 as members of the Scottish PPA, providing places for considerably more children than any other form of pre-school provision (PPA, 1983). The PPA also run training courses for parents and others wishing to increase their understanding of children: introductory courses of a few short talks; foundation courses taking a day a week for a year; further and more advanced courses on the same basis; and courses for those wishing to become tutors. These courses attracted nearly 38 000 parents and others during 1981 – 2, enabling mothers in particular to share and learn from their experience of bringing up children and build on this to run groups.

Involvement in playgroups has helped many hundreds of parents to understand better the needs of their own children and how to provide for them and the experience of being involved in running a community group has also provided many mothers with a new-found confidence in their own abilities. A small-scale study of parental involvement in playgroups in Leighton Buzzard concluded that a combination of involvement and responsibility were the keys to parent education, leading mothers to considerable learning about themselves and about their children and to the making of many new friends (Keeley, 1981). Yet even in playgroups learning tends to be incidental rather than heavily structured. As the Oxford Pre-school Project discovered, few parents were aware of pre-school groups as an educational experience for themselves, for the emphasis tended to be informal and couched in non-educational terms. There were no formal programmes for parents, or instructions in child development, and parents learned through exposure and by accident rather than through structured, programmed teaching. The research concluded that 'If the goal [of involving parents in pre-school groups] is the educational process and their role in it – then no group in our study achieved this totally, even those that tried' (Smith, 1980).

Although there are those who have doubted the value of play-groups other than in middle-class areas, a number of recent studies and developments have shown how playgroups can be sensitive to the needs of local areas. A National Children's Bureau study of playgroups in disadvantaged areas found that although the nature of some mothers' involvement might differ from the traditional rota-sharing and fund-raising, nevertheless the playgroup could play an important part in response to the mothers own need for relief, support and a break from home and children (Ferri, 1977). Elsewhere playgroups are developing by responding to local needs as for example in the Wirral, where the Woodchurch Family Support Project started as a playgroup and now includes a drop-in centre, a parents and toddlers group, an advice centre, a toy library and a home-visiting scheme (Robinson, E., 1982). In Lewisham the PPA has set up a neighbourhood visiting scheme to support families through home visits. The Scottish PPA's innovative Stepping Stones project in five priority areas in Strathclyde has also responded to the needs of local families. The project workers have seen their role as facilitators within the community and have developed family centres with the parents to include playgroups, drop-in facilities, mother and toddler groups, shared meals, workshops, adult education, social events and family outings (Overton, 1982). Parents are also involved in the 'users group', a specific attempt to give parents opportunities to plan things for themselves and take responsibility for them.

To meet the needs of rural areas and some inner city areas with little playgroup provision, the use of play-buses as a flexible response to community needs has been slowly growing since the first bus took to the road in 1969, and the National Play-bus Association now reports that there are 150 such buses throughout the country. A key role for these mobile playgroups may be to inspire the establishment of a permanent group where there is not one. A recent report for example, states that regular visits from a bus began to attract a group of local mothers, from which a leader emerged, and with the help of the social services department a permanent group was set up in a nearby house (Goulding, 1983).

Parent education groups The definition of parent education discussed in Chapter 2 noted the prevalence overseas of structured programmes such as Parent Effectiveness Training, and discussed some of the drawbacks of such approaches. Nevertheless these and other parent education programmes do enjoy considerable popularity. A survey undertaken by the Parent Education Centre in just three cities in the Boston area for example, found 400 parent education programmes and concluded that there must be several thousand throughout the United States (White, 1979). In other countries too, parent education tends to take a more formal pattern.

Sweden for example, passed a law in 1979 which made parent-training compulsory, in an attempt to 'increase knowledge, link parents with each other, and increase their involvement with and influence over their children'. At present this 'training' is centred mainly in ante- and post-natal clinics, but it is hoped to extend it to pre-school facilities and schools. The Mannerheim League in Finland is also building up a parent-education programme to be available to all parents at four key stages of their children's development, based on a synthesis of several theoretical approaches (Rönka, 1983).

New Zealand too has a long tradition of parent education through the work of its Marriage Guidance Council, its network of Parent Centres, through the work of the Plunket Society and its Family Support Service, and through the recently formed Family Life Education Councils in a number of areas (Social Development Council, 1977).

'Schools for parents' as started in France in the 1920s and promoted through the International Federation for Parent Education are popular in many countries, as for example in Brazil, one of several in South America to run these schools. They operate through weekly discussion groups led by parents, usually a husband and wife working together, an approach which, unlike most others, tends to encourage men as well as women to participate. Japan too has an ambitious programme of parent education classes, provided through adult education and aiming to attract 14 million parents in the next few years to a series of classes. These are backed up by a family education consultative service giving postal, telephone and television support in 41 of Japan's 47 prefectures.

Structured schemes and 'schools for parents' have never really caught on in Britain to the extent they have elsewhere. Schools for parents have been criticised for their restrictive appeal, tending to draw 'educated and conscientious middle-class élite' (Stern, 1960), and even parent-teacher associations in schools have played a minimum role in this respect in comparison with similar bodies elsewhere in Europe and in countries such as New Zealand and Japan. The DHSS report of the consultations in 1973 concluded 'The most common view was that the majority of parents would not participate in the parent education movement or attend formal further or adult education classes even if, as was suggested, they were given a financial incentive to attend... Some less formal approach was needed' (DHSS, 1974b).

What is happening today may not perhaps be described as a movement, but it is certainly not very formal. Parent groups are being set up by youth and community workers, by playgroup leaders, by adult education tutors, health visitors, counsellors, psychologists, teachers, clergymen and parents themselves. Two of the longest-running organisations are in Halifax and Gloucester. The Calderdale (formerly Halifax) Association for Parents, set up in 1968 for the 'promotion of parent education', has for many years been campaigning for a British Association for Parent Education to encourage the establishment of a national network of such groups and to draw attention to the importance of the parental role and the place of education in it. CAP runs discussion groups and lectures for parents, and has recently set up Mixenden Parents Centre, with funding from MSC and based on the Liverpool Home Link project, to provide a resource centre and toy library for parents. The Gloucester Association for Family Life, also started during the 1960s as an alliance of local organisations whose aim was to 'encourage an understanding of the importance of secure and happy family life, as the basis of a stable and civilised community'. GAFL runs discussion groups and provides speakers for other organisations, NAMCW courses for local schoolgirls and has published various materials for use in discussion (see Appendix 3).

One of the difficulties facing parents' groups has traditionally been the dearth of good materials for starting off and guiding the discussion. The publication over the last few years of the Open University's parent education courses has however provided a wealth of resource materials covering childhood from birth to late adolescence in four courses. Details of these are given in Appendix 3. As well as providing tools for learning in the form of booklets, leaflets, radio and television programmes, a key to the OU approach is the *process* of helping people to review their own experiences, values and resources in child-rearing and to make and implement decisions. Thus the television programmes on discipline and two-year olds, or toilet training, presents different families coping in different ways and encourages viewers to reflect on these approaches in the light of their own experience.

Although originally intended as structured learning materials for parents to use on their own at home, as part of a short course, the courses were found to have a much wider use. Chapter 3 looked at their contribution to work in schools. They have also been used extensively as the basis for group discussion by health visitors, social workers, teachers, adult education tutors, playgroup leaders and childminders, either as they are or in a modified form. They have often acted as a trigger in bringing mothers together and appear, on the whole, to have been well received. Comments such as 'The course gave me lots of ideas on handling the baby, like talking to her. It gave me some ideas on what to expect her to do as she grew older' were recorded in the Wirral (Cheshire) groups already described. The mothers in this project were offered sponsored places, and the availability of several thousand such 'free places' (funded by the Health Education Council and the Scottish Health Education Unit) has enabled the professionals working with parents to use them flexibly and with a wide range of groups.

In addition, a project funded by the Bernard Van Leer Foundation has been working with community groups in Birmingham, Coventry, Liverpool and the Western Isles of Scotland to produce materials which are a little less glossy and middle class and are more accessible to those who have difficulty with the written word. Three separate projects have also been funded jointly by the Open University and local education authorities in Buckinghamshire, Strathclyde and Cambridgeshire. Because the materials were originally intended for individual use, two packs of topic leaflets for use in groups have now been published, using some of the original material but with guidance for group leaders and group members. And a *Book of the Child* based on the materials has been given free to every pregnant woman in Scotland over a two-year period. Details of all OU materials are given in Appendix 3.

An organisation which has made a significant contribution to parent education through planning, setting up and evaluating several such groups in different settings is the National Marriage Guidance Council (NMGC). Unlike the MGC in New Zealand which sees education work as of equal importance to counselling, and runs parent education courses for up to 20 000 people each year, the NMGC in Britain is best known for its remedial work with those who are experiencing difficulties in their relationships. However, over the past three years (1980–3) NMGC has set up a number of education projects at different stages of the life-cycle, and three in particular have worked with groups of mothers and pre-school children: at a drop-in centre at Moorland Nursery in

Milton Keynes, at the nursery unit of an infants school in Telford (LeRoy, 1982) and at Medway Infants School in Leicester. Each project has been concerned to give parents opportunities to share each other's experiences, to contribute information, to understand parenting issues, to support each other within the group and often outside it, and to build up their own self-confidence and reduce their isolation (Torkington, 1982).

A key element in all these projects has been the role of the counsellor who has worked closely with the teachers and community workers. As we saw in Chapter 2 the need for appropriate skills and sensitivity when leading groups is particularly important. Marriage guidance counsellors are trained specifically in the development of sensitivity, self-awareness and increased understanding and awareness of others and some in addition have skills in understanding group dynamics. These are valuable assets in working with parents and it is encouraging to note the increasing involvement of NMGC in parent education work.

Projects under the general umbrella of the Family Life Education Ecumenical Project, set up in 1981 by the main Christian churches, are also relevant here. Compared with some countries, notably Germany where some 250 parent education centres are affiliated to the Catholic and Protestant churches, the influence of the church in parent education in this country tends to be fairly limited. However, the churches are all to some extent involved and three dioceses of the Church of England – Coventry, Leicester and Guildford – have set up specific family life education projects and more are planned. The Coventry project, as one example, in addition to work with local groups and individuals has produced a study course entitled *How's the Family* and a resource pack on marriage and family life. The Mothers Union is also involved through the work of its Young Families Department, which runs mother and toddler groups throughout the country.

Although there are few structured programmes or formal evening classes in parent education, there are a number of independent organisations and individual psychotherapists and psychologists beginning to offer courses on such topics as 'Becoming a mother' or 'Parents and children are people'. One such organisation is a charitable trust entitled Exploring Parenthood, which offers one-day seminars for parents. The Adlerian Society of Great Britain also runs one or two parents groups based on the teachings of Alder and Dreikurs. It is early days to gauge the success of these various enterprises, but after a rather shaky start some do seem to be drawing small groups of parents and professionals to their courses.

Advice and information

An essential part of any programme of parent education is the need to give parents access to information and resources and thus to some extent to a greater sense of control over their lives. Many of the approaches outlined in this chapter see the provision of information and – where it is sought – advice, as part and parcel of their work, but it is nevertheless worth re-emphasising the need to make information about services and resources widely available in places that parents use (post offices, supermarkets and laundrettes, as well as clinics and libraries) and in language that they can understand. It is of little use providing mother and toddler groups and toy libraries and then omitting to tell potential users where they are. The variety of services provided by different local authority departments and hundreds of voluntary groups, is confusing to parents and it is encouraging to find that a number of local groups have produced handbooks on services for under-fives and their families. Some areas have also set up specific advice and information services in addition to those provided by Citizens Advice Bureaux and the crisis phone services, for example the Parent Advice Service operated by the school psychological service once a week in Hartlepool, and the Under Fives Advice Clinic staffed by psychologists in two Islington health centres.

Working with vulnerable families

Whilst an attempt has been made to avoid labelling either families or the different approaches to working with them, the difficulty of organising the material presented in this chapter has necessitated grouping the schemes for ease of reference. Inevitably some schemes could be listed in several places but it is hoped that the grouping will be seen merely for the organisational purposes for which it is intended. Whilst most of the approaches described so far should be generally available to all families, some families may be more vulnerable than others, particularly when their children are small. A number of factors are known to have an adverse effect on parents' abilities to care for their children and there will be particular points of stress in many parents' lives when the traditional approaches may no longer be adequate. Problems might be presented by a difficult pregnancy and birth and a high degree of post-natal depression for example; an unsupported mother with several young children; very young parents whose own needs as adolescents have not been met; parents who have grown up in care with inadequate models of parenting; ill-health or unemployment.

Many of the groups and schemes in existence today reflect the current emphasis on self-help and, in the face of inadequate state provision, the need for families and neighbourhoods to provide their own support systems. In drawing together the papers from the original DHSS consultations on parenthood, Joan Cooper said:

The most effective policy to assist the family would lie less in precise educative work . . . than in community development aimed at engendering relationships between households within a local area in order to provide opportunities for people to act together to solve their problems rather than to meet them in isolation and to become over-dependent on specialised agencies. (DHSS, 1974a)

This theme was also central to the Barclay report (1982) on the role and tasks of social workers.

The report's commitment was to a community work approach which assumes that lay people have more potential, ability and commitment to care for each other than is generally accepted. Whilst this is undoubtedly true, some of the assumptions about the potential of the community are not based on clear evidence that all lay people are able or willing to care for each other. Many of the most vulnerable families find it difficult to rely on informal care networks, and as the schemes illustrated in this chapter show, professionals have a key role to play in helping families to learn the skills of setting up and managing groups and centres. The way in which these skills are learned should be built upon a concept of partnership and mutual respect between professionals and families, with a focus on individuals learning new skills and rebuilding their own confidence through opportunities to give as well as to take, for 'knowing you're being useful to somebody else is the best medicine in the world . . . this is one of the core features in self-help group work; the rebuilding of self-confidence through one's ability to actually help others' (Robinson and Henry, 1977).

Adult and community education

Adult education starts from a basis of mutual respect and teaching among equals, and it is thus ideally placed to respond to individuals who through lack of confidence may feel there is no way in which they can alter the circumstances of their own lives. In practice, however, it has tended to concentrate on traditional evening classes in pottery and car maintenance and attempts to set up similar classes on child development or 'parents and children' have not on the whole met with a flood of students enthusiastic to enrol. Some of the schemes already mentioned – notably playgroup courses and work with the Open University parent education materials – have been organised by adult education tutors, but on the whole the conventional adult education model has failed to reach vulnerable families. A report on education for women in Liverpool, for example, shows vividly how working-class women who left school at the earliest opportunity, are intimidated by the prospect of further education; have no confidence in their learning ability; often have no information on what is available; may find the cost prohibitive; have forgotten how to study; if ever they knew; and have no-one to look after young children while they are in classes (Cousins, 1982).

A study of parent education courses in adult education institutes in London showed that most of the participants were mothers with children under five (Scribbins, 1983). Whilst mothers such as these might be intimidated by a course at the institute every Monday night, they may well respond to a health group at the local school starting next week, with a crèche and a programme that can be planned from one week to the next. The organisation of adult education institutes and their emphasis on what one principal describes as wall-to-wall dressmaking, tends to militate against a flexible use of resources and an immediate response to local needs. But if they so choose it *is* possible for institutes to appoint tutors responsible for 'outreach' work, and developments within some areas over the last ten years show considerable sensitivity to working with people in local communities, building on their resources and skills, and devising groups and schemes in response to their specific needs. Table 6.1 illustrates the very wide range of activities currently available at one or other of the institutes within the Inner London Education Authority under the general title of parent education. The mothers do come to such schemes, and many do enjoy and benefit from them. As one mother said of Home Link, a community-based adult education scheme in Liverpool, 'When I started going to Home Link, the mist seemed to clear – I thought I HAVE got a brain, I'm NOT a cabbage' (Cousins, 1982).

Many of the schemes within adult education are building on parents' inherent interest and concern for their children. Speaking at a Bureau conference in Scotland about community education in Strathclyde for example, Helen Munro pointed out that contrary to the views expressed by some local professionals who said that

TABLE 6.1　*Parent education activities available at one or more of the adult education institutes within the Inner London Education Authority*

1. Pre-school playgroup leaders courses:
   doorstep
   introductory
   foundation
   further
2. Courses and drop-in centres for childminders
3. Courses for family group leaders
4. Family workshops in community centres and primary and secondary schools
5. Pre-school educational home visiting
6. Crèches as part of many of the courses
7. Mother and toddler groups and drop-in centres
8. Discussion groups and women's studies groups, including child development, parents' rights
9. Tutors for specific projects, e.g. in health centres, with tenants associations, in drop-in centres
10. Open University short courses using free places:
    First Years of Life
    Pre-school Years
    Childhood 5–10
    Parents and teenagers
    Health choices
11. Unemployment projects
12. Project with single, teenage mothers
13. School-based courses, with parents and with teenagers
14. Adult literacy and English as a second language courses.

mothers were only interested in 'booze and bingo', mothers were extremely interested in their children's development, but because of their lack of confidence in themselves as mothers, were almost terrorised by their 3- and 4-year olds (Munro, 1983). These particular mothers surprised the tutors by their enthusiasm for completing the OU courses and wanting a formal presentation of their certificates – perhaps their first education success and for many the first rung on the ladder of 'second chance' education.

Playgroup leaders courses, groups using Open University materials and educational home visiting schemes are all helping parents to understand and enjoy their children. This is also inherent in the ILEA family workshops. Since the first workshop was set up in 1969, others have been set up within ILEA in schools, community centres and church halls. Most are craft-based and all provide activities for parents and young children, sometimes together and sometimes separately. Each develops in response to the needs of the families involved and their contribution to parent education tends to be indirect, being concerned with reducing isolation, increasing confidence, self-respect and an enjoyment of parenting (Bennett and Stobart, 1981).

These various approaches have succeeded in offering women, particularly working-class women, a wider horizon, and have started many on a path towards greater self-fulfilment. But the Liverpool mother who said 'My husband doesn't mind but he doesn't want me to get too clever' highlighted an inherent difficulty. For most parent education activities within adult education – and indeed elsewhere – are geared exclusively to women, and work with women as mothers. As the ILEA policy document on parent education argued:

Parent education has its roots in role education and as such is in danger of fitting, or at least reinforcing, men and women into the stereotypic images created for them by the dominant ideology . . . [it] needs to make explicit the contradiction between the ideologically defined and traditional status of the women-in-the-home and the characteristics of subordination, isolation and dependence which 'staying at home' can create. It should also demonstrate that such an ideology, whilst disadvantaging women, does not benefit all men, for it places on the man in the family an 'obligation' to provide for his wife and family. (ILEA, 1983)

If parent education is genuinely to encourage women to increase their confidence and self-esteem and to explore the nature of their dependence and their roles as mothers, what are the implications of this for relationships within their families and society as a whole? Whatever the emphasis of the parent education group, the educational task will be as much concerned with helping people to understand themselves and their relationships, as with acquiring information and skills, and in this respect the 'educator' may need to rethink his or her relationship with the group. Allan Wellings described, for example, how the extension of a mothers' group programme from the Sheffield University campus to the community, where mothers accepted the tutors on their merits as group members rather than as educators, forced the tutors to rethink their role: 'We had to relinquish assumptions about the relevance of our academic kind of understanding of parenting and child development and our right to determine the direction and content of the group's activities' (Wellings, 1981).

Closer liaison between home and school

Nursery schools and classes are an obvious community resource and many are now seeing their role in terms of the families who use them and not just of the children. Parental involvement is no longer the prerogative of the playgroups, and indeed the Oxford Pre-school Research project found that the main difference in involvement was not between playgroups and nursery schools, nor related to the class and background of the parent, but depended on whether the group operated a 'partnership' as distinct from a 'professional' model (Smith, T. 1980). Parental involvement in schooling is considered in more detail in the following chapter, but one aspect of this involvement is the greater openness of the schools to community use. An increase in the number of mother and toddler groups and adult education classes attached to nurseries has already been noted, some of these in traditional subjects such as keep fit and flower arranging and others, such as those which have been running in Sheffield for many years, specifically concerned with being a parent and bringing up children (Hubbard and Wellings, 1979).

There are also a number of schemes, often in inner city areas, which are sensitive to the needs of parents whose own memories of schooling make dropping-in to a local school a real challenge.

Specific educational home-visiting schemes are described in more detail shortly, but many nursery teachers now see home-school liaison as part of their role and some schools and classes have appointed 'under-fives workers' with special responsibility for closer liason with families in the area. Drop-in centres, such as the South Harringay Pre-school Centre, and the parent education flat in Manchester, can also help to forge links between home and school, and as they tend to be open every day and responsive to the needs of those who use them, quickly become a centre for community activities. The Harringay centre is based in a multi-racial area of Tottenham and is used by at least twenty different ethnic groups. The educational home-visiting scheme is also based at the centre, which sees itself as providing equally for the needs of children and parents (Stacey, 1983). The Manchester flat grew from the work of home-school liaison teachers and in addition to a concern with involving parents more closely in the education system, has a specific brief to 'raise levels of parenting skills' (Crow, 1983).

The areas that were involved in Educational Priority Area (EPA) projects in the early 1970s still have a strong tradition of community education and a commitment to involving parents in school from the pre-school period onward. The Home and School Centre in Govan in Glasgow for example, has evolved from a long history of home-school liaison and draws parents of under-fives to a wide range of parent workshops, OU courses, group discussions and recreational activities (Grant, 1983). In Coventry the community education unit has been the base for educational home-visiting (Feeley and Karran, 1983) and local groups of parents have worked with the Open University in rewriting the parent education materials. The unit has also established a network of ten nursery annexes, linked to infant schools but run by local parents. Two teacher-leaders in charge of five annexes each, provide training and support for the annexe leaders, all of whom are local mothers. Although none of the twenty-three leaders have had any further education, their high level of skills has been remarked on by the teacher-leaders. Many more mothers applied for the training than there were places available, and the report on the scheme concludes that 'training opportunities in child development, parenting and the pre-school field are urgently needed in urban areas, where large numbers of women are able and likely to take advantage of them' (Coventry, 1979).

Toy libraries

Toy libraries have traditionally been seen as a resource for parents of handicapped children, but their potential as a basis for work with all children with special needs has led to an increasing number being set up as a preventive service within the community, offering information and support to parents before problems arise. This is an approach which has been pursued for example in Portsmouth, where six 'Connor's' Toy Libraries have been set up since 1973, providing a meeting place for parents, offering advice on play activities, providing a range of carefully selected toys which may be borrowed, advising on child development and the management of behaviour problems and offering an information service on local resources. Periodic courses for parents are also arranged by the psychologist who set up the libraries. The Toy Libraries Association has supported many such community toy libraries throughout the country, based in schools and community centres and many of the groups and centres described in this chapter include them amongst their resources for parents. Nursery and infant schools in particular have seen toy libraries as a way of drawing parents with pre-school children into the school and making it more accessible. In Belfast for example, twenty-six toy and book libraries for children under three were introduced into nursery schools in the first four years of the scheme.

Family groups

Nowhere are labels more inadequate than in the case of family groups and family centres, for both types of facility include informal community projects at one end of the spectrum and intensive therapeutic work at the other. One scheme which shares many of the underlying assumptions of adult and community education is Scope, an organisation which started in Southampton in 1976 to 'help families help themselves' and has now spread to Portsmouth, Basingstoke and Bordon. Scope attempts to offer a supportive network of care at times when families are functioning at a low ebb and the main focus of their work has been to establish a network of neighbourhood self-help groups for families with at least one child under five. About 100 families join local groups each year (Poulton, 1982). The groups, which are led by local mothers with training and support from the co-ordinator, meet weekly and whilst the children are cared for in a crèche, the mothers are able to share their experiences and anxieties and provide mutual support. One of Scope's main aims is to reinforce the role of parents as educators of their own children and discussion sessions frequently revolve around the behaviour and learning of young children. In line with other community projects, Scope is concerned to help parents gain a greater sense of power and control over their lives, and on a broader canvas it offers a model for services which do not create dependency but build on the existing strengths and resources within the local community. In addition to the groups Scope also operates a home-visiting scheme for those who find it difficult to join groups and has recently opened a family centre where any group member can stay, with or without their families, at times of particular stress for up to four nights. The co-ordinator also works in Basset Green First School with mothers and their pre-school children (Poulton, 1981) and secondary school pupils participate in the crèche and family groups.

Although attendance at groups is often considered to be the preserve of the middle classes, an evaluation of Scope shows that it did reach an exceptionally 'high stress' group of working-class women; and a study of one group over a period of nine months showed that group support could be effective in the face of major crisis, as when the child of one group member died unexpectedly (Hevey, 1982).

An organisation which has pioneered the establishment of rather different groups is the Family Groups Unit of the London Voluntary Service Council, now a separate unit working nationally and known as COPE. The first group was set up in 1951 as an 'experimental home advice centre' to teach basic home-making skills to women whose families were at risk because of poverty and low educational achievement, and there are now forty groups in Greater London and a number elsewhere. Family groups today are small neighbourhood-based groups, meeting regularly for mutual support and enjoyment. They are run by local people who are selected and prepared for their roles as group leaders and play leaders with the backing of professional workers. The groups aim 'to enable individuals to grow, to develop skills, to learn more about community resources and share troubles and celebrations'. Although they are intended for any people who are isolated, or looking after dependents at home, or who lack the confidence to join other groups, many of those who come are in fact mothers with young children. As with other community projects, the groups are able to create networks and help people find the neighbourhood support that they need as they cope with the normal stresses of family life, child-rearing, budgeting, health and housing problems (Knight *et al.*, 1980; Cowan, 1982). COPE itself acts as a national consultancy and training agency to promote this particular approach to family groups.

There are also many small one-off groups for parents – usually mothers – and young children, run along more structured, therapeutic lines by social workers, health visitors, psychologists, psychiatric nurses and others. Some of these, such as the group at the Thornbury Child and Family Guidance Centre in Bristol, work intensively with vulnerable mothers who are not using existing facilities, helping them to gain insight into themselves and their family relationships, with a particular emphasis on relationships with their children. This group was found to provide a new sense of security, which led to growing confidence and initiative in both mothers and children (Searing, 1980). The Child and Family Centre at Bethel Hospital, Norwich, has run groups for mothers and small children for nearly ten years. Some of these focus on the needs of particularly vulnerable mothers (those who are depressed, have abused their children, and are lonely, isolated or immature) whilst others are for mothers who are having difficulties in handling their pre-school children. Some social workers also run groups for parents, including both therapeutic approaches and the more practical basic skills of budgeting, cooking simple meals etc.

Family centres

Family centres are another form of provision which has multiplied rapidly in the last decade and there appear to be as many methods of working as there are centres. But generally speaking the centres work with parents and children together rather than providing day-care for children of parents who are not coping well. A small-scale study of thirty-three family centres, set up in association with our own project, found that they had developed in response to three main factors (Birchall, 1982). One was a shift in emphasis in the work of the main voluntary child-care organisations – such as the

Children's Society, National Children's Home, Save the Children and Barnardo's – away from residential work and towards working with the child and the family within the community. Second, some social services departments were rethinking the nature and purpose of their day nurseries, and were involving parents more closely in the care of their children by offering supportive and modelling help. Third, a small group had been established by education authorities as an alternative to or extension of their nursery provision.

Although there are inevitably differences in the way the centres operate, in that each attempts to build up a programme of work in response to the needs of the local area, the Bureau study and an evaluation of twelve of the Children's Society's family centres (Phelan, 1982, 1983) show that the overall aim of each centre is to strengthen families, to help to improve the quality of parenting, and prevent children being separated from their families and the community by being received into care. Some centres provide structured schemes or individual therapy focussed on parent-child relationships for a small number of families, as for example Orchard House, the NSPCC centre in Wellingborough, which is working with parents who have abused, or are at risk of abusing, their children. Others, including many of the twenty centres set up by the Children's Society, adopt a community work approach, encouraging self-help within families and neighbourhoods, capitalising on the strengths and skills of local people and setting up a wide range of clubs, groups and activities for children, adolescents, parents, elderly people, the unemployed and the handicapped. Bob Holman in a study, entitled *Resourceful Friends*, looking at techniques, aptitudes and attitudes amongst staff in a number of family centres, speaks of the basis of the work as being friendship and reciprocity, with both workers and families giving and taking (Holman, 1983).

One difficulty which became apparent in the Bureau's study of family centres is that of staffing, and of the need for broader and more relevant training and support, a problem not unique to family centres. Many of the workers whose training had prepared them for work with young children but not with adults, and who had been employed by a traditional day nursery found difficulty in working with mothers, some of whom were living in conditions of considerable stress. Attempts to meet the mothers' needs were being made, in some of the centres at the expense of work with the children, who were equally in need of individual attention and stimulation, and required a programme geared to their particular level of development (Birchall, 1982). It is encouraging that the issue of training is one of the main concerns of the newly-formed Young Family Day Care Association.

Home-based programmes

Although many of these community programmes are drawing in some of the most vulnerable families, there is a body of evidence now in relation to health, social welfare and educational provision, that those who might most benefit from services tend to use them least. The low take-up of immunisation and vaccination for example led the Children's Committee (1980) to suggest that certain criteria be established which would entitle some families automatically to receive a domiciliary visit, and a number of health authorities have now adopted a practice of health visitors undertaking health surveillance by routine visits to the home. Social service departments and voluntary agencies such as Family Service Units are sometimes also able to provide family help or home aides to stay with families at times of particular crisis, to prevent the children being taken into care.

Although ease of access, the times at which they open, their cost and attitudes towards 'educational' facilities are obviously factors in the take-up of services, a recent study concluded that 'even if financial resources were available to provide free and splendidly flexible institutionalised provision, the hoped-for goal of reaching over-stretched mothers who lack confidence would not be achieved' (Shinman, 1981). The isolation and sense of alienation from 'authority' which these mothers exhibited could only be overcome, it is suggested, by an informal one-to-one approach offered by a volunteer, who could build up confidence and help such mothers reach the point where they *are* able to use local resources.

A number of such home-visiting schemes are now in operation, some using volunteers and others attached to schools and community centres, using teachers. A book entitled *Perspectives in Pre-school Home Visiting* describing six of the longest running schemes (educational home-visiting in Lothian and Haringey, the ILEA Adult Education Programme, the work done by community education in Coventry and Birmingham and the extensive volunteer networks set up by Home-Start) and looking both at the evolution over the past decade and how it might develop in the years ahead, was published last year as part of the Bureau project (Aplin and Pugh, 1983).

Home-Start is a scheme which offers families the volunteer to which Shinman referred. Since Margaret Harrison set up the first Home-Start scheme in Leicester in 1973, more than twenty-five similar schemes have been set up elsewhere in the country and as many again are at the planning stage or awaiting funding. Home-Start uses volunteers, all of them parents, and some who have themselves been visited in the past, to offer support, friendship and practical assistance to families with children under five who are experiencing difficulties. What many parents need is someone to whom they can relate and who really cares about them and this is what Home-Start aims to provide. Whilst offering support to the parent, the volunteer is also offering a positive stimulus to the child, and in encouraging parents' strengths and emotional well-being is working towards the point where parents feel able to widen their network of relationships and use community support and services effectively. Holman's definition of the 'resourceful friend' could equally well apply to the Home-Start volunteer, who because of the non-statutory nature of her work and her lack of professional status, can offer to 'be with' rather than 'do things to' the family with whom she works. A study of Home-Start distinguishes between the professional, who is problem-orientated and delivers a service, and the volunteer who can be person-focussed and act as a support (Van der Eyken, 1982). For those who are concerned with cost-effectiveness it is also an extremely economical form of family support, particularly when a volunteer is able to help the family stay together and prevent children being taken into care.

Educational home-visiting was first introduced in this country in 1970 as part of the educational priority area project in the former West Riding of Yorkshire. It was strongly influenced by the Head Start programme in the USA which showed that the cognitive performance of children in disadvantaged families could be improved by systematic structured curricula for young children, and that strategies which include parents were more effective in the long term than those which did not (Bronfenbrenner, 1974). Where many American projects tended to be compensatory and concentrate on raising levels of children's performance, the British schemes have aimed at increasing parents' self-confidence and encourage them to feel that they have an important part to play in their children's development. Most of the schemes are available to all the families with pre-school children in a carefully defined area, such as the school catchment area, and most are based in inner city areas where there is considerable deprivation.

Although the emphasis of schemes varies, depending on where they are based, the responses from more than fifty schemes to a questionnaire sent out as part of our study of home visiting, confirmed the focus on family support rather than an exclusive concern with children's cognitive and social performance. Their aims included not only 'helping parents to understand the importance of play as a learning tool and of their role as educators of under-fives' but also 'to improve the links between home and school' and 'to encourage parents' own strengths, to reassure parents, to improve their network of contacts, to promote independence and self-confidence'.

Such research as has been done on the effectiveness of pre-school home-visiting from the *parents'* point of view, shows that schemes have encouraged parents to take a closer interest in their children's education and general development (Armstrong and Brown, 1979); that parents have come to discover 'how interesting their children were . . . they began to believe that it was more possible to influence the sort of person their child would become' (McCail, 1981); that they have increased take-up of pre-school facilities (Jayne, 1976); and perhaps most important of all, have increased confidence in their own abilities as parents. As one parent in London said 'Her coming has helped me and Paul a great deal. I think I'm not so nervous with people now, and I'm able to cope with the children better. It's really good to have someone to sit and talk to – someone who listens to you. Lots of the time you are doing the right thing for the children – but talking it over makes you feel more sure' (Aplin and Pugh, 1983).

The study of Home-Start also showed that the scheme achieved remarkable success in supporting families to the point where 'control' was restored and the family could, perhaps for the first time, function as a healthy child-rearing environment (Van der Eyken, 1982).

Crisis phone services

Acute problems with children who won't feed or won't sleep or won't stop crying, or deeply distressing personal problems, may not wait until the doctor's surgery is open or until the next group meeting or home visit. A service which has therefore been welcomed in many areas is a confidential crisis phone service. Most social work offices have an emergency out-of-hours service, although many parents are reluctant to ring social services, and in some parts of the country there are now 24-hour telephone services specifically related to the needs of parents with young children. Some are run by midwives from the local maternity hospital. In Bethnal Green social workers and psychiatrists run such a service from the London Hospital; health visitors operate a crying baby/advisory relief service in Huddersfield, where calls are put through to the local ambulance station and then referred to the health visitor on duty, and similar schemes have been set up in Portsmouth, Enfield, Barnet and Richmond. A new organisation with a number of local groups is CRYSIS, set up by a group of mothers in north London to support the parents of babies who cry excessively.

In addition to these individual initiatives there are two networks of crisis support services operating on a national basis, OPUS and Family Network. The biggest is that provided by self-help groups for parents who are at risk of harming their children. The first of these groups was set up in the early 1970s following the success of Parents Anonymous in America and Canada, and in 1980 some fifty groups with names such as Parents Helpline, Family Lifeline and Parents Anonymous, came together to form OPUS (Organisations for Parents Under Stress). The groups are run by parents for parents, and although the majority have professional advisers and work closely with the local statutory services, few have paid staff. The services they offer vary, but almost all the groups run a 24-hour telephone helpline which offers a confidential service, anonymous if the caller wishes. Some groups also offer a home-visiting scheme, small contact groups for parents who want on-going support, drop-in and day centres (such as the one in Eaton Socon in Cambridgeshire) and practical help with such things as transport. A recent survey of phone calls to eighteen OPUS groups found that the average caller was in her early thirties, married with young children and with her own phone (Meacher, 1982). Not all the calls were child-centred, many being related to the parents' personal problems or environmental problems.

The lack of statutory responsibility and the 'open door' approach means that OPUS groups can respond to requests for help with speed and with a range of flexible services. The study also found that the groups were able to make effective therapeutic relationships with parents whose resistance to authority and whose feelings of guilt prevented them seeking help from statutory agencies. But the report concluded that without some paid staff the resources of time and energy were likely to become exhausted, and that much better training and supervision was required for a difficult and tiring job (Meacher, 1982).

Family Network, set up by the National Children's Home in 1979 as its contribution to the International Year of the Child, also provides a network of telephone support and referral services, with phone-in centres in each of the eight NCH regions. It was an ambitious plan which aimed at providing a listening post, a bank of information, a support service for people with chronic family problems, and a catalyst for setting up self-help or action groups in many parts of the country, and inevitably it was more successful in some areas than others. Some fourteen centres were set up and the network has received thousands of calls. These calls consistently showed unrealistic expectations of relationships, difficulties in communication and lack of insight into an individual's capacities (Kidd, 1981, 1982). Family Network has also collaborated with local radio stations, notably in Swansea, Cardiff and Leeds and with Piccadilly Radio in Manchester, which went into partnership with Family Network and became known as Careline. The phone service provided the radio station with topics upon which they based special programmes, and a number of self-help groups have been set up.

Collaboration with local radio stations has also been a successful venture for a number of other voluntary organisations. The National Children's Centre 'child-care switchboard' experiment for example, showed both the extent of the need for advice and information on child-care issues, and also the potential of local radio for meeting this need (Jackson, 1982). The experiment evolved from Brian Jackson's earlier education shops in local high streets and at Butlin's Holiday Camps, as another way of making 'professional help' more accessible to families. During the summer of 1977 the BBC local radio stations in Nottingham, Manchester, Bristol, Derby, Leeds and London ran an experimental phone-in service on child-care problems, usually for an hour or so a day for a week in each city, and combined this with a private hot-line open for longer hours. During a total of 127 hours of access, some 508 calls got through, though lines were jammed and it was estimated that a considerable number of callers were unsuccessful. The report points out that schemes such as these are modest and cost very little, yet fulfil a very real need, for many of the callers were fairly desperate in their cries for help. Amongst the report's recommendations, are the suggestion that every telephone directory should list on its front cover all the key services (American and Australian directories for example list police, fire, ambulance, and a number to ring about suspected baby-battering); that a crying baby service be considered by every health authority; and that child-care switchboards should be run on a regular basis by local authorities and voluntary organisations in collaboration with local radio stations.

Intensive work with families

Although some families who are experiencing severe problems or where individual members are exhibiting pathological behaviour may well benefit from more intensive work with social workers, psychologists and therapists, an examination of such techniques as behaviour modification, psychoanalysis and family therapy, whether in day or residential centres, is beyond the remit of this book. Few local authority social service departments have the resources to offer long-term intensive support to families, although their statutory responsibility for the welfare of children does mean that they must work with the families of children who are at risk and if necessary take the children into care. Local authority day nurseries and family centres are increasingly working with families, but much of the therapeutic work with the most disadvantaged families is done by voluntary agencies such as Family Service Units, Barnardos, the Family Welfare Association and Home-Start, either in family centres or in the families' homes. There are a few residential family centres run by organisations such as Scope, Arbours, the Richmond Fellowship, the Children's Society and Save the Children, and one or two funded by social services departments such as Broadlands Family Centre in Northamptonshire, which offers a family skills programme over a nine-month period in the centre and three-month follow-up at home. On the whole, however, most intensive work with families takes place within their own homes or at least within their own communities.

Summary

The first five years of a child's life are important ones for the new parents, the young child and the growing relationship between them. A central factor in this relationship is the emotional stability of the parents, and particularly the mother, and this chapter has examined a range of schemes and services which aim at responding to parents' needs for companionship, for increased self-confidence, and for greater knowledge and understanding of themselves and their children. Some of these schemes, for example post-natal groups and parent and toddler groups are very informal, offering parents opportunities to meet together and learn from one another in the course of conversation whilst watching their children playing. Some, such as playgroups, have started from parents' wish to provide facilities for their children, and have moved on, through opportunities for training and running groups, to broaden parents' own horizons. The publication of the Open University parent education materials has provided a focus for many groups to look at being a parent and bringing up children in a rather more structured way, and these materials are now widely used in groups throughout the country. There is still little evidence, however, of working with parents to develop specific skills or of the type of 'parent effectiveness training' that is popular elsewhere in the world.

Some approaches have attempted to work with more vulnerable families. Adult and community education appear to have a particular contribution to make here, as do the growing number of family groups and family centres. Nursery and infant schools are using a variety of strategies to effect a closer relationship between parents and teachers, and home-visiting schemes have an obvious potential for supporting families who tend not to use existing groups and facilities. The best of these approaches attempt to work *with* parents rather than do things *to* them, helping to build up their confidence by giving them opportunities that they may not often have had before, to make decisions and take responsibility. There has been criticism that parent education is simply role education, reinforcing mothers' roles as the chief home-maker and carer of children. However, some of these schemes have shown that involvement in a home-visiting scheme or mother and toddler group has given to many mothers who had left school at the earliest opportunity, a chance to go on to PPA and OU courses and often to further education and employment.

Although few professionals or para-professionals see parent education and support as the main thrust of their work, a very considerable number are in a position to increase this aspect of their work if they so choose. The importance of sensitivity and of appropriate skills and knowledge in those who work with parents is, however, particularly important. The relationship between professional and parent was found to be most effective when it built on partnership and mutual respect, with an emphasis on reciprocity that allowed people to give as well as to take. Many schemes have found that parents are well able to lead groups, given adequate training and support and that the professional role is often that of a catalyst or enabler. The enthusiastic response to home-visiting schemes and crisis telephone services using volunteers, indicates that for some parents another local parent may be more acceptable and appropriate than 'someone from the welfare'.

Many new developments have taken place during the course of the Bureau project and there has been a considerable expansion since Stern's survey in 1960, but this provision is still uneven, both in terms of its geographical spread and in the kind of support that is available. There is still a lack of continuity between the antenatal and post-natal periods and too few facilities for parents with children under one year. There are also insufficient attempts to include fathers in these schemes, and not enough approaches reaching out to particularly vulnerable families. And whilst the strength of many approaches lies in their informality and their ability to provide companionship, ease isolation and increase confidence, there are still not very many schemes which are thinking through the *educational* component of their work, or focussing on the skills of parenting.

7
Parents of School-age Children

Introduction

Education and support for parents of pre-school children may be inadequate, but compared with the availability of schemes for parents of school-age children, it provides a richness and diversity that leaves older parents looking back wistfully to the days of health visitors and informal groups. The increase in published information, advice and support groups for parents of under-fives has not as yet been paralleled with a realisation that parents of school-age children, too, might welcome the opportunity of discussing their growing children, how they are developing and moving towards independence, what they are learning at school and how relationships in the family may be changing. As more mothers return to work the opportunities for parents to meet informally decrease. Indeed, there are few natural meeting places for parents as children get older, since part of the parenting task is to encourage independence and that in itself often prevents opportunities of meeting with the parents of children's peers. When looking for groups of parents to use its pilot material for the *Childhood 5–10* and the *Parents and Teenagers* courses, for example, the Open University could find few groups already in existence, apart from those linked to Family Network and the National Housewives Register. They had to rely on local OU co-ordinators to set up groups especially for the purpose and on their own student network.

Even after the age of five, children spend considerably more of their waking life at home than they do at school and the great majority of parents are concerned to do their best for their children even if they are not always sure what this might be. There can be few parents, as children begin to move away from the influence of the family towards peer groups and eventual independence, whose progress through the school-age years is trouble-free. Adolescence is inevitably a time of change, and change in itself almost always brings some anxiety and difficulties. This can put a strain on the most stable of family units and parents' ability to help and guide their children, and to cope with problems, can play an important part in the successful transition of a young person from childhood to adulthood.

Parent education for parents of school-age children needs to build on to the parenting skills and abilities outlined in the previous chapter, to prepare parents for the growing influence of the school and for those particular events that are likely to occur during their child's pre-adolescent and adolescent development. The focus of this chapter is therefore twofold. The first part examines some aspects of the relationship between home and school and looks at a number of ways in which schools can help to continue the network of support which has grown up informally in the community in the pre-school years. We look at approaches where professionals are building upon parents' inherent interest in their children, and helping to raise their understanding of how their children develop and learn; and at attempts to focus on parents' own personal growth and development. The second part of the chapter looks at the quality of the relationship between parents and their school-age children, the areas of relevance for parent education and at the emergence of schemes which offer parents some practical and emotional support.

An additional point is the need to see such provision in the context of the wider social and economic issues of employment, housing, financial support and child care. Child care is a particular problem at this stage. The majority of mothers of school-age children either go out to work (see Table 7.1) or would like to do so, and schooling from 9 a.m. to 3.30 p.m. for thirty weeks of the year is not compatible with most jobs.

Provision for children of working parents after school and in the holidays – a group sometimes known as 'latchkey' children – is totally inadequate. A particularly vulnerable group in this respect are lone parents, many of whom have to bear the burden of earning

TABLE 7.1   *Percentage of mothers aged 16–59 who go out to work (1980)*

Age of youngest child	Mothers at work Full-time %	Part-time %	All work %
0–4 years	7	23	30
5–9 years	14	47	61
10 years and over	29	41	70

SOURCE   *General Household Survey*, 1980.

an income and finding and paying for child care single-handed – a major expense on which there is still no tax allowance. Ginger-bread, a national organisation supporting a network of local self-help groups for single parents, runs eleven projects which provide holiday and after-school care at Croydon, Keighley, Bristol and elsewhere, but these are a drop in the ocean in the face of national need. Although it is difficult to present accurate statistics on children left unsupervised, a study in 1978 estimated that approximately 15 per cent of 5 to 10 year olds (or 225 000 children) and 20 per cent of 11 to 15 year olds (300 000 children) are left alone after school (Simpson, 1978). A Bureau paper on latchkey schemes points out that one of the main problems has been that responsibility for provision does not lie within one government or local authority department, and indeed many of the existing schemes are run by voluntary organisations (Robinson, 1982).

Parents and schools

Background influences

Over the last thirty years a great deal of research has underlined the importance of parental attitudes and interest in education, in particular Douglas (1964; 1971), Plowden (1967) and Davie *et al.* (1972). The Plowden report was the first to promote the concept of parents as equal partners with teachers in the education of their children and suggested a minimum programme of action by schools to involve parents as a means, primarily, of influencing parental attitudes towards education, and thereby children's attainment. As a direct result of the report the Educational Priority Area (EPA) research project was set up in five areas of the country with the overall aim of raising educational standards in primary schools in these areas and enabling schools to 'supply a compensating environment'. A key factor in the low educational achievements of working-class children was felt to be the difference in life experience and in values between home and school, and a focus of the project thus became the community school which Plowden had defined as being beyond ordinary school hours for the use of children, their parents, and exceptionally for other members of the community. In this respect schools can readily be seen to contribute to parent education.

A second focus in the home-school area has been the growth of parents' pressure groups. As educationalists became concerned at apparent lack of interest on the part of *parents*, so the concern of some parents at *teachers'* attitudes led to demands for greater involvement in, consultation on, and information about their children's schooling. In 1967, the year in which the Plowden report was published, three such groups – the Advisory Centre for Education (ACE) the Confederation for the Advancement of State Education (CASE) and the National Confederation of Parent Teacher Associations (NCPTA) – came together to form the Home and School Council. Although predominantly middle-class in their appeal, the campaigns of these organisations have had a considerable impact on recent legislation as enshrined in the 1980 and 1981 Education Acts (see p. 174). There have also been a number of more broadly-based initiatives, notably the 'education shops' set up by ACE; and the Newham Parents Centre in London's East End dockland which over the past ten years has provided advice, support and information for parents, so that they can be 'informed and thoughtful about education'. The Centre describes much of its work as a self-help programme of adult basic education (Phillips, 1980) and as such it has much in common with the community approaches described in Chapter 6.

A third potential influence is the extensive involvement of parents in the provision of services for pre-school children. This experience suggests that as children reach full-time schooling there is a considerable body of parental goodwill, enthusiasm and expertise on which to build. As the previous chapter suggested, many parents – particularly mothers – find that involvement in playgroups and community groups gives them increased self-confidence and a greater understanding of their children. However, there is little evidence as yet of primary schools making substantial efforts to capture and extend this enthusiasm, involvement and awareness.

Recent developments

The State assumed responsibility for universal primary schooling over a hundred years ago, yet the point that schooling, to be effective, must depend upon the intelligent support and co-operation of parents still has to be argued. Parents and teachers often view each other's worlds a little differently, and research studies have suggested a divergence of opinion as to what education is about, and a certain deference and lack of confidence on the part of parents. Studies have found that whilst parents are happy to help their children (educationally) before school, once the child starts school they are not sure how to support their child (McCail, 1981). Others have found that parents felt the home counted for very little in terms of children's development, and concluded that because of the lack of information and communication, parents and teachers saw the aims of education very differently (Lynch and Pimlott, 1976). This point was evident too in Tizard's study of parental involvement in nursery and infant schools, where Asian parents in particular had difficulty in understanding the purpose of many of the 'messy' activities in the nursery class when their concerns were with language development and reading (Tizard *et al.*, 1981).

Studies of home–school relationships are almost universal in portraying parents who are anxious to help their children but not very clear of their role. As the Newsons conclude in their study of parents of seven-year olds:

> The help parents give now may be ill-directed; it may be too tentative to be effective, out of fear of what 'the school' may say; it may be too little, too late, or too fragmented, but if 81 in every 100 parents are trying to help their children with reading and most of them don't know how to, schools are not only failing dismally in their educative role but wasting the most valuable resource they have. (Newson, Newson and Barnes, 1977)

In his 1960 survey of parent education Stern stated that:

Close co-operation between home and school is advocated in Great Britain; but compared with those countries where parents go freely into schools, visit classes or make direct contact with teachers, the contact between parent and school in the UK is customarily more restricted. (Stern, 1960)

The OECD/CERI project on the 'educational role of the family' has provided evidence that the uneasy relationship between home and school is by no means peculiar to Britain. The need to work towards a closer partnership between parents and teachers was one of the main themes of the contributions made by twenty countries to that project. A number of governments (for example, Netherlands, Finland, Norway) had published policy statements intended to strengthen home–school links. Belgium reported a network of PMS centres (psycho-pedagogical-medical-social centres) which served as a model for orderly and systematic parent–school co-operation; and the United States reported on its government-funded Families as Educators project, in which parents were being involved as teachers and managers in twenty-five major programmes at upper elementary and lower secondary school levels. But the French comment reflected the overall difficulties encountered in most countries:

Each camp blames the other for the loss of authority over children, the parents complaining that the school syllabus does not match real needs and the teachers complaining of apathy amongst school children. The lack of effort by children is attributed by parents to slack discipline in the classroom and the teachers put the blame on lack of parental control. Meanwhile, the child can at times end up spending the best part of the learning phase of his existence in that no-man's land between family and school. (OECD/CERI, 1982)

Such evidence as we have in this country suggests that in some respects matters have improved. Over half the primary school teachers interviewed in a recent national study for example, felt that parental involvement *had* increased and attitudes changed, but that classroom involvement became less as children got older and were sent rather than brought to school (Cyster *et al.*, 1980). On the whole however, research suggests that there is still an uneasy partnership in many schools and that 'despite appeals for greater mutual understanding, communications between home and school serve as much to reinforce distance between parents and teachers as they do to unite them in the educational enterprise' (Open University, 1981a).

Further impetus for parental participation comes in two pieces of recent legislation on the relationship between home and school. The 1980 Education Act was a direct development from the Taylor report on school governors *A New Partnership for our Schools* (DES and Welsh Office, 1977), which made a forceful statement on parents' rights: 'We believe that every parent has a right to expect a school's teachers to recognise his status in the education of his child by the practical arrangements they make to communicate with him and the spirit in which they accept his interest'. The 1980 Act introduced three measures which go some way towards improving in practice this concept of communication and involvement: the inclusion of parents on the governing bodies of schools; the right of parents to choose the school which their child will attend; and the requirement that all schools should publish basic information about the curriculum and structure of the school.

The 1981 Education Act is a major piece of legislation in the field of special education, following as it does the far-reaching recommendations of the Warnock report. The concept of partnership between professionals and parents of children with special needs is more deeply rooted in special education than it is in main-line schooling, and Warnock's proposals for sharing knowledge, skills and experience have found many practical expressions, initially in the pre-school field but now increasingly in primary, secondary, and further education (see Pugh, 1981; Mittler and McConachie, 1983). Under this new legislation not only do parents have access to all records on their children's educational progress, but they must, of right, be involved in assessment procedures and decisions on the most suitable form of schooling. It will be interesting to see how long it is before parents of all children are accorded such rights.

Parental involvement in schooling

What can research and practical developments tell us about the school's role in helping parents to understand, and perhaps be more closely involved in their children's educational progress, and at the same time develop their own skills and awareness? An underlying assumption of much of this work has been that teachers need to change parents' attitudes and behaviour in order to improve the educational attainment of their children. The terms have therefore usually been laid down by teachers rather than by parents, and it is questionable whether this assumption is a sound base for true partnership. There are four main areas under which initiatives intended to improve home–school relations can be grouped, and these will be examined in turn.

Giving information to parents and increasing access to schools   The recommendations of the Plowden committee have now been enshrined in law and every school must publish a prospectus outlining its organisation and curriculum. Evidence suggests that the majority of schools do send written information to parents (Cyster *et al.*, 1980) and one school in Cambridge estimated that parents received on average 30 000 words a year (Elliott *et al.*, 1981). Receiving written information, however, often does little to increase parents' understanding. In one study in Sussex middle-class parents who were quite closely involved in the school, were found to have little knowledge of what actually happened in the classroom – what reading schemes were used, how maths was taught and so on (Becher and Eraut, 1980). It also has little effect on broadening teachers' perceptions of what they are doing, and they tend to be better at producing information than at receiving comments or criticisms (Elliott *et al.*, 1981). These studies also suggest that the exchange of information may not always be very helpful and that parents soon become frustrated by their inability to influence quite minor decisions.

Direct contact between teachers and parents at open meetings and parent workshops is now possible in most schools. Some 92 per cent of schools in a national survey reported that parents were invited to visit the school before the children started, and a similar proportion reported holding parents' evenings and open days, so attempts are certainly being made to increase access (Cyster *et al.*, 1980). But evidence consistently shows that it tends to be the same highly motivated parents who come to these occasions. The availability of teachers for individual discussions with parents is also crucial – and indeed Tizard describes individual consultations as 'the single most important opportunity for parental involvement. If the school can manage nothing else it should at least attempt to hold regular, worthwhile discussions about every child with his parents' (Tizard *et al.*, 1981).

Parent-Teacher Associations are an obvious means of establishing closer relationships between home and school, and in countries such as New Zealand PTAs run meetings and courses for parents on aspects of child-development and family relationships. Reaction to PTAs in this country has been a little more guarded. The Plowden report for example, suggested that in the hands of a small group of parents PTAs frightened many parents away. They found that about 33 per cent of all schools had a PTA, whilst 26 per cent had informal committee or 'friends of the school' groups. Some 5000 home–school organisations are now affiliated to the NCPTA. The parents in the Cambridge study saw PTAs as an élitist group and had little faith in them as vehicles for expressing their real concerns, and the schools themselves found that the existence of a parents' association tended to reduce the wider commitment of other parents and of the community (Elliott *et al.*, 1981). As regards meetings with a wider parent-education brief, a study in Newcastle (1982) found very few PTAs were 'actively involved in educational matters', tending to concentrate on fund-raising, and the Open University did not find PTAs to be a useful network for the circulation of their parent education materials.

Whilst the much publicised notices which read 'No parents beyond this point' have on the whole been removed, schools where parents feel they have complete ease of access, other than by appointment or for special meetings, are still in the minority. Booklets which offer advice on how to make schools readily accessible to local parents give examples of home visiting; of welcoming letters and publicity; of the availability of a parents' room; of social and educational events; of adult education activities for parents, based in the school; of ready-for-school groups for new parents and their children; of maths, science and reading workshops and of inviting parents to join assembly one day every week (CEDC, 1982a; Lingard and Allard, 1982).

Inviting help from parents in the school Parent associations have traditionally been seen as raisers of money to supplement the school capitation allowance, to build luxury items such as swimming-pools or to top up essentials in time of cut-backs. But there are many other 'non-educational' tasks with which parents are asked to help. Cyster (1980) found that by far the most popular methods of parental participation were helping on school visits and outings, with sewing and cookery and minor repairs to equipment. Although these tasks undoubtedly help the school and may well be a first step towards more active involvement, they tend to have a limited educational value on their own in helping parents to understand and support learning.

Involving parents in the curriculum is, in the words of a recent report, 'the most demanding but potentially the most profitable area of parental involvement' (Wood and Simpkins, 1982) and the authors outline many ways in which parents can be involved in both home-based and school-based activities. One important area is the teaching of reading, with about a quarter of schools in the Cyster study allowing parents to hear their children read. The researchers expressed surprise at this number, pointing out that it is this issue over which many battles have been fought, with widely expressed professional misgivings on the part of teachers and their unions (Cyster *et al.*, 1980). Teachers in the study felt that parents should never be involved in helping children who were having difficulty in reading and yet the majority of parents are, quite understandably, concerned to help their children to acquire this basic skill.

It is in the field of reading that a number of recent projects have shown the potential of a true partnership between home and school. Following some earlier research in Barking, parents in twelve Haringey primary schools, a multi-ethnic inner city area, were asked to hear their children read several times a week over a two-year period, from books sent home from school (Hewison, 1981; Tizard *et al.*, 1982). The reading progress of these children was compared with a control group who received no help and a third group who were given tuition from a specially appointed teacher. At the end of the project the children who had received help from the parents were reading considerably better than either of the other two groups, and there were other benefits. Teachers and advisors claimed that the project had changed their views about parental involvement, and that where the focus of the relationship is centred on the child and his learning a true partnership evolves between home and school.

Similar approaches have met with success elsewhere, at Belfield Community School in Rochdale for example (Jackson and Hannon,

1981) and in Northamptonshire (Friend, 1981). A project in Hackney which started by involving parents in the teaching of reading has now expanded under the title of PACT (Parents Children and Teachers) to more than 100 primary schools, some of them involving almost every parent. PACT and a parallel project on 'family co-operation in the development of literacy' in Hackney and Lewisham found, as others had before them, that parents were concerned to help their children, but were unsure of what to do for the best and found difficulty in recognising progress. However, despite the evident success of these schemes, the approach has not spread as rapidly as might have been expected, even within the immediate neighbourhood of the experimental schools (Hagedorn, 1983).

Reports of these reading projects suggest that teachers found their professionalism enhanced rather than eroded by this sharing of skills and expertise. This may in some measure be due to the fact that on the whole parents did their 'teaching' at home, leaving the classroom to the teachers. But there are also a number of examples of parents working in the classroom, helping with basic skills of reading, writing, numeracy and language development; sharing experience of their jobs, of being parents; or taking cooking and football. A report from CEDC (1982b) points to the value of this approach for teachers, parents and their children alike, but also stresses the need for careful planning, preparation and support. If parents are to increase their understanding of educational development, teachers may also need to be more explicit. For example, whilst parents involved in one study learned that play materials aided learning and that messy play had some value, they did not know *what* learning was being aided (Tizard, 1981). Approaches which involve parents in reading and mathematics workshops, where they can work through problems as their children have and where there is a relaxed atmosphere for discussing all aspects of schooling, have an important part to play if parents are to increase their understanding and their confidence in involvement (McGeeney, 1980).

Consulting parents or involving them in management While teachers do not on the whole find it easy to consult parents, it is also true to say that parents seldom assume their rights as taxpayers and ratepayers and attempt to exert control over schools as they do for example in the United States. The inclusion of a parent governor on each school's governing body should at least in theory ensure that the parents' voice is now heard in decision-making, albeit collectively. The 1973 Act which recommended the establishment of Schools Councils (to include parents) in Scotland to 'manage and supervise schools' seems however, not to have met with the success in this respect that one might have hoped for. Nearly three-quarters of head teachers in a recent study felt that the Schools Councils had not improved home–school liaison (Macbeth, 1980). This was partly due to a lack of understanding on the part of most parents of the function of Schools Councils and partly to the fact that many councils serve a group of schools. The new English and Welsh governing bodies would do well to learn from this experience.

Reaching out into the community The potential of community education for reaching a wide cross-section of parents, many of whom have unhappy memories of school themselves, was described in the previous chapter. Although 'reaching out into the community' is by no means the prerogative of community schools, and certainly not of community education, the reluctance of many schools to blur the boundaries between school, home and community suggests that community education has a particular contribution to make to the home–school debate. The Cambridgeshire Village Colleges set up in the 1920s and 1930s (see Rée, 1973) and community colleges in Cumbria, Leicestershire, Nottinghamshire, Derbyshire, Oxfordshire, Telford, Milton Keynes and elsewhere, have aimed at providing in one place adult and further education, youth clubs, social and recreational facilities and sometimes health and social welfare provision, in addition to the traditional primary or secondary education. During the 1960s community education also began to take root in some inner city areas – notably Coventry – and with the setting up of the EPA programmes in Liverpool, Birmingham, London and Glasgow.

Community education covers a multitude of different beliefs and practices (see for example Fletcher and Thompson, 1980) and it is not easy to gauge the extent of its influence. Although the spread of ideas has been slow and patchy, and some would say disappointing, there are some interesting examples of 'good practice'. The work of the Home and School Centre in Glasgow for example and the Family Learning Unit based in a number of secondary schools has grown out of an earlier 'experiment in education' in Govan, a small inner city area of Glasgow, which aimed to improve the education of the children by working with all the significant adults in their environment (Wilkinson *et al.*, 1978). The project worked on a number of fronts simultaneously: in the community through the establishment of parent discussion groups, family workshops, home visiting and the establishment of a library which attracted up to 150 people a day; in the schools, through the appointment of home link teachers; with school leavers and with teachers and other professionals.

Coventry, too, has a strong tradition of community involvement in the education process. The local education authority commitment is such that, as from 1984, where other authorities are closing down schools as roles fall, Coventry is redesignating all its secondary schools as 'neighbourhood learning centres'. Coventry, Leicester, Liverpool and Sheffield have also pioneered a 'new generation of pupils' in schools, where adults are returning to classrooms to study side by side with the pupils. This is not the strange phenomena that some may think, for a CEDC survey found that thirty-nine local education authorities reported some instances of adults attending secondary classes, although only eight reported schemes involving ten or more adults (CEDC, 1982c). Sheffield for example plans to open the doors of all its comprehensive schools to anyone over school-leaving age from September 1983.

Much of the Liverpool work has developed through its Parent Support programme, a scheme which started in 1979 in seventeen primary schools and which has subsequently been extended to a further nine, plus one secondary school. Each school has set up a parents' centre staffed by a teacher key worker and an outreach worker, and the twin aims have been to help parents to understand their children's education and to continue their own. This approach has encouraged a dramatic increase in the take-up of adult education through the primary schools – sewing, cooking, child development and even some O-levels – and the schools have also built in sessions where parents have worked with their children in maths, reading, cooking and so on. Again, teachers have been surprised to find that they have underestimated the skills of parents and children alike, that the confidence of both have grown through involvement in the project, and that inner city parents have been found to be neither apathetic nor incompetent. The evaluator does report, however, that despite the scheme's evident success, progress is still slow in persuading teachers to 'make the most of the myriad opportunities they have for involving parents in existing curriculum work' (Davis 1982).

A final example is the expansion of the Inner London Education Authority's family workshop programme, described in Chapter 6, into primary schools, through the workshops in Wandsworth and the Fleet Community Education Centre in Camden, and into secondary schools, as in Pimlico Comprehensive School in Westminster. The opportunity for teachers, parents, pupils and adult education tutors to work together for one afternoon a week within the school may take a considerable amount of time and energy to establish but it provides an excellent bridge between home and school. It offers parents, teachers and children alike, opportunities to get to know each other informally in a relaxed and unthreatening atmosphere, and to be both teachers and learners of new skills. It also provides an important link between the worlds of adult and school-based education.

There are then many examples of attempts to reach out to parents, some involving teachers and others using additional professionals such as the family workshop tutors in London, employed by adult education; home–school link teachers or home–school liaison officers as in Liverpool, Glasgow, Birmingham, Northern Ireland and elsewhere; school-based social workers as in Haringey; educational welfare officers and the educational home visitors (see Chapter 6). There are also some initiatives based within the community which attempt to help parents understand and use the education system better – the Newham Parents Centre for example, and the Manchester Parents Centre, and the education shop run by the city council's education welfare department.

Community education, with its belief in social change and increasing opportunities for the whole community, has a fundamental contribution to make to parent education throughout the life cycle. The school is an obvious and central resource within the community, although paradoxically, as the recent NUT document on home–school relations pointed out, the exercise of parental choice in schooling does tend to lead to difficulties in establishing links, when homes are so widespread that they cannot really be said to constitute a community (NUT, 1983).

The evidence presented here underlines the need for teachers and parents alike to realise that they both have an important role to play in the education of children and for parents to be seen as partners in the system rather than clients or recipients. This should not reduce the teacher's professional role, but will certainly change its emphasis and call for new skills and knowledge. Because most learning takes place at home, the family, as a commentator on the Belfield reading scheme said, 'is the glue that holds education together'. Whilst it may be easy enough to make schools open to parents and make friendly contact, 'if parental involvement means giving parents a real understanding of school education, helping them to contribute to it and exchanging information and opinions with them, there are serious obstacles in the way' (Tizard *et al.*, 1981). There are few examples of schools involving parents in the educational process or of the broader commitment to extending parents' own horizons as in Liverpool, but it may be that schools on their own are insufficient and that a broader-based approach incorporating adult and community education, as in the pre-school field, would meet with greater success.

A recurrent problem is the attitude of teachers, who have no training or role definition for working with parents. This is despite the fact that a very high number of head teachers – 90 per cent in nursery schools and 80 per cent in primary schools – find their advice is being sought by parents on social and domestic problems. The combination of the time involved in this increasing 'counselling' perspective and in working more closely with parents in the classroom, has led some teachers to fear that the broadening of their professional role 'may lead to its dilution, with their energies being expended in a variety of ways peripheral and debilitating to their main task of educating children' (Cyster *et al.*, 1980).

Parents and pre-adolescents

There are aspects of the parents' role in addition to relationships with schools which are important for parent education. In many ways the years between 5 and 10 years old are a fairly relaxed, happy and stimulating time for parents and children alike, and parents may not appreciate that they have a particular role as educator during these years, not only in relation to the school but also at home. Children are ready to undertake family tasks and learn to be responsible for others, perhaps by looking after a younger brother or sister, or by taking care of a pet. They are also developing and exploring new physical skills which require instruction, guidance and patient reassurance and practice. Fathers often find this one of the easiest stages of family life in which to find a definite role as sons and daughters take up swimming, cycling, football, cricket and other sports.

Attitudes towards the wider family and friends, school and ouside activities are formed at this stage. Children become aware of other adult models, or rules and behaviour that may be different to those of home. Social activities become important in encouraging children to develop an identity separate from their parents. Leisure centres and community centres offer a variety of experiences both for the family as a whole and for individual members – from family workshops to specific sessions on gymnastics, dancing, pottery, judo, fencing, drama and many others. Parents may find this a physically exhausting stage as they deliver and collect their children from school to clubs and activities or to play with friends, but such opportunities for increasing independence and social interaction are important in developing their children's self-confidence and autonomy.

Children often start to conform with their peers at this stage and parents begin to discover the advantages and disadvantages of the peer groups. The familiar phrase 'everyone has/does/is going to . . . ' is a challenge by the child to seek some control over their world. Over one and a quarter million children are currently enrolled in the two best-known organisations for young people – the Girl Guides Association, with its Brownies, and the Scouts Association with its Cub Scouts. This desire to belong to their 'own' group is also acted out in gangs and clubs in the school playground and the local neighbourhood. Parents may have to channel such enthusiasm and energy so that children develop respect for others and self-responsibility rather than insist on a restrictive regime which stifles the opportunities for children to develop their own skills and talents.

Wherever the child comes in the family, parents will need to be sensitive to the impact of new events on children in this age-group. The arrival of a new baby, a change of house or school, mother starting work or father becoming unemployed, all result in changes which may be difficult for the pre-adolescent child to cope with alongside other developments in their own personal world. Separation and divorce can be particularly disturbing at this stage and children often feel they are to blame or have in some way provoked the split between their parents. Self-help groups of parents can offer valuable support and guidance on how to cope with a child who appears to be reacting badly to such a situation.

There is little in the way of parent education or formal support services at this point in the family life cycle, apart from the Open University course. The majority of books are concerned with settling the child into school and it is as if there will be no more problems until adolescence. Parents do have the opportunity to build up informal contacts at the school-gate but as more parents work and more local schools are closed, even this opportunity is not always available.

Parents and adolescents

Since individual children mature at very different rates, puberty (which is what is commonly thought of when talking about adolescence) may start as early as ten or as late as sixteen years of age. The uncertainty of what is going to happen next and when, together with the actual physical and hormonal changes adolescents are experiencing make this a demanding time for parents. Parental confidence and patience can be severely tested as adolescents fluctuate between wanting total responsibility for themselves or none at all, complaining of interference one moment and lack of interest the next. It is a time when family life can be exhausting, tense and stressful but also enriching, stimulating and fun. As we have seen, there is very little direct formal or informal support for parents of school-age children. Even in books on child-rearing or child development, information or advice is likely to be tucked at the end in one chapter. Yet the successful transition from child to young adult is greatly influenced by the young person's family and the ability of his parents to cope. And, in turn, the turbulence of adolescence can lead to enormous stresses and strains on the parents' marital relationship and their ability to support one another.

A number of studies have shown a significant association between different styles of parenting and their children's social behaviour in adolescence: different forms of parental supervision (Wilson, 1980) and different disciplinary styles (Newson, 1982) in relation to juvenile delinquency and in relation to schoolgirl pregnancies (Cox, 1982). The patterns of behaviour already developed in relation to the way the family deals with power, intimacy, communication, problem-solving and respect for individual values and attitudes will also influence how the family will tackle issues like sexuality, dependency, stress, crisis, new roles and new responsibilities.

The information and services which do exist often focus on the physical 'growing-up' period and particular problems rather than looking at what is happening in the parents' lives and the family as a whole. The role of parent education could be to provide both information and emotional support to enable parents to understand their adolescent children and develop appropriate 'coping' strategies, to understand and participate in educational and employment decisions and appreciate the impact of youth unemployment on the self-esteem and confidence of their children, and to help their children leave home as competent and caring adults.

Parents also have their own needs which may restrict their ability to cope with their many responsibilities. As the middle generation, parents of older children may be caught between the demands of aged parents on one side and rebellious children on the other. It is likely to be a period of transition for everyone as part of the normal pattern of the life cycle. The young people are developing new bodies and new minds; making choices about school and work; developing new friendships and more intimate relationships; experimenting with sexual activities; learning to set their own limits and take on more responsibility for themselves and their behaviour. For their parents, it may be a period of questioning their role as a parent, as a spouse or as a worker, often referred to as the mid-life crisis (Fiske, 1979). Many mothers will have returned to work. But whilst this middle generation may gain freedom and relinquish some of the responsibilities for younger members of the family, they may lose it by taking on new responsibilities for the older members as grandparents and great-grandparents become more dependent and demanding. Thus parents find that they are both nursing their frail and elderly parents, and at the same time continuing to support their unemployed teenagers, in houses which are seldom designed to accommodate three generations. The implications for loss of personal and sexual freedom of young people of 19, 20 and older, still living at home, are likely to be a rising source of depression, frustration and conflict within the family home.

The generation gap and family relationships

The many changes in society emphasise the generation gap between the parents' experience as youngsters and that of their own children and this may affect current and future family relationships. Values, attitudes and expectations have altered in social, sexual, educational and economic patterns; legal rights and responsibilities may highlight conflicting needs of parents and children; changing patterns of family structure mean that many parents and children are confronted with situations for which there is little advice or help – particularly in divorce, remarriage, youth unemployment and women as the sole breadwinners.

Parents of teenagers will range in age from their late twenties to their late fifties. Not only will their own childhood and adolescent experiences be shaped by the society in which they grew up, but their tolerance and stamina may also differ dramatically. This 'generation gap' can affect the relationship between parents and children and also the amount and form of advice and support that parents can give to each other. As at other stages of the life cycle, the focus of parent education will need to vary according to the particular needs and circumstances of each parent.

It would seem that on the whole most young people get on well with their parents and a happy family life is the rule rather than the exception. The Bureau's NCDS found that 86 per cent of 16-year-olds got on well with their mother and 80 per cent with their father (Fogelman, 1976). Another study, of 15-year-olds followed up again at 17, found that the majority saw their parents as acceptable sources of advice and guidance and relations with parents generally were positive and rewarding (Porteous and Fisher, 1980). In a Gallup Poll on European attitudes, British parents were said to feel closest to their children but were also ranked as the strictest (*The Times*, 1981).

Services for parents and adolescents

Services for adolescents are ambiguous and piecemeal so that there is neither provision for the particular needs and development of adolescents themselves nor a system of support to which their parents could turn for information and advice. Parents' concerns during the adolescent period range from wanting to know what is usual behaviour in adolescence and how to handle emotional issues, to coping with actual or potential problems. Many parents also find it difficult to accept or adapt to current social pressures or to relinquish their own cultural values and traditions. Others find it hard to reconcile their personal expectations for their children with reality. The following five areas in which parent education and support could be offered highlight the limited nature of existing provision.

Information. One of the major differences between today's adolescents and their own parents' experience as adolescents is the substantial increase in information. Knowing more about contraception, abortion, venereal disease, homosexuality, barbiturates and heroin (learnt partly in school and partly from the media) does not necessarily prevent them from experimenting, leaving the parents, who do not have the knowledge, to cope. One useful publication for parents is the Open University's *Parents and Teenagers* which contains a comprehensive guide to sources of information and help from people, places and books. This is also the nearest equivalent to a 'child-care manual' on teenagers.

Several national organisations, such as the National Children's Bureau and the National Youth Bureau, keep lists of organisations and institutions concerned with young people – from runaways to children's rights, solvent abuse to homelessness. Such organisations in turn produce their own information and guidance, for example, the Children's Legal Centre and the Institute for the Study of Drug Dependence.

Many of the informal and informative booklets circulated at schools, clinics, social services and health authorities are not easily available for parents. The recommended routine medical check-up by family practitioners of all 13-year-olds, as distinct from school medicals, would provide an opportunity for such printed information to be distributed to parents.

Emotional support. Many parents' concerns are related to emotional issues. Knowing that their daughter has selected the most up-to-date and (statistically) reliable form of contraception does not necessarily make parents any happier about her using it, especially if she is under 16-years-old. Knowing that spiked green hair, pierced ears and hobnailed boots on their living-room floor are only natural expressions of youthful self-identity does not stop parents bursting into tears or ordering their children out of the house. There are very few opportunities for parents of young people to meet informally to discuss these problems. The natural grouping that takes place at health clinics, playgroups or primary-school gate no longer exist when adolescents are being encouraged to be independent and make their own arrangements. Knowledge and skills are important but actual personal support systems, opportunities for talking and sharing experiences, exchanging anxieties and rejoicing in successes, can be the key to sanity and survival when it seems that values and attitudes are being challenged daily.

Some innovative schemes, groups and activities have been set up by individual workers in adult education, community education and youth services, realising that parents of adolescents need as much help and support as the adolescents themselves. Creating opportunities for parents to come together can support parents in understanding and coping with what is already happening in their adolescent child's development, advise and prepare them for future stages, and encourage a network of help for others. For some organisations this is a natural continuation of the education and support offered to all families throughout the parenting years. For example, the Open University courses, the Mothers' Union, the Family Life project in the Coventry Diocese and the Gloucestershire Association for Family Life have all produced materials for families with pre-adolescents and adolescents (see Appendix 3).

For other organisations, working with parents of teenagers extends their role and function in a new way. Family Network moved beyond listening to problems over the telephone and began creating supportive networks and opportunities for parents to meet (Kidd, 1982a and b). In Glasgow, the community education service began with a brief to improve adult literacy which led to parents' groups studying OU courses and an active involvement in the testing of the materials for the parents and teenagers course. The National Children's Centre extended its opportunities for discussion and support beyond the teenagers and young people to include their parents, sometimes helping parents with their own problems as well as with their teenagers.

At the Riverside Child Health Project the multi-disciplinary team has extended its original brief of working with schools and parents of young children to include parents of teenagers. Their eight-week course *Calling All People with Teenagers* particularly emphasises the importance of looking back to when parents were teenagers, of examining what triggers off their annoyance or anxiety (clothes, hair, smoking, drugs) and different ways of communicating and dealing with conflict. In an area of high unemployment for all family-members the sessions do not look at educational and occupational choices which are irrelevant for so many of the parents and their teenagers. Instead they focus on how best they can learn to live together in such circumstances through understanding each others' feelings and needs and developing positive coping strategies.

Developing courses or groups for the parents of older children has often arisen from an orginal intention to provide such opportunities for the children themselves. Indeed, in New Zealand a school meeting called to inform parents of a course on exploring communication skills, coping-strategies and decision-making, resulted in the parents wanting to take the course first, and the publication of a *Handbook for Parents of Teenagers* (Shaw and Matthews, 1981) which is now available in this country. In England, the National Marriage Guidance Council has been instrumental in creating similar opportunities through its education work. A six-session course on *Family Life in the Twentieth Century* in Dudley brought together pupils, parents and teachers with the aim of increasing their knowledge, understanding and competence to make more informed choices (Proctor, 1983). Another NMGC project worked with 120 parents and 20 teachers in Luton to explore the three main areas of adolescent development, relationships and responsibilities. In Oxfordshire a detached youth worker, caught as a mediator between parents and young people, was prompted to bring together a multi-disciplinary team from adult and community education, from the health and education authroities, to provide courses for parents of teenagers. The next step was to run programmes for young people in parallel with such groups for their parents (Collins, 1982). The Workers Educational Association (which has 21 districts and 900 branches) has also supported several courses in response to similar requests from youth workers, social workers, community workers, teachers and probation officers.

Much of the family conflict arising at this stage of the life cycle stems from parents' failure to understand the adolescent's desire and need for privacy and independence compounded by an inability to communicate openly. The Youth Charter Conference in 1977 highlighted the need to help parents informally before such problems and conflicts became severe and pointed out how rarely youth workers, teachers and other workers are able to meet informally to discuss such initiatives (National Youth Bureau, 1977).

Coping with problems. Research suggests that in most families problems amongst parents and teenagers are a question of negotiation and usually relate to such matters as choice of friends, time of coming in, hairstyles and clothes, drinking and smoking and use of leisure time (Fogelman, 1976; Porteous and Fisher, 1980). As far as more serious problems are concerned, it is often the parents' own fears and anxieties that provoke additional personal and behavioural problems by insisting on rigid or inappropriate rules. One of the main anxieties that parents of older children express is that problems will become entrenched before they know about them. For example, truancy may have become a habit long before the school informs the parents or the educational welfare officer calls to discuss how to cope with it. Many of the large chainstores now have an aggressive policy of contacting parents immediately, at work or at home, no matter how small the offence or incident, to emphasise the criminal nature of shoplifting in the hope of preventing a recurrence.

For some parents, however, their fears are justified and few schemes are available to alleviate the problem or offer information or support. On the whole, services for the parents of teenagers and for young people themselves are designed to cope with the consequences and symptoms of problems rather than offer any preventive measures. Psychiatric services, hospitals, clinics and counselling agencies do little more than help parents and youngsters cope with their predicament through treatment, medication or therapy and few offer continuing support through parent- or family-groups. There are some areas of particular concern to parents where education and support could sensitively and effectively help them in coping with the actual problem identified. They are related to alcohol and drugs, sexual activity, mental illness and death.

Although there have been numerous official reports and recommendations stressing the importance of supporting and involving parents it is primarily the voluntary and self-help groups that offer what little support is available. The recent report from the Advisory Council on the Misuse of Drugs (1982) has called for a multi-disciplinary approach to the problems of addiction and has recommended the establishment of family groups. In the meantime, Families Anonymous help parents cope with the additional side-effects which can include marital break-up, severe depression, financial chaos and attempted suicide. The Lifeline Project in Manchester, a voluntary agency working with solvent-abusers, has also stressed the importance of working with parents.

Abortion and birth statistics tell us that many young people are sexually active. As we saw in Chapter 4, although schoolgirl pregnancies have remained fairly steady there has been a steep rise in the number of legal abortions. There is little support for parents – emotional, financial or educational, when faced with an unexpected grandchild or the knowledge of an abortion.

Schizophrenia, anorexia and depression are especially prevalent during adolescence and are extremely harrowing for parents. The increase in the suicide rate is another alarming symptom of the pressures and mental stress experienced by many young people. Family therapy is increasingly favoured as a way both of involving and supporting parents in coping with and acknowledging the problems or the loss of their child, but few NHS services are able to provide this opportunity. Compassionate Friends is a self-help group for parents who have lost a child, whether through illness, accident or suicide. Half of all motorcyclists killed or seriously injured are teenagers.

Social change. A major concern for all parents is the shortage of jobs and higher and further education opportunities. This creates stress for many parents and young people and perhaps the most important aspect for parent education is to emphasise the need for more understanding between parents and their teenagers.

Changes in family patterns and in patterns of care have highlighted the lack of help for those acting as parents to adolescents. Whilst studies on the effects of separation and divorce have shown that pre-adolescents may cover up their pain and distress, adolescents tend to show overt depression, withdraw from the family and form other relationships outside the home (Richards and Dyson, 1982). In step-families issues of discipline and authority, of sexual tension and provocation, can arise from a socially ambiguous 'parent–child' relationship (Maddox, 1980). Many parents are deeply upset by their children's behaviour and are unable to differentiate between what is 'normal' adolescent behaviour and what is related to the 'new' family structure. The newly-formed Stepfamily Association hopes to provide information, advice and a supportive network similar to that created by Gingerbread for single parents. The move to place adolescents in foster homes rather than in institutions led to a training course for foster-parents, recognising the particular problems associated with this transition period, *Added to Adolescence* (NFCA, 1977).

The media – television, radio, newspapers and magazines – have been quick to respond to parental anxiety. Not only has information been generated on numerous problem areas but the very process of parenting has been aired, shared and discussed. Radio and television programmes range from *Living with Teenagers* and *Working with Teenagers* to *What are we doing to the children?* on the effects of divorce. Many local radio stations now have a family-care line or parents-link line with both confidential off-air services and particular slots given to problems of adolescents and parents questions. Increasingly articles are appearing in newspapers and magazines detailing the experiences of parents coping with such problems as heroin addiction, anorexia, suicide attempts, the anger and frustration of unemployment, the increasing apathy and cynicism towards acquiring educational qualifications and the dilemma posed in Asian families when a daughter prefers to pursue her education rather than accept an arranged marriage.

Coming to terms with personal expectations. Parents may well be re-assessing their own lives while their children as adolescents, pursue their quest for personal identity. The questioning of parental values and attitudes, and the impact of adolescent problems can have severe effects on the parents' relationship as a couple. Marriage-enrichment courses are one attempt to ease the couple through this transition phase, to help them understand themselves as a couple without children, as well as supporting them in 'launching' their children as young adults.

Acceptance of reality and of the loss of their cherished hopes and dreams for their children can also be a severe emotional adjustment for parents. Youth unemployment, cut-backs in higher education, teenage abortions and unwanted pregnancies – few parents want this or expect it to happen to their children.

This may also be a particularly difficult time for parents of handicapped children who suffer new anxieties in trying to plan for the future, especially with the renewed emphasis on community care (Russell, 1983). Adolescent siblings may start to resent the restrictions placed on the family activities and many parents are torn between creating a normal upbringing for them without denying the handicapped child the participation in family life.

Summary

Parents of school-age children have a demanding and important role to play in the social, psychological and educational development of their children. The parents' ability to help and guide their children is crucial for the successful transition from childhood to young adulthood, from school to work or unemployment. This period often coincides with a similar transition process for parents often referred to as 'mid-life crisis'. Parents of older children are also a middle generation having to cope on the one hand with the younger generation demanding more freedom and taking more responsibility for their own actions, and, on the other hand, with the older generation requiring more help and becoming more dependent and relinquishing their former responsibilities.

Compared with developments in the 'under-fives' area, there is little parent education available and very few opportunities for parents to obtain help, advice or support. Although children spend more of their waking life at home than at school, well over half the mothers of children of primary school age and nearly three-quarters of secondary school age are working.

The importance of the home background and of parental interest in their children's education has been a primary focus for involving parents in their children's schooling. Such involvement can be initiated in a number of ways: giving parents more information; increasing access to the school and encouraging more informal contact with teachers; inviting parents into the school in both a teaching and non-teaching capacity; consulting with parents and incorporating their views and presence within the management structure of the school; extending the role of the school, by designating it a community school and linking with parents, community networks and other forms of provision. Although parents are universally interested in and concerned to help with their children's education, they are seldom made to feel they have the confidence or expertise to do so. There are few examples of schools involving parents in the educational process or of the broader commitment to help parents extend their own horizons.

The pre-adolescent period is also a significant time for parents as educators of their children in terms of physical, social and emotional development. Children are learning new skills, expanding their social networks and learning how to take some responsibility for themselves, for household tasks and for others.

Puberty and adolescence may start as early as 10 or as late as 16 and can be a turbulent and stressful time for all members of the family. Most parents and teenagers get on well together but many parents worry about health, educational, social, behavioural and employment problems which often tend to overlap. There are few natural meeting places for parents of older children and there is a need for informal, positive opportunities to meet with other parents, to share experiences, discuss common concerns and develop a better understanding of themselves and young people.

Services for adolescents are ambiguous and piecemeal and are not designed to play a mediating role between parents and their children. On the whole there is little information or support for parents of this age-group and the services rarely plan an educative, preventive or supportive role. Numerous self-help groups have formed to help parents cope with identified or potentially stressful situations, for example, bereavement, lone parents, foster-families, step-families. Other groups have formed – though more are needed – to help parents cope with the day-to-day management of particular problems, for example, solvent, drug- or alcohol-abuse. The media has proved to be an important vehicle for informing parents, providing a forum for an exchange of views and fears, and highlighting the dual nature of the issues in relationships between parents and their children.

Part III

A POLICY FOR PARENT EDUCATION

8
Parent Education and Support: Summary of Main Issues and Recommendations

Summary of main issues

In looking at what it is like to be a parent in the 1980s we have taken a bird's eye view of current developments to present a national picture of preparation, education and support for parents. Although this approach has certain shortcomings, it has enabled us to paint a unique picture – or at least construct a rather complex jigsaw – of parent education in Britain, to detect some of the main trends and pick out some of the key issues. We have noted, for example, the pressure that is put on parents through increasing knowledge of how children develop and through society's high expectations of the part that they should play in this development. The tendency of professionals to undermine parents' self-confidence with their 'expertise' and the isolation felt by many bringing up young children were also seen to be contributing to the difficulties experienced by many parents. In discussing the tasks and skills of parenting, particular emphasis was put on the importance of adequate social and economic conditions in which to bring up children, and on parents' need for information and knowledge, for social and practical skills, for self-awareness and for an understanding of how their values affect the way in which they bring up their children. Styles of parenting were seen to be affected by a number of personal and family characteristics and social and environmental constraints. Amongst these were the effect of their own childhood experiences, the role of the father, social class, cultural background and the children's influence on parents' behaviour. Basic living conditions and the strength of community support were also important.

The changing nature of the family and of the society in which it operates were also examined and it was apparent that whilst the family as an institution may be changing it is not disappearing. The changes in family patterns, in structure and in roles have important repercussions for family life education. For the 'traditional' British family upon which much of our thinking and many policy decisions appear to be based, in which the man is breadwinner and his wife is at home looking after two dependent children, now accounts for only a small proportion of all households. The effect of increasing divorce rates, the changing role of women and increasing poverty and unemployment have had a considerable impact on families, on the relationships within them and on the roles played by men and women alike. These changes have perhaps had a particular impact on women, who may find themselves torn between idealised views of motherhood and child-rearing – which suggest that they should stay at home with the children – and a commitment to greater equality of opportunity and the financial need for two incomes – which urges them to return to work as soon as possible, in the face of totally inadequate day-care facilities.

In tracing the historical development of parent education in this country and abroad, evidence was presented which showed many similarities between concerns and developments in Britain and elsewhere. In this country recommendations that parent education be more generally available have been made in a series of reports from government departments and elsewhere, covering topics ranging from children in care, to violence in the family, and from pregnant schoolgirls to child health, recommendations seldom if ever matched with resources and certainly never developed into a coherent policy. In presenting the case for parent education it was suggested that whilst most parents manage very well most of the time, parenting is at times a difficult and lonely job, and that society has a responsibility both to help young people develop an understanding of what is likely to be involved in bringing up children *before* they decide whether or not to become parents; and to provide parents with information, support and education as and when it is needed and particularly at critical periods of the life cycle, such as the birth of a first child.

The information on current developments presented in the main body of the book shows a considerable increase in provision in many areas but suggests that much remains to be done. Where interesting and relevant work is in progress it is all too often due to the energy and enthusiasm of an individual worker, rather than as the result of a policy decision to commit resources to preventive and educational work, and in many such instances the scheme stops if the worker moves on.

A summary of the main points is given at the end of each chapter. In brief, the evidence on the extent of family life education in schools shows that whilst this is still not a part of every schools curriculum, some schools are beginning to adopt a more coherent approach to the social and emotional development of their pupils. Courses whose primary aim is family life education tend to fall within the ambit of child care and development, and, as optional subjects offered at CSE or O-level, are taken almost entirely by girls and often less-able girls. Where relevant courses are a compulsory part of a core curriculum taken by all pupils, they are often a secondary aim of broad-based non-examined courses in personal, social or health education. Despite numerous recommendations in reports from the DES and HMI, there is no central government policy on family life education, and few local authorities have thought about its implications across the curriculum. There are as yet few courses which offer to boys and girls alike an opportunity to develop self-confidence and self-knowledge, to build up satisfactory relationships, to consider whether or not they wish to become parents, to discuss values and attitudes towards parenting, to develop some insight into child development, and to gain some first-hand experience of life with young children.

Outside the school classroom, such opportunities are even more limited. Despite the fact that 33 per cent of all women and 20 per cent of all men marry before they are 21, and that teenage marriages have a particularly high breakdown rate, neither the youth service nor further education seem to see family life education as part of their brief. Social education is a primary goal of the youth service, and social and life skills are an important feature of the new Youth Training Scheme, yet the current emphasis in both these services is on skills related to work rather than to personal relationships and

family life. At a time when many young people are becoming
involved in long-term relationships and embarking on parenthood
there seem to be virtually no opportunities for them to consider and
discuss family life in the light of their own needs, desires, life-styles,
personal characteristics and potential. For teenagers who are already parents, many of whom will be particularly vulnerable in
respect of both their own and their children's development, there is
also very little evidence of education and support for them either as
young people, or in their new role as parents.

In preparing for parenthood, attention is now beginning to focus
on the need for pre-conceptual care and on the importance of those
planning and embarking on pregnancy being fit and healthy and
continually mindful of the needs of the developing foetus. Although
antenatal clinics and classes are now widely available they are
attended by only about half of all pregnant women. They have been
consistently criticised for failing to reach the most vulnerable
women – the young, the single, the ethnic minorities; for the fact
that they are often at times and in places which are inconvenient to
many prospective users; and because their content is not always
relevant to the needs of pregnant women and their partners. Their
main focus is still too often on physical preparation for the birth and
although some involve prospective fathers there are few opportunities to discuss the fundamental changes in life-style that a new
baby will bring. There have been some attempts to meet these
criticisms, many of them in the voluntary sector. These include
schemes such as those which link prospective parents with new
parents and attempts to provide continuity of professional care
from the antenatal to the post-natal period. The availability of this
continuity and of a network of supportive friends and health
personnel have been found to be key factors in a happy and
successful transition to parenthood.

The early years of parenthood are a time of learning and growing
for parents and children alike and there are many who find this a
particularly stressful period. Although the provision of supportive
schemes and services is still unevenly spread across the country,
there are now many ways in which parents' needs for companionship, increased self-confidence and greater knowledge and understanding are being met. An appreciation of the value of the support
that parents can give each other is reflected in the growing number
of informal post-natal and mother and toddler groups, and of parent
education groups some of which use the materials from the OU

parenthood courses as a trigger for discussion. Adult and community education, family groups and family centres are developing
strategies for working with more vulnerable families, and along with
playgroups are often offering mothers both increased insight into
their own children's development and opportunities for widening
their own horizons and developing their own confidence as parents.
Home-visiting schemes and crisis telephone services are also growing in response to the needs of those who find difficulty, for
whatever reason, in using existing groups and facilities. Many of
these approaches have found that given adequate preparation and
support, parents are well able to lead groups, visit other families and
run 24-hour crisis telephone services.

Parents of school-age children have an important role to play in
guiding their children through childhood and adolescence, at a time
when they may also be taking on responsibilities for elderly parents.
There is, however, little parent education or support available at
this stage of the life cycle, and few opportunities for parents to
obtain help or advice. Schools could provide such opportunities, but
there are few examples of schools involving parents in their children's education, or of a broader commitment to the personal
growth and development of parents. Adolescence can be a particularly difficult time, as young people grow towards independence in
ways that may well conflict with their parents' views, values and
attitudes. Parents' ability to help their children and to cope with
these problems can play an important part in easing a successful
transition from childhood to adulthood, yet many parents have no
knowledge of what is 'normal' adolescent development and there
are few opportunities to discuss common concerns with other
parents or to develop a better understanding of themselves and
their teenage children.

Some common themes

Lack of policy for parent education

It has been possible to detect a number of common themes amongst
these often very disparate attempts at parent education. One of the
most important of these has been the lack of a coherent policy on
parent education in this country, be it within schools, the antenatal
service or in community support. Such a policy would need to be

carefully devised, for as we have seen many of the most successful programmes are those small informal groups which develop in response to the needs of local parents and acknowledge the skills and abilities that they bring to parenting. If policies are devised and resources made available, they will need to be structured in such a way that decisions on their use are made within local communities. At the very least statutory and voluntary agencies working with families must commit themselves much more strongly to preventive work rather than crisis or remedial work and to realise that a fence at the top of the cliff is far more effective in human and financial terms than an ambulance at the bottom. Positive steps will need to be taken to maintain established schemes and to set up new ones.

Role of professionals

Related to the question of policy and commitment is the issue of professional involvement in parent education, for we have noted on the one hand the very wide range of workers involved in these schemes, and yet on the other, the fact that few see it as an integral part of their work-load. Individual energy and enthusiasm are important ingredients in any successful scheme, but if a commitment to parent education is not built into policies at local authority or health authority level, the scheme tends to be ephemeral and short-lived. The life-cycle approach we have traced in the book also illustrates vividly the need for close co-operation between professionals working with families at different stages of this life cycle. There was little evidence of such a co-operative approach, although the publication of *A Job for Life* (Pugh *et al.*, 1982) did encourage the development of initiatives such as the series of working parties set up by the Area Health Education Officers in Northumberland involving all relevant professionals. A recent development is the three-year project to be undertaken jointly by the NCB, Hampshire County Council and Winchester District Health Authority, which will attempt to develop a coherent approach to parent education at all the stages outlined in this book.

Parents as family workers

Whilst professional workers have an important role in parent education, many of the schemes presented in Chapters 5, 6 and 7 point to the value of peer group support. The playgroup movement, family groups, many informal antenatal and parent and toddler groups, voluntary home-visiting schemes, and telephone services for anxious parents have all demonstrated that parents themselves, given adequate preparation and ongoing support, are well able to lead groups, visit homes and offer support to other parents. Where parents are involved in this way, the professional role may need to be re-defined to include the provision of training and support, or to act as a catalyst in helping to start new schemes, rather than taking responsibility for actually running the scheme.

Responding flexibly to different needs

The preceding chapters have made their own case for the importance of responding to parents' needs in a variety of different ways, for not only will an individual's needs change throughout the life cycle, but no two parents – or their children – will be completely alike. Whilst a mature, confident parent may simply want to meet other local parents, a young, single, teenage mother may find even the simplest of tasks difficult and frustrating – and even a self-assured parent will find there are times when screaming pitch is reached. Any policy on parent education will have to respect the very different needs of families and will have to respond to them in such a way that schemes and services are not only available but also accessible, appropriate and above all acceptable.

Self-confidence and self-image

Key concepts at each stage of the life cycle have been those of self-confidence and self-image. Our view of ourselves is significantly affected by the feedback we get from those around us and in this respect we have seen the importance of the ethos of the school and have looked at the crushing effect that professional 'expertise' has often had, albeit unwittingly, on many parents' views of their own capabilities. The best parent education schemes have found how important it is to value the experience that individuals bring to each situation, and have recognised the need to work *with* parents rather than do things *to* them. Effective relationships between professionals and parents were built on partnership and on mutual respect, with an emphasis on reciprocity that allowed people to give as well as to take. This approach has important implications for the methods used in parent education, and for the training of those professionals who work with parents.

Methods in parent education

The advantages and disadvantages of different methods and approaches were reviewed in Chapter 2. Whilst the mass media undoubtedly reached the largest number of people and could contribute to their knowledge, it was less successful in increasing understanding or skills, and offered few possibilities for asking follow-up questions unless it was linked to other forms of parent education, such as phone-in programmes or group discussion. Groups were found to be particularly successful as a way of sharing experiences, making friends and learning from each other and, importantly, in giving people the confidence to question the 'experts'. But they did require skilled leadership and such skills appeared to be in short supply. It has also become evident during the course of the project that there are few groups which are systematically attempting to help parents develop specific skills in relating to each other and to their children and few opportunities for increasing their sensitivity to their own values and attitudes and the way these affect their children. The educational content is often in the group, but is less often exploited. Some of these more structured approaches are not without their problems, however, for as one American commentator observed 'Parent education, while attempting to improve the quality of family life, can impair functioning by undermining confidence and creating dependency' (Hess, 1980).

Training

The training of professionals working with families was also mentioned in Chapter 2. From the evidence presented throughout the book it is clear that very few of those working with families have, through their training, an experience of seeing families as a whole, tending to focus either on some members – usually the children – or on pathology and dysfunction. There are also a number of specific areas where too often family workers are not in a position to provide the kind of service that parents need – where they have inadequate or irrelevant knowledge; where they do not fully understand their own attitudes, values and feelings, and may be insensitive to those with whom they work who may hold different values from their own; and where they may not have the skills to handle sensitive issues in group discussion. A specific recommendation about a core training for family workers is made at the end of this chapter.

Evaluation

It has also become evident during the course of this study that we still know very little about the effectiveness of these various approaches to parent education. While a number of small-scale studies have been mounted which look at the extent to which individual schemes are meeting their own objectives, there are still many unanswered questions. There have been no long-term follow-ups of the recipients of specific parent education programmes, although the difficulties inherent in isolating the many variables involved in the development of either parents or their children would present enormous problems to researchers. Even measuring changes in attitude and behaviour resulting from programmes concerned to increase self-confidence and coping-skills is a task fraught with problems. Nevertheless there are many areas in which further research could usefully increase our understanding of parent education. Fuller understanding is needed of exactly what skills are required in parenting and in how parental competence is acquired. It would be valuable to know more about the comparative effectiveness of different kinds of approach, and of different types of leadership. We need to know more about which kinds of programme work for which parents, and to develop further strategies for reaching the more vulnerable families; and we need to know more about what parents actually need and use during the life cycle, and how the education and support they receive affects their abilities as parents.

Personal development and parental development

Central to the debate on parent education is the distinction between the development of an individual as a person, who is, one hopes, growing towards maturity as a coping and caring adult, and the development of skills specifically related to parenting. This was vividly portrayed in the section on schoolgirl mothers who were struggling to find and enjoy their lost adolescence at the same time as having to learn the responsibilities of caring for a new-born baby. It was evident too in many of the schemes described in Chapter 6, where, in reaching out through adult education to largely working-class women, a conflict was detected between their role as mothers (by focussing on the needs of their children through parent education) and their needs as individuals to take some of the new-found possibilities offered by the education system and develop their own interests. The needs of parents and their children will not always coincide and one of the major challenges to parent education is to help parents to understand and reconcile these often conflicting needs.

The individual and the state

A related dilemma which has been apparent at every stage of the life cycle is that posed by the family's right to privacy and self-determination as against the State's need for healthy and productive citizens. This is a dilemma which reflects different political and ideological viewpoints, and one on which parent educators cannot turn their backs. Is parent education basically a means of social control, whereby for example, existing role stereotypes are reinforced and women are seen as home-makers whilst men support their family economically? Is it a means of encouraging adolescents to conform to socially-accepted norms of behaviour, and of encouraging mothers to prepare their children to fit neatly into the education system? Or can it be a means to social change and personal growth, whereby individuals are given increased encouragement and self-confidence to take greater control over their lives, to break out of traditional roles and to question the status quo? If women – for it relates particularly to women – are to explore and question the nature of their dependence and their roles as mothers, what are the implications for relationships within their families and society as a whole? For many women parent education is likely to intensify the conflict between their dual roles as mother and worker.

The status of parenting

The traditional male and female roles may be beginning to change, speeded in many instances by the impact of unemployment, but parenting is still too often seen as mothering, as is evident from the ways in which schools present child-care options almost entirely to girls, and in the difficulty experienced by almost every parent education scheme in attracting men. The need to involve boys and men in parent education at every stage is a pressing issue, and until it is resolved it is difficult to see how the generally low status of parenting in Britain might be improved. Motherhood is idealised and yet denigrated. The emphasis on equal opportunities, which we would heartily endorse, has left many women feeling that in an attempt to maintain an equal status with men at work, their roles and abilities as mothers are being under-valued. If shared parenting were a reality, and if men's roles as fathers were seen to be as important as their roles as workers, this might go some way towards giving parenting the value it deserves.

Family policy

Closely connected to the status of parenting is the concept of a family policy which looks at legislation and at the way that society is ordered and organised with an eye to how it supports or underlines family life. Throughout the book we have referred to the need for what in Chapter 1 we called 'permitting circumstances', and a considerable body of evidence now points to the adverse effect on family relationships of such factors as bad housing, unemployment, poverty, isolation and depression. It is surely unrealistic to expect that parent education and support can, on its own, relieve complex social problems and alleviate stress. Policies are needed that will enable *all* families to enjoy a basic level of income, commensurate with what is acceptable within a developed society, that will give them some genuine choice in how they live their lives and bring up their children. This will need to include a redistribution of resources through improved benefits and a reorganised system of taxation, and a swift rethinking of current policies which assume, as public services are cut back, that all families are able to be self-sufficient and that all citizens are equally well able to stand on their own two feet. Family policy has been interpreted in many different ways, but at the very least a family perspective on legislation might 'involve a greater sensitivity within the policy process to changing family patterns; the development of a positive partnership between family and state; and the monitoring and evaluation of the impact of public policy on families' (Craven, Rimmer and Wicks 1982).

Recommendations for policy-makers and practitioners

On the basis of this evidence we conclude with a definition of parent education based on a synthesis of the best programmes that we have seen, and with a number of proposals which could form guidelines for action. Some of these are of a general nature; others relate to specific stages of the life cycle.

General recommendations

1. Our main recommendation is that parent education, as defined below, should be available to all who wish to take advantage of it. An overall definition of parent education and of its aims and objectives is as follows:

    > Parent education comprises a range of educational and supportive measures which help parents and prospective parents to understand their own social, emotional, psychological and physical needs and those of their children and enhances the relationship between them. It should be available to all parents and prospective parents. It is a lifelong process and as such will have a different emphasis at different stages of the life-cycle. Its emphasis should be on individuals' roles and relationships in the here-and-now, as well as with their future roles and relationships.

    > The overall aim of parent education is to develop self-aware and self-confident parents. It should do this by:

    > providing people with access to *information* and *knowledge* about:
    >   human health and development;
    >   different stages of child development, marriage and family life
    >   sources of help within the community, including welfare rights and benefits;

    > helping them develop *social skills*:
    >   in understanding themselves and relating to others
    >   in communicating;
    >   in making decisions and accepting responsibility for them,

and *practical skills* in managing a home and family;

offering opportunities and encouragement in *understanding* how to apply this information and these skills in relation to their own needs, desires, life-styles, personal characteristics and potential;

helping them to identify their own *values* and *attitudes* and acknowledge how these affect the way in which children are brought up.

We further recommend that:

2. Parent education should be based upon the general principles suggested in Chapter 2 and in particular that

    there is no single right way of parenting, no blueprint for a perfect family, and diverse family patterns should be respected;

    the ability to parent reflects each individual's level of self-confidence and sense of worth. Education and support should therefore acknowledge, value and build on parents' and prospective parents' existing skills, experience and abilities;

    programmes should be sensitive to the diverse social, ethnic and cultural backgrounds of families;

    in order to fulfil their obligations, parents need adequate social and economic support.

3. Parent education is a lifelong process and as such will have different emphasis at different stages of the life-cycle (see specific recommendations on pp. 211–17).

4. In every locality there should be a range of schemes and services available reflecting the different needs and circumstances of individual parents and prospective parents. For young people this should include appropriate courses in schools and further education establishments, and groups in youth centres, churches etc. For prospective parents it should encompass a more flexible and relevant approach to antenatal education. Parents should be offered a continuum of support

from informal post-natal groups and readily available information, through parent education groups, playgroups, community and adult education, home-visiting schemes and closer involvement in schooling.

5. Because parent education and support is not always seen as a high priority amongst many of those who work with parents, health authorities, local authorities and voluntary organisations should seek to strengthen their commitment to *preventive* rather than crisis work with families. A valuable approach would be through the setting-up of schemes such as those described in this book.

6. In the best interests of parents and their children, professionals should support parents in their task and work in partnership with them. The underlying assumption of the best parent-education schemes is of the need to build on parents' skills, experience, competence and self-confidence, rather than provide 'expert' advice on how to bring up children. In the words of the Court report 'We have found no better way to raise a child than reinforce the ability of his parents to do so'.

7. If schemes and services are to make sense to families, and are to make best use of limited resources, there will need to be much closer co-operation than is at present the case between professionals and para-professionals working in health, education and social services, and between statutory and voluntary organisations.

8. There are certain core elements which should be a part of the training of all those working with families. These include:

    opportunities to understand their own *attitudes, values and feelings* about marriage, family life and parenthood and develop sensitivity to those with whom they work, and who may hold different values and attitudes from their own;

    an extension of their *knowledge* about and *understanding* of family patterns, human and child development, and relationships;

development of their *skills*, (i) in teaching and particularly in the sensitive and enabling approach required for working with groups; and (ii) in working with parents and with colleagues from different professional backgrounds.

Included as Appendix 4 is the outline of a suggested training package for education workers, proposed by the Educational Advisory Board of the National Marriage Guidance Council, which gives a useful summary of the kind of core training we have in mind.

9. Further thought should be given to the educational content of existing parent-education programmes.

10. Research studies should look at the comparative values of different approaches to parent education and support; at the skills involved in parenting and how they are acquired; at the skills required in leadership of parent education schemes and at how leadership affects the scheme; at which approaches work for which families; and at what parents actually need and use during the life cycle.

11. Specific attempts should be made to involve boys and fathers in parent education programmes.

Education for family life: work with children and young people in schools, further education and the youth service

1. Family life education should be part of a co-ordinated approach to personal, social and health education, in primary and secondary schools, in further education (and in particular on the Youth Training Scheme), and in correctional settings such as intermediate treatment schemes and prisons.

2. A basic course should be devised which is available to all young people at some stage of their education. The main aims of the course should be to equip young people with *skills* in understanding themselves and relating to others; with *opportunities* for developing self-confidence and for discussing values and attitudes; and with *knowledge* about human and

particularly child development, methods of contraception, about family life and parenting and about how to find out and use such resources as may be available – in order that they can make balanced and informed decisions about the choices that affect their own lives.

3. In addition to the basic core course, there should be optional subjects available to those who want to specialise, for example, in child development, and these options should be so organised that they present genuine choices to boys and girls alike. The child-development option should include opportunities for working with and observing young children.

4. Because the education system forms only a small part of the social and physical environment in which young people are growing up, family life education should be particularly sensitive to the home background of children and young people, and wherever possible the parents of the pupils to whom it is to be offered should be consulted.

5. Family life education should be based on the needs, interests, experience and abilities of the pupils here and now. Much of the current work in this area takes a white, protestant, middle-class approach to family life, ignoring the multi-cultural society in which we live and the different ethnic and social backgrounds from which many of the pupils come. It also tends to focus on the practical skills of child care, which are more appropriate later in the life cycle, rather than working from the experience of the pupils.

6. Every school or college of further education should devise a clear policy for family life education and be clear about its aims and objectives.

7. In order to increase the status of the course a senior member of staff should be appointed co-ordinator of family life education.

8. Those teachers with specific pastoral responsibility should be involved in the work.

9. In-service training provision and continuing support should be available to all members of the teaching team, who may not only find themselves dealing with unfamiliar content, but also using new methods of teaching, particularly informal group discussion. This training needs to include examination of aims and objectives, and of values and attitudes, knowledge and understanding, and the development of specific skills, and provide support for the implementation of these new ideas in schools.

10. Social education should be available through the youth service to young people up to 21 years of age, and this should include opportunities for family life education.

11. These same opportunities should be provided for all those in residential settings away from their own family home – for example, in community homes, detention centres, Borstals, armed forces.

12. Every local education authority should develop a policy for schoolgirl mothers and devise a suitable range of measures to ensure that their needs for formal education, for personal and social education and for parent education are met, whether in the schools, in special units or in voluntary projects.

13. Youth and community workers should develop a policy for providing a range of activities and provisions for teenage mothers and teenage couples. This will require facilities for toddlers, as well as opportunities for personal and social education and parent education.

Preparation for parenthood: pre-conceptual care, pregnancy and the transition to parenthood

1. Schemes and services should be available in each local area which meet the aims of parent education at two stages – before and after conception. During a committed relationship parent education should:

    Offer as much information as possible about parenthood to those who have not made decisions about their adult roles;

give them opportunities to consider and discuss this information in the light of their own needs, desires, life-styles, personal characteristics and potential;

encourage them to develop to the maximum their self-awareness and self-confidence;

support them in the resulting conscious choices they make about their lives and the results of actions for which they were not offered a choice or did not exercise it.

Once the pregnancy is under way it should:

involve prospective fathers as well as mothers;

give realistic information about pregnancy, childbirth and parenthood;

provide opportunities for couples to talk with each other and with other couples about the experience of pregnancy, childbirth, and babyhood, fatherhood and motherhood.

2. Pre-conceptual counselling should be available in all health clinics and particularly at family planning clinics.

3. Health visitors should be informed of every confirmation of pregnancy in their area, and at this point should make available information on diet, smoking, drugs, etc.

4. Antenatal services should respond to research findings by introducing appointments systems, the provision of facilities for young children, more privacy, personal attention, improved communication and more explicit information.

5. Particular attention should be given to encouraging those who tend not to use antenatal services to make use of them – particularly the young, the single, and women from ethnic minorities.

6. Antenatal services should be made more accessible through the setting up of walk-in clinics, evening and weekend clinics and classes, mobile or local community-based services; and

more relevant to the needs of individual mothers by providing opportunities to meet parents with newly-born babies, and to share feelings and anxieties about pregnancy, childbirth and parenthood.

7. Local support networks should be created to include prospective parents and new parents, health visitors, GPs, community midwives, and any local voluntary groups that parents might want to contact after the birth.

8. Continuity of care between the antenatal and post-natal stages should be provided by midwives and health visitors, ensuring that consistent advice and guidance is given to parents and that health professionals are alerted to the needs of particularly vulnerable women.

Education and support for parents

1. A range of schemes and services should be available in each local area which meet the overall aims of parent education and support. For parents of young children this should:

   provide parents with sufficient social competence and information to enable them to have some measure of control over their own lives and to retain their individuality as people and as a couple;

   provide support for parents who may feel depressed or isolated;

   increase parenting skills so parents can enjoy their children and become models of good parenting to their own children;

   support and develop parents' self-confidence in making decisions about their children's future.

   For parents of older children it should also:

   provide information and support to enable parents to understand their adolescent children and develop appropriate 'coping' strategies;

enable parents to 'allow' their children to leave home;

provide parents with sufficient information that they may understand and participate in educational and employment decisions.

2. Resources should be made available through the statutory services and voluntary organisations to local communities to set up parent-education schemes appropriate to their needs.

3. Professionals working with families should consider providing preparation and support for parents who wish to lead groups, become involved in home-visiting schemes or run other support services.

4. Priority should be given to work with vulnerable families, and adult education and community projects in particular should look to see what their contribution could be.

5. Whilst self-help groups and community-based schemes have considerable potential in terms of the individual growth of those involved in them, such projects have demonstrated the need for professional workers to act as catalysts or enablers, helping parents to develop community networks, find and use resources, to share and build on their own experiences, and identify and solve their own problems.

6. Whilst voluntary schemes have a key role to play in the provision of services for families, they should supplement and not substitute for statutory services.

7. High priority should be given to work with parents of children under the age of one and particularly in the first few months after the birth.

8. In addition to those elements in a core training programme recommended under *General recommendations* (8), a high priority should be to broaden the base of training for those who work with children (particularly teachers and workers with pre-school children) to enable them also to work with parents.

9. Teachers should be encouraged to work in closer partnership with parents, building on their evident wish to be more closely involved in their children's schooling.

10. There is a pressing need for parent education for parents of school-age children, in terms of increasing parents' understanding of what is 'normal' development for each age group; in providing opportunities for discussing issues relating to their children's education, health, employment, etc; and in looking at changing relationships within the family.

11. Schools and adult education should work more closely together in order that schools can become a real community resource, offering opportunities to parents to increase both their understanding of and involvement in their children's development, and to continue their own personal growth through adult education.

Bringing up children in the 1980s is a demanding and at times difficult task. It requires not only inner resources of empathy, resilience, confidence and appropriate skills and knowledge but also the external resources of support provided by a caring community. Whilst the majority of parents manage well for most of the time, many would welcome further opportunities for increasing their knowledge, understanding and enjoyment of family life. If society continues to have high expectations of parents then it must also provide opportunities for young people to make realistic choices about becoming parents and provide an adequate network of information, support and education for parents as and when it is needed. As Mia Pringle (1975) has said 'Modern parenthood is too demanding and complex a task to be performed well merely because we have all once been children'.

Appendix 1

Organisations and Individuals Consulted*

All-Party Parliamentary Group on Children
Association of Advisers for Under-Fives
Association of Educational Psychologists
Association of Family Therapy
Association for Jewish Youth
Aston University: Department of Educational Enquiry: Preparation for Parenthood in the Secondary School Curriculum Project

Balsall Heath Health Centre, Birmingham
Barnardo's
Barnet Social Services
Bath Working Party on Preparation for Parenthood
Berkshire Local Education Authority – Home Economics Teachers
Birmingham Parent and Child Centre
Birmingham Under-Fives Consultative Group
Birmingham University: Department of Psychology
                              Board of Graduate Clinical Studies
Bristol Home Plus
Bristol University: School of Applied Social Studies
                        Department of Community Health
British Association for Adoption and Fostering
British Association for Early Childhood Education (BAECE)
British Broadcasting Corporation: Schools Radio and Television
                                        Continuing Education Department
British Youth Council
Brunel University
Buckinghamshire Local Education Authority – Home Economics Teachers

Calderdale Association for Parents

* Addresses of these and any other organisations mentioned in the book are available from the National Children's Bureau.

Cambridge University: Institute of Education
Early Parenthood Project, Hughes Hall
Education for Parenthood Project
Child Care and Development Group
Channel 4
Children's Society
Church of England Children's Society
Churches Television Council (CTVC)
Community Education Development Centre (CEDC), Coventry
Connors Toy Library, Portsmouth
Contact Health and Teaching (CHAT), Pinner
COPE
Council for Education and Training of Health Visitors (CETHV)
Croydon College, Health Visitors Course
Curtis Family Centre, Barnet

Department of Education and Science (DES):
    Members of HM Inspectorate
    Under Fives Dissemination Project
Department of Health and Social Security: Children's Division
Durham University, Adult Education Department: Exploring Parenthood
    Course

Family Forum
Family Life Education Ecumenical Project (FLEEP)
Family Planning Association (FPA)
Family Service Units:
    Brent, Edinburgh, Coventry, Leicester, Waltham Forest
    Training Workshop for Unit Organisers
Family Start, Oldham
Family Welfare Association (FWA)
Fellowship of St Michael

General Synod of Church of England Board of Education
Gingerbread
Girl Guides Association
Glasgow University
Gloucester Association for Family Life (GAFL)

Hackney 'Off Centre' Youth Project
Hampshire Local Education Authority
Hampshire Social Services Department
Haringey Local Education Authority – Home Economics Teachers
Health Education Council (HEC)
Health in Homerton
Health Visitors Association
Home and School Centre, Govan, Scotland
Home Start: Leicester, Melton Mowbray, Nottingham, Ripley
Home Start Consultancy

Independent Broadcasting Association (IBA): Education Department
Inner London Education Authority (ILEA):
   Adult Education and Youth Inspectorate
   Home Economics Inspectorate
Inner London Education Authority (ILEA): Islington Division
In-Service Training and Education Panel (INSTEP): Youth and
   Community Work
Institute of Group Analysis
Institute of Marital Studies: Transition to Parenthood Project
Institute of Psychiatry
Islington Social Services Department

Kettering Divisional Review Committee for Child Abuse and Neglect

Leeds University: Career and Counselling Development Unit
Lincolnshire Local Education Authority – Home Economics Teachers
Lisson Grove Project for Prospective Parents
London University: Institute of Education
London Voluntary Service Council
London Youth Advisory Centre
Lothian: Home Visiting Scheme

Marlborough Day Hospital, St John's Wood
Milton Keynes, College of Education
Moorland Nursery, Milton Keynes
Mothers Union

National Association for Maternal and Child Welfare (NAMCW)
National Association of Young People's Counselling and Advisory
   Services (NAYPCAS)
National Childbirth Trust (NCT) – Education Committee
                               Post-natal Support Committee
National Childminding Association (NCMA)
National Children's Centre, Huddersfield
National Children's Home (NCH), Family Network
National Council for One Parent Families
National Council for Voluntary Organisations: Antenatal Project
National Council for Voluntary Youth Services (NCVYS)
National Council of Women
National Foster Care Association (NFCA)
National Marriage Guidance Council (NMGC)
National Nursery Education Board (NNEB)
National Society for the Prevention of Cruelty to Children:
   Advisory Service
   School of Social Work
   Family Centre, Farnborough
   Special Units: Wellingborough, Nottingham
National Youth Bureau
Nene College, Northampton

Network, Watford
New Grapevine, Islington and Camden
Newcastle University School of Education
Newham Parents Centre
Newpin
Norfolk and Norwich Hospital, Parentcraft Co-ordinator
Northumberland Area Health Education Unit
Northumberland Working Party on Education about Parenthood
Nottingham Health Education Unit
Nottingham University Child Development Unit

Open University: Community Education Unit
                Education for Family Life Project
Organisation for Economic Co-operation and Development/Centre for
    Educational Research and Innovation (OECD/CERI)
Organisation Mondiale pour L'Education Prescholaire (OMEP)
Organisations for Parents under Stress (OPUS)
Oxford University: Pre-School Research Project

Parents, Children and Teachers (PACT), Hackney
Policy Studies Institute: Home-school relationship project
Portsmouth Toy Libraries Association
Portsmouth Under Fives Forum
Pre-School Playgroups Association:
    Working Party on Education for Parenthood
    Training Committee
    Welsh PPA
Priority Area Playgroups, Birmingham

Radford Family Centre, Nottingham
Redbridge and Waltham Forest Area Health Authority
Riverside Child Health Project, Newcastle
Royal College of Midwives
Royal College of Nursing

Salford Local Education Authority – Nursery and Infant Teachers
Save the Children
Schools Council: Parents Liaison Group
                 Group Work Skills Group
SCOPE, Southampton
Scouts Association
South Glamorgan Local Education Authority
South Harringay Pre-school Centre
Southwark Institute of Adult Education
Southwark Wel-care
Stantonbury Campus Community School, Milton Keynes
Stepping Stones Project, Glasgow
Strathclyde Community and Adult Education Department
Study Commission on the Family

Surrey University
Sussex Youth Trust

Thomas Coram Research Institute: Transition to Parenthood Project
Toy Libraries Association

Under Fives Research Dissemination Group
United Nations International Children's Emergency Fund (UK)
(UNICEF)

Voluntary Council for Handicapped Children
Voluntary Organisations Liaison Committee for the Under Fives
(VOLCUF)
Volunteer Centre: Media Project

Waltham Forest Social Services Department
Widnes Health Centre

Appendix 2
Examinations in Child Care and Development, 1982 (1978 figures in brackets)

1. CSE and CEE

Examining Board	Mode 1 and 2	Mode 3	CEE
Associated Lancashire Schools	*Child Care and Development*	*Child Studies* 317 (190)	*Child Studies* 9 (21)
East Anglian	*Child Care and Development*	—	—
East Midland Regional	*Child Care and Development* 3219 (231)	—	—
London Regional	*Child Development and the Family* 2824 (2200) *Child Care and Development* 400	*Child Care and the Family* 875 (549)	—
North Regional	—	*Child Development* 1485 (750)	
North West Regional	*Child Care and Development* First exam 1983	—	—
South East Regional	*Child Development and Care* 4446 (2200)	*Child Development and Care* 53 (–)	*Family Centred Studies* 196 (–)
Southern Regional	*Parentcraft* 2735 (2084)		
South Western	*Child Care and Development* 2742 (1185)	—	

West Midland	*Child Care and Development* 5936 (4582)		
Welsh Joint Education Committee		*Child Care* 205 *Child Care and Development* 94 *Child Development and the Family* 471 (100)	*Family Welfare* 23 *Child Development* 109 *Child Development and Care* 41
Yorkshire and Humberside Regional	*Child Care* 765 (–)	*Child Care* 413 (114) *Parentcraft* 347 (129) *Child Care* 1840 (1653) *Home Management and Family Care* 25 (50) Other child care exams – (227)	*Child Care* 61 *Family and Society* 16
Total Candidates	27 858 (13 252)	6125 (3762)	455 (21)

Overall Total: 33 983 (17 014)

2. GCE O and A Level

Examining Board		
Associated	(O/A) *Psychology: Child Development* starting 1983	
	(O) *Family and Community Studies*	1200
Joint Matriculation	(A) *The Home, Family and Society*	1066
Oxford Local	(O) *Child Care and Development* starting 1983	
Southern Universities Joint	(O) *Child Development*	354

3. NAMCW

Human Development and Family Life Basic and General Parts 1, 2, 3	10016

4. City and Guilds

Community Care Foundation Course	4173

Appendix 3

Resources for Parent Education

In addition to the many books and articles on parent education listed in the bibliography, a number of organisations have produced lists of books and audio-visual material for use in parent education, and some have published materials for use in group discussion. Many of these books and materials will be available locally at health education units or at teachers' centres.

Bibliographies of books and audio-visual material for parent educators

British Broadcasting Corporation,
The Langham, London W1A 1AA.
Radio and television programmes relevant to parent education in schools and colleges are listed in the *Annual Programme: Radio and Television for Schools and Colleges*. Adult education programmes are listed in *Insight*, available annually from BBC continuing education. (See also under IBA.)

Birmingham Education Committee,
Council House,
Margaret Street,
Birmingham B3 3BJ.
Child Development and Family Related Courses (1981) A guide for teachers.

Catholic Marriage Advisory Council,
15 Lansdowne Rd,
London W11 3AJ.
Resources for Relationships (1979) A selection of teaching materials.

Development Education Centre,
Gillett Centre,
Selly Oak Colleges,
Bristol Road,
Birmingham B29 6LE.
Values, Cultures and Kids (1983) Approaches and resources for teaching child development and about the family.

Further Education Curriculum Review and Development Unit,
Elizabeth House,
York Road,
London SE1 7PH
A selection of publications on personal and social education in further education.

Health Education Council,
78 New Oxford Street,
London WC1A 1AH.
Detailed bibliographies of publications and teaching aids on:
  Child development (including preparation for parenthood), Family planning, Personal relationships, Relationships and sexuality, Sex education.
Most of the publications and teaching aids can be viewed at the HEC's resources centre.

Independent Broadcasting Authority,
70 Brompton Road,
London SW3.
Radio and television programmes relevant to parent education in schools are listed in the *Annual Programme Booklet* available from each of the 14 IBA regions. Adult education programmes are listed in *TV Take Up* which includes ITV and Channel 4. The IBA also publishes a useful document entitled *Parent Education Programmes* which draws together all the child studies and parent education programmes from the BBC, the IBA and the Open University.

Inner London Education Authority,
c/o Essendine Home Economics Teachers Centre,
Essendine Road,
London W9 2LR.
  Resources for child development (1983)
  Child development courses: films and visual materials (1983)

International Planned Parenthood Federation,
18–20 Lower Regent Street,
London SW1Y 4PW
Approaches to Population Awareness, Family Life and Sex Education
Selected resource materials.

National Association for Maternal and Child Welfare,
Tavistock House North,
Tavistock Square,
London WC1H 9JG.
Parentcraft Education Teaching Aids – sources, notes and guide for teachers.

National Children's Bureau,
8 Wakley Street,
London EC1V 7QE.
Booklists:
  Education for Parenthood (34)
  Adolescent pregnancy and parenthood (115)
  Drug taking in pregnancy (119)
Booklists are also available on more than 100 other topics relating to children's care and development.
Filmlists:
  Adolescent sexual and personal relationships (13)
  Adolescence (1)
  Early child care (9)
  Play (7)
  Pregnancy and Childbirth (15)
  Preparation for Parenthood (14)
  Pre-schooling (6)

Royal College of Midwives,
15 Mansfield Street,
London W1M 0BE.
Antenatal Education A selected reading list
Parentcraft Education A selected reading list

Royal College of Nursing,
Henrietta Place,
London W1M 0AB.
Bibliographies on:
  Parentcraft, Parenting, Preparation for Parenthood

Materials for use in parent education

Community Education Development Centre,
Stoke School,
Briton Road,
Coventry CV2 4LF.
Coping with kids A collection of materials for use with individuals or in group discussion.
Working Together A set of ten leaflets on early childhood (discipline, temper tantrums etc)
What would you do? Situational flip charts

Early Years A pack of child-development materials for use in groups with parents, giving information about stages of development and suggestions for how parents might stimulate their children.

Coventry Diocese Family Life Project,
3 Brooke Close,
Warwick.
How's the Family? Material for use by groups looking at contemporary family life over five sessions.

Family Planning Association,
27–35 Mortimer Street,
London W1N 7RJ.
Films, videos and other teaching materials on contraception and sexuality. Also courses in personal relationships and sexuality for community workers, social workers and teachers.

Gloucester Association for Family Life,
2 College St,
Gloucester
Spare the Time for Family Life
Adolescence
The Family and the Pre-Adolescent
An Elderly Person in the Family.

Mothers Union,
Mary Sumner House,
24 Tufton Street,
London SW1P 3RB.
Various discussion materials with a Christian perspective on family life.

Open University,
Centre for Continuing Education,
Walton Hall,
Milton Keynes MK7 6AA.
Four parenthood courses, which are also available in book form:
    The First Years of Life (also published by Ward Lock)
    The Preschool Years (also published by Ward Lock)
    Childhood 5–10 (also published by Harper & Row)
    Parents and Teenagers (published by Harper & Row)
A new updated series is now in production. Available shortly
    Getting Ready for Pregnancy
    Understanding Pregnancy and Childbirth
Packs of materials specifically prepared for use in discussion groups are:
    Parents Talking: The Developing Child
    Parents Talking: Family Relationships
which use some of the original material but with additional guidance for group leaders, and

Women and Young Children: Learning through Experience
produced by the Van-Leer-funded project.
Book of the Child – Pregnancy to 4 years is based on the courses and
published by the Scottish Health Education Unit, 21 Landsdowne Cres-
cent, Edinburgh.
Materials are also in preparation for use in schools, developing from the
Education for Family Life Course (P532), and for youth workers developing from *Parent and Teenagers*.

Schools Council,
Newcombe House,
5 Notting Hill Gate,
London W11 3JB.
Many curriculum development projects are relevant (see Chapter 3). These
include:
　All About Me and *Think Well* (Health Education 5–13) Nelson
　Health Education 13–18 Forbes Publications
　Home and Family 8–13 Forbes Publications
　Moral Education Project Longman
　Humanities Curriculum Project, Heinemann Educational Books

Scriptographic Publications,
92 Carnwath Road,
London SW6 3HW.
Information booklets for parents:
　Your child's emotional health
　Understanding Adolescence

Appendix 4   Basic Training Package

Affective Aspect – Attitudes, Values and Feelings
This pervades all other aspects of training, with the aim of enabling workers:

To absorb, understand and respond critically to information, knowledge and insights which may touch and often challenge the attitudes values and feelings about such material, which as people they bring to training.

To use – i.e. apply skilfully in practice situations, the information, knowledge and insights which they encounter through training.

Cognitive Aspect

Topics
Human growth and development
Physical   ⎫
Psychological ⎬ perspectives
Sociological   ⎭

Personal relationships education
Friendship
Sexual relationships, sexuality and sexual orientation
Community relationships
Class, race and religion

Skills Aspect

Development of:
Communication skills – verbal and non-verbal
Teaching skills through practice
Groupwork skills – leadership and analysis of groups
Observation, listening, diagnostic & referral skills
Skills in using techniques which increase learning such as visual aids (film, video, overhead projector)
role play
games and exercises
social skills and other educational programmes
Skills in preparing one's own teaching materials
Skills in course planning and contract-making
Skills in recording, monitoring and evaluating work

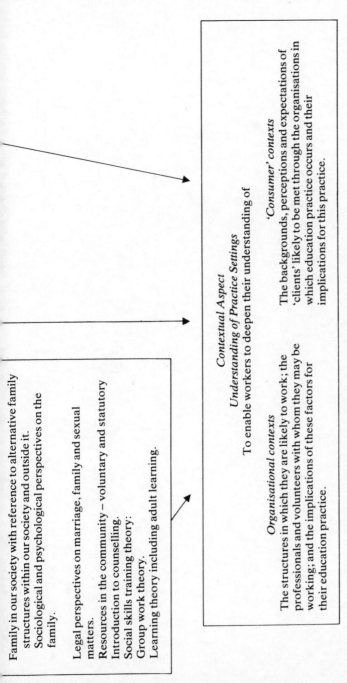

Family in our society with reference to alternative family structures within our society and outside it. Sociological and psychological perspectives on the family.

Legal perspectives on marriage, family and sexual matters.
Resources in the community – voluntary and statutory
Introduction to counselling.
Social skills training theory:
Group work theory.
Learning theory including adult learning.

Contextual Aspect
Understanding of Practice Settings
To enable workers to deepen their understanding of

Organisational contexts
The structures in which they are likely to work; the professionals and volunteers with whom they may be working; and the implications of these factors for their education practice.

'Consumer' contexts
The backgrounds, perceptions and expectations of 'clients' likely to be met through the organisations in which education practice occurs and their implications for this practice.

SOURCE   *An Education Strategy for MG*, National Marriage Guidance Council April 1983
Reprinted by permission

References

Numbers in **bold** refer to pages on which references can be found

Adams, L. (1980) *Survey into Antenatal and Parentcraft Education* (Redbridge and Waltham Forest Area Health Authority Health Education Service). **126, 128**

Advisory Council on the Misuse of Drugs (1982) *Treatment and Rehabilitation* (London: HMSO). **191**

Allen, R. and Purkis, A. (1983) *Health in the Round: Voluntary Action and Antenatal Services* (London: NCVO, Bedford Square Press). **122, 127**

Aplin, G. and Pugh, G. (eds) (1983) *Perspectives on Pre-School Home Visiting* (London: National Children's Bureau and Community Education Development Centre). **161, 162**

Armstrong, G. and Brown, F. (1979) *Five Years On* (Oxford Social Evaluation Unit, Department of Social and Administrative Studies, Oxford University). **162**

Balding, J. (1979) 'Health topics research', also published in *Education for Family Life* (Milton Keynes: Open University Press (1981)). **70**

Baldwin, J. and Wells, H. (eds) (1979–81) *Active Tutorial Work Books 1–5* (Oxford: Basil Blackwell). **82**

Barclay, P. M. (1982) *Social Workers: their role and tasks* (London: National Institute of Social Work, Bedford Square Press). **35, 150**

Barker, P. (1981) *Basic Family Therapy* (London: Granada Publishing). **52**

Barnett, R. (1981) 'The importance of being a parent', *Marriage Guidance Journal*, 19, 6, 267–75. **77, 78**

Baxter, B. (1981) 'A secondary school course in education for parenthood', in *Education for Family Life*, source book P532 (Milton Keynes: Open University Press). **86**

Beail, N. (1982) 'The role of the father during pregnancy and birth', in Beail, N. and McGuire, J. (1982). **21**

Beail, N. and McGuire, J. (eds) (1982) *Fathers: Psychological Perspectives* (London: Junction Books). **21**

Becher, R. A. and Eraut, M. R. (1980) *Accountability in the Middle Years of Schooling* (Brighton: Sussex University, Department of Education). **175**

Bennett, D. and Stobart, T. (1981) *A Paper about our Work 1974–81* (Wandsworth: Family Workshop Unit). **153**

Birch, K. and Chambers, M. (1979) 'Preparation for parenthood', *Health Visitor*, 52, 12, 507 – 10. **128**

Birchall, D. (1982) 'Family centres', *Concern*, 43, 16–20. **5, 158, 160**

Birmingham Education Committee (1981) *Child Development and Family Related Courses: a guide for teachers.* **76, 78**

Bone, M. (1977) *Pre-school Children and the Need for Day Care* (London: OPCS, HMSO). **31**

Borg, S. and Lasker, J. (1982) *When Pregnancy Fails: coping with miscarriage, stillbirth and infant death* (Routledge & Kegan Paul). **133**

Bowlby, J. (1953) *Child Care and the Growth of Love* (Harmondsworth: Penguin Books). **12, 31**

Boyd, C. and Sellers, L. (comps) (1982) *The British Way of Birth* (London: Pan in assoc. with Spastics Society). **122, 128**

Breen, D. (1975) *The Birth of a First Child* (London: Tavistock Publications). **119, 132**

Breen, D. (1981) *Talking with Mothers: about pregnancy, childbirth and early motherhood* (London: Jill Norman). **116**

Brierley, J. (1982) 'Health education in schools', in West Midlands RHA *Health Education in Schools* (Birmingham). **75, 84**

Bronfenbrenner, U. (1974) *Is Early Intervention Effective?: A report on longitudinal evaluations of pre-school programmes*, vol. 2 (Washington DC: DHEW Office of Child Development). **161**

Brown, G. and Harris, T. (1978) *Social Origins of Depression: A study of psychiatric disorders in women* (London: Tavistock Publications). **31**

Brown, G. W. *et al.* (1975) 'Social class and psychiatric disturbance among women in an urban population', *Sociology*, 9, 225 – 54.

Brown, M. and Madge, N. (1982) *Despite the Welfare State* (London: Heinemann Educational Books).

Busfield, J. and Paddon, M. (1977) *Thinking about Children: sociology and fertility in post-war England* (Cambridge University Press). **116**

Button, L. (1974) *Developmental Group Work with Adolescents* (University of London Press). **82**

Button, L. (1981, 1982) *Group Tutoring for the Form Teacher*, Books 1 and 2 (London: Hodder and Stoughton). **82**

Callias, M. (1980) 'Teaching parents, teachers and nurses', in Yule, W. and Carr, J. (eds) *Behaviour Modification for the Mentally Handicapped* (London: Croom Helm). **52**

Cameron, R. J. (ed.) (1982) *Working Together: Portage in the UK* (Windsor: NFER – Nelson). **52**

Cartwright, A. (1979) *The Dignity of Labour? A study of childbearing and induction* (London: Tavistock Publications). **118, 132**

Central Advisory Council for Education (England) (1959) *15 to 18* (Crowther report) (London: HMSO). **67, 93**

Central Advisory Council for Education (England) (1963) *Half Our Future* (Newsom report) (London: HMSO). **67**

Central Advisory Council for Education (England) (1967) *Children and their Primary Schools* (Plowden report) (London: HMSO). **170**

Central Health Services Council, standing Maternity and Midwifery Advisory Committee (1970), *Domiciliary Midwifery and Maternity Bed Needs; report of the Sub-committee* (Peel report) (London: HMSO). **120**

Central Policy Review Staff (1980) *People and their Families* (London: HMSO). **31**

Chapman, J. B. (1982) 'Helping the new mother with her baby', *Maternal and Child Health*, March, 96–9. **141**

Children's Committee (1980) *The Needs of Under-Fives in the Family* (London: HMSO). **137, 160**

Clark, J. (1973) *A Family Visitor* (London: Royal College of Nursing). **128**

Clark, M. (1981) *Child Care and Development Courses for Secondary Pupils*, University of Nottingham, MPhil thesis, unpublished. **77**

Clarke, A. M. and Clarke, A. D. B. (eds) (1976) *Early Experience: Myth and Evidence* (London: Open Books). **136**

Clulow, C. *et al.* (1982) *To Have and To Hold* (Aberdeen University Press). **47, 57, 115, 118, 120, 131**

Coleman, J. (1980) *The Nature of Adolescence* (London: Methuen).

Collins, N. (1982) 'The Family Service', *Youth in Society*, 65, April, 8–9. **94, 189**

Committee on Child Health Services (1976) *Fit for the Future* (Court report) (London: HMSO). **14, 37, 41, 68, 128, 138, 139**

Committee of Enquiry into the Education of Handicapped Children and Young People (1978) *Special Educational Needs* (Warnock report) (London: HMSO) (Cmnd 7212). **174**

Community Education Development Centre (1982a) *Parents in the Primary School* (Coventry: CEDC). **176**

Community Education Development Centre (1982b) *Parents in the Classroom* (Coventry: CEDC). **178**

Community Education Development Centre (1982c) 'Adults in school: results of enquiry', *Network*, 2, 7, 3. **180**

Community Service Volunteers (1978) *Teenagers in Playgroups*. **78**

Coombe Lodge Further Education College (1983) *Planning Local Education Authority Support for YOP: MSC Exemplary Projects* (London). **100**

Council for Science and Society (1980) *Childbirth Today: Policy making in the National Health Service – A case study*. **130**

Cousins, L. (1982) *I'm a New Woman Now: Education for women in Liverpool* (Liverpool: Priority). **151, 152**

Coussins, J. and Coote, A. (1981) *The Family in the Firing Line* (Child Poverty Action Group and National Council for Civil Liberties). **32**

Coventry Education Department and van leer Foundation (1979) *Nursery Annexes in the Inner City* (Coventry). **155**

Cowan, J. (1982) *People Cope* (London: COPE). **158**

Cowley, J. and Daniels, H. (1981) *A Feasibility Study concerning the Viability of Developing Parenthood/Child Development/Family Life Education Courses in Schools through In-service Education of Teachers.* (Milton Keynes: Open University) Part I. **71, 89**

Cox, K. (1982) *Pregnancy and Parenthood in School Age Pupils.* Paper delivered at NCB seminar, 13 May. **107, 185**

Craven, E. *et al.* (1982) *Family Issues and Public Policy* (Study Commission on the Family). **207**

Crow, G. (1983) *An Evaluation of the Manchester Low Cost Pre-School and Parent Education Unit.* Coventry: Community Education Development Centre. **155**

Cyster, R. *et al.* (1980) *Parental Involvement in Primary Schools* (Windsor: NFER Publishing Co). **174, 175, 177, 181**

Dally, A. (1982) *Inventing Motherhood* (London: Burnett Books). **13, 118**

David, K. and Cowley, J. (1980) *Pastoral Care in Schools and Colleges* (London: Edward Arnold). **82**

David, K (1982) *Personal and Social Education in Secondary Schools* (London: Longman). **81**

David, M. (1982) *Sex Education and Social Policy: towards a new moral economy*, paper given at Westhill conference on 'Class, gender and race', 4–6 January. **44**

Davie, R. *et al.* (1972) *From Birth to Seven* (London: Longman). **170**

Davies, B. (1979) *From Social Education to Social and Life Skills Training: In Whose Interests?* occasional paper, 19 (Leicester: National Youth Bureau). **104**

Davis, J. (1982) *Parent Support Programme: Evaluation end of year 1982.* Liverpool Education Department. **181**

De'Ath, E. (1982) 'Tomorrow's parents – a job for life?'. *Youth in Society*, 73, 20–1. **5**

De'Ath, E. (ed.) (1983a) *Supporting Parents in the Community: Parent–Professional Partnership in Scotland*, Parenting Paper 6 (London: National Children's Bureau). **6**

De'Ath, E. (ed.) (1983b) *Evaluating Parenting Groups*, Parenting Paper 7 (London: National Children's Bureau). **5, 62**

Department of Education and Science (1977) *Education in Schools: A Consultative Document* (London: HMSO). **67**

Department of Education and Science (1977) *Health Education in Schools* (London: HMSO). **77**

Department of Education and Science (1979) *Aspects of Secondary Education in England: A Survey by HM Inspectors of Schools* (London: HMSO). **81, 82**

Department of Education and Science (1980) *A View of the Curriculum* (HMI Series: Matters for Discussion II) (London: HMSO). **68**

Department of Education and Science (1981) *The School Curriculum* (London: HMSO). **68**

Department of Education and Science. Review Group on the Youth Service in England (1982) *Experience and Participation; report* (Thompson report) (London: HMSO) Cmnd 8686. **93**

Department of Education and Science and Welsh Office (1977) *A New Partnership for our Schools* (Taylor report) (London: HMSO). **174**

Department of Employment (1982) *New Earnings Survey* (London: HMSO). **36**

Department of Health and Social Security (1974a) *The Family in Society:*

Dimensions of Parenthood (London: HMSO). **2, 15, 16, 17, 19, 41, 68, 150**

Department of Health and Social Security (1974b) *The Family in Society: Preparation for Parenthood* (London: HMSO). **2, 17, 19, 41, 68, 145–6**

Department of Health and Social Security (1978) *Violence to Children: a response to the first report from the select committee on violence in the family* (1976–77). (London: HMSO) Cmnd 7123. **139**

Department of Health and Social Security (1980a) *Reply to the Second Report from the Social Services Committee on Perinatal and Neonatal Mortality* (London: HMSO) Cmnd 8084. **117**

Department of Health and Social Security (1980b) Townsend, P. and Davidson, N. (eds) *Inequalities in Health; the Black Report* (Harmondsworth: Penguin Books) (Original edition, London: HMSO, 1980). **34**

Development Education Centre (1983) *Values, Cultures and Kids* (Birmingham: DEC).

Devon County Council (1978) *Health and the School.* **72**

Dinkmeyer, D. and McKay, G. (1976) *Systematic Training for Effective Parenting* (Circle Pines, Minnesota: American Guidance Service Inc). **49**

Docherty, S. (1978) *Do Pupils want Health and Social Education? A Reanalysis* (Edinburgh: Scottish Health Education Unit). **70**

Doherty, W. J. and Ryder, R. G. (1980) 'Parent Effectiveness Training: criticisms and caveats'. *Journal of Marital and Family Therapy*, 6, 4, 409–19. **49**

Dominian, J. (1968) *Marital Breakdown* (Harmondsworth: Penguin Books).

Douglas, J. W. B. (1964) *The Home and the School* (London: MacGibbon and Kee). **170**

Douglas, J. W. B. *et al.* (1971) *All Our Future* (London: Panther). **170**

Draper, J. (1983) *An Experiment in Community Antenatal Care*, Early Parenthood Project (Hughes Hall, Cambridge). **124**

Draper, J. *et al.* (1981) *Early Parenthood Project Report of the First Year* (Hughes Hall, Cambridge). **115, 120, 125, 132**

Dreikurs, R. and Soltz, V. (1970) *Happy Children* (London: Souvenir Press). **49**

Dykins, M. (1982) *Widening Opportunities for Parents, Children and Adolescents* in Pugh, G. (1982a). **78**

Eggleston, J. (1976) *Adolescence and the Community* (London: Edward Arnold). **93**

Elbourne, D. (1981) *Is the Baby All Right? Current trends in perinatal health* (London: Junction Books). **118**

Elliott, J. *et al.* (1981) *School Accountability* (London: Grant McIntyre). **175, 176**

Elliott, S. (1982) *Some Psychological Measurements in Pregnancy and their Relationship to Postnatal Depression*, paper presented at Marcé Society Inaugural Conference on Motherhood and Mental Illness, 21–23 July, London. **132**

Equal Opportunities Commission/National Union of Students (1980) *Nur-*

series in Colleges and Universities (Manchester: EOC/NUS). **110**

Equal Opportunities Commission (1982) *Parenthood in the Balance: An Assessment of Benefits and Leave around the Time of Childbirth* (Manchester: EOC).

Essen, J. and Fogelman, K. (1979) 'Childhood housing experiences', *Concern*, 32, 5–10. **34**

Fabes, R. (1980) 'Personal view', *Youth in Society*, June, 43, 24. **111**

Fantini, M. D. and Cardenas, R. (eds) (1980) *Parenting in a Multicultural Society* (New York: Longman).

Farrell, C. (1978) *My Mother Said: The way young people learned about sex and birth control*. Routledge & Kegan Paul. **70, 86**

Feeley, G. and Karran, S. (1983) 'The Coventry experience', in Aplin and Pugh (1983). **155**

Ferri, E. (1976) *Growing Up in a One-Parent Family* (Windsor: NFER Publishing Company). **26**

Ferri, E. (1977) *Disadvantaged Families and Playgroups* (Windsor: NFER Publishing Company). **144**

Ferri, E. (1984) *Stepchildren; a national study* (Windsor: NFER–Nelson). **26, 27**

Fine, M. (ed.) (1980) *Handbook of Parent Education* (London: Academic Press). **49**

Fiske, M. (1979) *Middle Age: The Prime of Life?* (London: Harper & Row). **185**

Fletcher, C. and Thomson, N. (eds) (1980) *Issues in Community Education* (Lewes: Falmer Press). **179**

Flynn, S. (1983) 'The changing definition of intermediate treatment', *Youth in Society*, 76, March, 10–11. **103**

Fogelman, K. (ed.) (1976) *Britain's Sixteen-Year Olds* (London: National Children's Bureau). **24, 186, 190**

Franklin, A. W. (ed.) (1977) *Child Abuse: Prediction, Prevention and Follow-up* (Edinburgh: Churchill Livingstone). **18**

Free Church Federal Council and The British Council of Churches (1982) *Choices in Childlessness*.

Freire, P. (1972) *Pedagogy of the Oppressed* (Harmondsworth: Penguin Books). **52**

Friend, P. (1981) 'Backing up the parents', *Times Educational Supplement*, 30 October. **178**

Frommer, E. (1973) 'The importance of childhood experience in relation to problems of marriage and family building', *British Journal of Psychiatry*, 123, 573, 157–66. **20**

Garcia, J. (1981) *Findings on Antenatal Care from Community Health Council Studies* (Oxford: National Perinatal Epidemiology Unit). **126**

Goodwin, S. (1982) 'Health visitors: help or hindrance?', in Pugh, G. (1982c). **138**

Gordon, T. (1970) *Parent Effectiveness Training* (New York: Peter Wyden). **49**

Gorell-Barnes, G. (1979) 'Infant needs and angry responses – a look at violence in the family', in Walrond-Skinner, S. (ed.) *Family and Marital Psychotherapy* (London: Routledge & Kegan Paul). **18**

Goulding, J. (1983) 'Playbuses in the Community', *Links*, 8, 2, 17–21. **144**

Grafton, T. *et al.* (1982a) *The Preparation for Parenthood Curriculum in Five Secondary Schools*, paper presented to BERA Annual Conference, St Andrews, September. **72, 77, 82, 83, 84, 85, 88**

Grafton, T. *et al.* (1982b) 'Getting personal – the teachers' dilemma', *International Journal of Sociology and Social Policy*, 2, 3. **72**

Grafton, T. *et al.* (1983a) 'Gender and curriculum choice in relation to education for parenthood'. In Hammersley, M. and Hargreaves, A. (eds) *Curriculum Practice: Sociological Case Studies* (Lewes: Falmer Press). **69, 72**

Grafton, T. *et al.* (1983b) *Preparation for Parenthood in the Secondary School Curriculum* (a report to the DES). (Birmingham: University of Aston Department of Educational Enquiry). **41, 72, 74, 76, 88**

Graham, H. and McKee, L. (1980) *The First Months of Motherhood* (London: Health Education Council) (7 vols or 1 vol summary report). **56**

Grant, Sister Doreen (1983) 'Home/school/community links in Glasgow', in De'Ath, E. (1983a). **155**

Greaves, K. *et al.* (1982) *Off-the-Job Training on YOP: Summary of Research Findings in Work Experience Schemes 1979–1982* (Sheffield: Manpower Services Commission) (Research and Development Series No. 12). **100**

Guardian (1983) 'Thatcher team plot their future for the family', 17 February. **69**

Hagedorn, J. (1983) 'All quiet on the home front', *Times Educational Supplement*, 11 March, p. 20. **178**

Hardy, M. *et al.* (1979) 'Prevention of baby battering', *Practitioner*, 222, 1328, 243–7. **137**

Hardyment, C. (1983) *Dream Babies*, (London: Jonathan Cape). **38**

Harman, D. and Brim, O. (1980) *Learning to be Parents: Principles, Programs and Methods* (London: Sage Publications). **49, 53**

Harrison, M. (1982) 'Do parents respond to a supportive rather than a didactic approach?' in Pugh, G. (1982d). **17**

Haskey, J. (1983) 'Marital status before marriage and age at marriage: their influence on the chance of divorce', *Population Trends*, 32, 4–14. **25**

Haystead, J. *et al.* (1980) *Pre-school Education and Care* (London: Hodder and Stoughton). **31**

Health in Homerton, *Annual Report* (London, 1983). **125**

Health Visitors Association/Royal College of Midwives (1982) *Joint Statement on Antenatal Preparation*, June. **124**

HM Inspectorate (1978) Curriculum 11–16. *Health Education in the Secondary School*, working paper by Health Education Committee of HM Inspectorate. **67**

Heron, A. (1952) 'Adolescents and preparation for parenthood', in *British Journal of Educational Psychology*, 22, 3, 173–9. **66**

Hess, R. D. (1980) 'Experts and amateurs: some unintended consequences of parent education', in Fantini and Cardenas (1980). **204**

Hevey, D. (1982) 'The wider issues of support and planning', in Pugh, G. (1982c). **157**

Hewison, J. (1981) 'Home is where the help is', *Times Educational Supplement*, 16 January. **177**

Hibbard, B. M. (1979) 'The effectiveness of antenatal education', *Health Education Journal*, 38, 2, 39–44. **128**

Hicks, M. W. and Williams, J. W. (1981) 'Current challenges in educating for parenthood', *Family Relations*, 30, 579–84.

Hiskins, G. (1976) 'Health education in schools and the community', *Health Visitor*, 49, 4, 115–17. **87**

Hiskins, G. (1981) 'How mothers help themselves', *Health Visitor*, March, 54, 3, 108–11. **140**

Hoffman, L. W. and Hoffman, M. (1973) 'The value of children to parents', in Fawcett, J. (ed.) *Psychological Perspectives on Population* (New York: Basic Books). **21**

Holman, R. (1983) *Resourceful Friends* (London: The Children's Society). **159**

Home Office (1979) *Marriage Matters* (London: HMSO). **41, 68**

Home Office (1982) *Criminal Statistics, England and Wales 1981* (London: HMSO) Cmnd 8668. **104**

Hopson, B. and Scally, M. (1980) *Lifeskills Teaching* (Maidenhead: McGraw Hill). **83**

Hopson, B. and Scally, M. (1981, 2) *Lifeskills Teaching Programmes No 1 and No 2.* (Leeds: Lifeskills Associates). **83**

House of Commons (1979) *Youth and Community Bill*, (Skeet report) (London: HMSO) Sections 1 and 2. **93**

House of Commons. (1980) Social Services Committee *Perinatal and Neonatal Mortality, Vol 1: Report.* (Short report) (London: HMSO). **121**

Hubbard, D. and Wellings, A. (1979) 'Mothers' groups in the school setting', *Education 3–13*, 7, 2, 38–42. **154**

Hughes, M. *et al.* (1980) *Nurseries Now* (Harmondsworth: Penguin Books). **31**

Inner London Education Authority (1979) *Practical Experience with Young Children*, ILEA Home Economics Inspectorate, Guidelines for use in child development courses. **78**

Inner London Education Authority (1983) *A Policy for Parent Education* (ILEA). **51, 153**

Isaacs, Susan (1930, 1933) *The Behaviour of Young Children*, 2 vols (London: Routledge). **38**

Jackson, A. and Hannon, P. (1981) *The Belfield Reading Project* (Rochdale: Belfield Community Council). **177**

Jackson, B. (1982) *The Child Care Switchboard* (Huddersfield: National Children's Centre). **164**

Jamieson, L. (1982) *The Challenge of Helping Professionals Respond to New Parents*, paper at National Children's Bureau study day, 25 May. **128**

Jayne, E. (1976) *Deptford Educational Home Visiting Project*. RS 645/76 (Inner London Education Authority). **162**

Jenkins, C. G. and Newton, R. (1981) *The First Year of Life* (Edinburgh: Churchill Livingstone). **138**

Johnson, D. (ed.) (1980) *Disaffected Pupils* (Brunel University). **108**

Jones, L. (no date) *The Case for More Parent and Toddler Groups within the Health Service* (West Glamorgan AHA: mimeo). **140**

Katz, L. (1982) 'Contemporary perspectives on the roles of mothers and teachers', *Australian Journal of Early Childhood*, 7, 1, 4–15. **53**

Keeley, B. (1981) *The Effect of Pre-School Provision on Mothers of Young Children* (Cranfield: Institute of Technology) mimeo. **143**

Kenny, M. (1981) 'When the experts take over from parents', *Daily Telegraph*, 11 February. **43**

Kidd, J. (1981) *Parenthood – Child's Play, Or Is It?* (London: National Children's Home) mimeo. **164**

Kidd, J. (1982a) 'Practical partnerships', in Pugh, G. (1982c). **188**

Kidd, J. (1982b) *Practical Partnerships* (London: National Children's Home). **42, 164, 188**

King, Sir Frederick Truy (1921, 1924) *The Expectant Mother, and Baby's First Months* (New Zealand, 1921; London: Macmillan, 1924). **38**

Knight, B. *et al.* (1979) *Family Groups in the Community* (London Voluntary Service Council). **158**

Lambert, L. (1977) 'Measuring the gaps in teenagers' knowledge of sex and parenthood'. *Health and Social Service Journal*, 87, 4536, 668–9. **86**

LaRossa, R. (1977) *Conflict and Power in Marriage: Expecting the First Child* (London: Sage). **21**

Leach, P. (1977) *Baby and Child* (London: Michael Joseph).

Leach, P. (1983) *Babyhood*. 2nd edition (Harmondsworth: Penguin Books).

Leff, J. R. (1983) 'Birth of the blues', *AIMS Quarterly Journal*, Spring, 7. **129**

LeRoy, M. (1982) *Ketley Family Life Project Evaluation*. (Rugby: National Marriage Guidance Council). **56, 57, 148**

Lewis, J. *et al.* (1976) *No Single Thread: Psychological Health in Family Systems* (New York: Brunner & Mazel). **23**

Liffman, M. (1978) *Power for the Poor. The Family Centre Project: An experiment in self-help.* (London: Allen & Unwin). **52**

Lilley, P. (1982) *Health Education Diploma* (Leeds University). **101**

Lingard, A. and Allard, J. (1982) *Parent/Teacher Relations in Secondary Schools* 2nd edition (Gravesend: Home and School Council). **176**

Lockwood, R. (1982) 'Education for family responsibility – the role of the school', in Pugh, G. (1982a). **71**

Lord Chancellor's Office. Committee on the Age of Majority (1967) *Report* (Latey report) (London: HMSO) Cmnd 3342. **93**

Lynch, J. and Pimlott, J. A. (1976) *Parents and Teachers* (London: Macmillan Education for Schools Council). **172**

Macaskill, H. (1982) 'How to bath babies and make a fluffy animal doesn't have a great deal of value in the long term', *Guardian*, 7 April. **77**

Macbeth, A. *et al.* (1980) *Scottish School Councils: policy-making, participation or irrelevance?* (Scottish Education Department, HMSO). **179**

McCafferty, I. (1982) *Co-ordinating Secondary School Health Education*

(Nottinghamshire Health Education Unit/Nottingham University Adult Education Department). **84, 86, 89**

McCail, G. (1981) *Mother Start* (Edinburgh: Scottish Council for Research in Education). **162, 172**

McCleary, G. F. (1933) *The Early History of the Infant Welfare Movement.* (London: H. K. Lewis). **38**

McGeeney, P. (1980) 'The involvement of parents', in Craft, M. *et al.* (eds) *Linking Home and School*, 3rd edition (London: Harper & Row). **178**

McGlaughlin, A. and Empson, J. (1979) 'Mother plus child = future', *Community Care*, 16 August, 277, 25. **136**

McKee, L. (1982) 'Fathers' participation in infant care: a critique', in McKee, L. and O'Brien, M. (1982). **21**

McKee, L. and O'Brien, M. (eds) (1982) *The Father Figure* (London: Tavistock Publications). **21**

Maddox, B. (1980) *Step-parenting. How to live with other People's Children* (London: Unwin Paperbacks). **27, 192**

Madge, N. (1983) 'Unemployment and its effects on children'. *Journal of Child Psychology and Psychiatry*, 24, 2, 311–19. **34**

Manpower Services Commission (1973) *Instructional Guide to Social and Life Skills Training* (London). **105**

Mansfield, P. (1982) 'Getting ready for parenthood: attitudes and expectations of having children of a group of newly weds', *International Journal of Sociology and Social Policy*, 2, 3. **47, 116**

Martin, C. (1982) *Psycho-social Stress and Puerperal Psychiatric Disorders*, paper presented at Marcé Society Inaugural Conference on Motherhood and Mental Illness, 21–23 July, London. **132**

Maternity Alliance (1981) *Policy Statement* (London). **122**

Maternity Alliance (1982) *Getting Fit for Pregnancy* (London). **117**

Maternity Services Advisory Committee (1982) *Maternity Care in Action, Part I – Antenatal Care* (London: DHSS). **121, 122**

Meacher, M. (1982) *Self-help Groups for Parents Under Stress: a contribution to prevention?* (London: Mental Health Foundation). **163–4**

Miller, J. *et al.*, (1983) *Towards a Personal Guidance Base* (London: Further Education Unit). **99**

Ministry of Education (1956) *Health Education: a handbook of suggestions for the consideration of teachers and others concerned in the health and education of children and young people.* Pamphlet 31. (London: HMSO). **66**

Ministry of Health (1932) *Final Report of the Departmental Committee on Maternal Mortality and Morbidity.* (London: HMSO). **117**

Ministry of Health (1960) *Youth Service in England and Wales.* (Albemarle report) (London: HMSO) Cmnd 929. **93**

Mittler, P. and McConachie, H. (eds) (1983) *Parents, Professionals and Mentally Handicapped People* (London: Croom Helm). **174**

Monson, S. (1983) *Welcoming Teenagers into PPA Groups* (London: Preschool Playgroups Association). **78**

Montague, J. (1979) 'Teaching teenagers about child development', *Midwife, Health Visitor and Community Nurse*, 15, 4, 150–1. **78**

Moss, P. and Fonda, N. (eds) (1980) *Work and the Family* (London: Temple Smith). **13**

Moss, P. (1982a) 'Transition to parenthood: the antenatal period' in Pugh, G. (1982a). **42, 55, 56**

Moss, P. *et al.* (1981) *Transition to Parenthood Project, Report on Second Interview* (London: Thomas Coram Research Unit). **41, 126, 128**

Moss, P. *et al.* (1982b) *Transition to parenthood project, Report on Fourth Interview* (London: Thomas Coram Research Unit). **132**

Mother Magazine (1981) 'Antenatal Clinics', November 1981, 547, 11–14. **122**

Mother Magazine (1983) 'What would you like to have known before becoming a parent?', April, 552, 21–2. **18**

Mount, F. (1982) *The Subversive Family: An Alternative History of Love and Marriage.* (London: Jonathan Cape).

Munro, H. (1983) 'Supporting parents in the community: the role of adult education', in De'Ath, E. (1983a). **153**

National Childbirth Trust (1981) *Change in Antenatal Care: A Report of a Working Party* (London). **122**

National Council for One Parent Families (1979) *Born Poor* (London). **110**

National Council for One Parent Families and Community Development Trust. Joint Working Party on Pregnant Schoolgirls and Schoolgirl Mothers (1979) *Pregnant at School* (Miles Report) (London: National Council for One Parent Families). **41, 68, 108**

National Foster Care Association (1977) *Added to Adolescence.* (Sole distributor in UK – NFCA.) **192**

National Union of Teachers (1983) *Home–School Relations.* **181**

National Youth Bureau (1977) *Youth Charter towards 2000.* (Leicester: NYB). **190**

Newcastle-upon-Tyne, City of (1982) *Performance and Review Subcommittee Report of the Director of Policy Services: Parental Involvement in Schools – discussion document.* **176**

Newson, J. and Newson, E. (1963) *Infant Care in an Urban Community* (London: Allen & Unwin). **22**

Newson, J. and Newson, E. (1974) 'Cultural aspects of Childrearing in the English-speaking world', in Richards, M. P. M. (ed.) *The Integration of a Child into a Social World* (Cambridge University Press). **38**

Newson, J. and Newson, E. (1976) *Seven Years Old in the Home Environment* (London: Allen & Unwin). **12, 21**

Newson, J., Newson, E. and Barnes, P. (1977) *Perspectives on School at Seven Years Old* (London: Allen & Unwin). **172**

Newson, J. (1982) 'Bringing up children in a changing world: disciplinary styles and moral outcomes', in Pugh, G. (1982b). **184**

Nottinghamshire County Council Education Department (1981) *Guidelines for the Teaching of Health Education in Secondary Schools.* **72**

Oakley, A. (1979) *Becoming a Mother* (Oxford: Martin Robertson). **116, 120, 130**

Oakley, A. (1980) *Women confined: Towards a Sociology of Childbirth* (Oxford: Martin Robertson).   **47, 118, 119, 132**

O'Brien, H. and Smith, C. (1981) 'Women's views and experiences of antenatal care', *The Practitioner*, 225, 123–5, February.   **121**

Office of Population Censuses and Surveys (1982) *Monitor AB 82/5* (London: HMSO).   **100**

Ong, B. (1983) *Our Motherhood: Women's Accounts of Pregnancy, Childbirth and Health Encounters*. (London: Family Service Units).   **119, 126**

Open University (1981a) *Contemporary Issues in Education 2.6 Parents and Teachers*. E200. (Milton Keynes: Open University Press).   **174**

Open University (1981b) *Education for Family Life: A planning pack for teachers*. (Milton Keynes: Open University Press) P532.   **78, 86, 89, 174**

Organisation for Economic Co-operation and Development/Centre for Educational Research and Innovation (1982) *The Educational Role of the Family: a thematic analysis of existing country policies, positions and programmes*. (CERI/ERF/82.01).   **39, 40, 173**

Orton, A. (1979) 'Parentcraft – a teacher's view', In Cowley, J. *et al.*, *Parenthood Education in Schools* (Manchester: TACADE).

Orton, A. (1982) *A Study of Education for Parenthood in Secondary Schools* (Newcastle University) mimeo.   **88**

Overton, J. (1982) *Stepping Stones Projects* (Glasgow: Scottish PPA).   **142, 144**

Palfreeman, S. (1982) *Valuing Mothers. A health visiting study of the effectiveness of mother and toddler groups amongst at risk families* (Cheshire A. H. A.) mimeo.   **56, 140**

Parsons, W. D. and Perkins, E. R. (1980) *Why Don't Women Attend for Antenatal Care?* Leverhulme Health Education Project (University of Nottingham) Paper 23.   **121**

Pearson, R. and Lambert, L. (1977) 'Sex education, preparation for parenthood and the adolescent', *Community Health*, 9, 2, 84–90.   **70**

Perfrement, S. (1982) *Women's Information on Pregnancy, Childbirth and Babycare* (Brighton: Centre for Medical Research).   **55, 120, 122**

Perkins, E. (1978) *Attendance at Antenatal Clinics: A District Study*. Leverhulme Health Education Project, (University of Nottingham) Paper 13.   **110, 126**

Perkins, E. (1979) 'Defining the need: an analysis of varying goals in antenatal classes', *International Journal of Nursing Studies*, 16, 275–82.   **125**

Perkins, E. and Morris, B. (1979) *Preparation for Parenthood: A critique of the concept*. Leverhulme Health Education Project (University of Nottingham) Paper 17.   **71**

Perkins, E. (1980) *Education for Childbirth and Parenthood* (London: Croom Helm).   **55**

Phelan, J. (1982) 'What's in a name', *Social Work Today*, 13, 5, 20–1.   **159**

Phelan, J. (1983) *Family Centres* (London: Children's Society).   **159**

Phillips, R. (1980) 'Towards a pedagogy of the oppressed. Newham Parents Centre as a resort for adult basic education', *Basic Education*,

May. **171**

Porteous, M. A. and Fisher, C. J. (1980) *Adolescent Problems: A Factual and Descriptive Account.* (Social Work Research Unit, University of Bradford). **104, 186, 190**

Poulton, G. and Couzens, L. (1981) *Scope for Parents and Children,* (Southampton: Scope). **50**

Poulton, L. (1981) 'Bassett Green first school family education project' in *Outlines* (Coventry: CEDC). **157**

Poulton, L. (1982) 'Support? Who gives it and when?', in Pugh, G. (1982a). **87, 156**

Prendergast, S. and Prout, A. (1980) 'What will I do? Teenage girls and the construction of motherhood', *Sociological Review,* 28, 3, 517–35. **47, 70**

Pre-school Playgroups Association (1981) *Parents and Playgroups* (London: Allen & Unwin). **141**

Pre-school Playgroups Association (1983) *Facts and Figures 1982–83* (London). **78, 141, 143**

Pringle, M. K. (1975) *The Needs of Children* (London: Hutchinson). **2, 18, 47, 217**

Pringle, M. K. (1980a) 'Aims and future directions', in Pugh, G. (1980). **2**

Pringle, M. K. (ed.) (1980b) *A Fairer Future for Children* (London: Macmillan). **2, 31**

Pringle, M. K. (1982) 'A fairer future for children', in Pugh, G. (1982b). **2**

Proctor, M. (1983) *Family Life in the Twentieth Century* (Rugby: National Marriage Guidance Council) mimeo. **96, 189**

Pugh, G. (ed.) (1980) *Preparation for Parenthood* (London: National Children's Bureau). **3, 14, 46, 59, 78, 87**

Pugh, G. (1981) *Parents as Partners: Intervention Schemes and Group Work with Parents of Handicapped Children* (London: National Children's Bureau). **52, 174**

Pugh G., Kidd, J. and Torkington, K. (1982) *A Job For Life* (London: National Children's Bureau, National Children's Home, National Marriage Guidance Council). **4, 202**

Pugh, G. (ed.) (1982a) *Parenthood Education and Support: A Continuous Process* (London: National Children's Bureau) Parenting paper 1. **6**

Pugh, G. (ed.) (1982b) *Parenting in the Eighties* (London National Children's Bureau) Parenting paper 2. **6**

Pugh, G. (ed.) (1982c) *Supporting Parents in the Community* (London: National Children's Bureau) Parenting paper 3. **6**

Pugh, G. (ed.) (1982d) *Can Parenting Skills be Taught?* (London: National Children's Bureau) Parenting paper 4. **6**

Pugh, G. (ed.) (1982e) *Working with Families: Services or Support?* (London: National Children's Bureau) Parenting paper 5. **6**

Pugh, G. (1982f) 'Broadcasting support for parents', *Media Project News,* January, 2–4. **5**

Rapoport, R. *et al.* (1977) *Fathers, Mother and Others* (London: Routledge & Kegan Paul). **11**

Rapoport, R. *et al.* (eds) (1982) *Families in Britain* (London: Routledge &

Kegan Paul).

Rathbone, B. (1973) *Focus on New Mothers: A Study of Antenatal Classes* (London: Royal College of Nursing). **128**

Reading, A. *et al.* (1982) 'Health beliefs and health care behaviour in pregnancy', *Psychological Medicine*, 12, 2, 379–83. **123**

Rée, H. (1973) *Educator Extraordinary* (London: Longman). **179**

Reid, D. (1981) 'Into the mainstream', *Times Educational Supplement*, 17 April. **75**

Rice, W. (1979) 'Teaching parenting skills', in Cowley, J. *et al. Parenthood Education in Schools* (Manchester, TACADE). **71**

Richards, M. (1982) 'How should we approach the study of fathers?', in McKee, L. and O'Brien, M. (1982). **119**

Richards, M. and Dyson, M. (1982) *Separation, Divorce and the Development of Children: A Review* (Cambridge: Child Care and Development Group, University of Cambridge). **27, 191**

Richman, J. and Goldthorp, W. O. (1978) 'Fatherhood: the social construction of pregnancy and birth', in Kizinger, S. and Davis, J. (eds) *The Place of Birth* (Oxford University Press). **119**

Rimmer, L. (1981) *Families in Focus: Marriage, Divorce and Family Patterns* (London: Study Commission on the Family). **24, 116**

Rimmer, L. and Popay, J. (1982) *Employment Trends and the Family* (London: Study Commission on the Family). **33**

Robertson, J. and Robertson, J. (1982) *A Baby in the Family* (Harmondsworth: Penguin Books). **38**

Robinson, A. (1982) *Latchkey schemes* (London: National Children's Bureau). **170**

Robinson, D. and Henry, S. (1977) *Self Help and Health* (Oxford: Martin Robertson). **151**

Robinson, E. (1982) 'Helping Merseyside parents', *Contact*, October. **144**

Rönka, T. (1983) *Developing New Methods in Family Education* (Paris: OECD/CERI). **145**

Rousseau, Jean Jacques (1762) *Emile, ou l' education* (Amsterdam/London). **37**

Royal College of General Practitioners (1982) *Healthier Children – Thinking Prevention* (London: RCGP). **139**

Royal College of Obstetricians and Gynaecologists (1982) *Report of the RCOG Working Party on Antenatal and Intrapartum Care* (Macnaughton report) (London: RCOG). **117**

Rubinstein, V. (1979) *Results of Questionnaire on Education for Parenthood* (London: British Federation of University Women). **79**

Ruel, A. and Adams, G. (1981) 'A parenting group in general practice', *Journal of the Royal College of General Practitioners*, 31, 496–9. **141**

Russell, P. (1983) 'The parents' perspective of family needs and how to meet them', in Mittler, P. and McConachie, H. (1983). **193**

Rutter, M. (1972) *Maternal Deprivation Reassessed.* (Harmondsworth: Penguin Books). **20**

Rutter, M. and Madge, N. (1976) *Cycles of Disadvantage* (London: Open Books). **19, 21, 40**

Rutter, M. *et al.* (1979) *Fifteen Thousand Hours* (London: Open Books). **65**

Satir, V. (1972) *Peoplemaking* (London: Souvenir Press). **118**

Schaffer, R. (1977) *Mothering* (London: Fontana/Open Books). **7, 48, 136**

Schleicher, K. (1982) *Preparation for Family Life* (Strasbourg: Council of Europe). **39**

Schools Council (1970) *The Humanities Project: an introduction* (London: Heinemann Educational Books). **80**

Schools Council (1976) *Health Education in Secondary Schools.* Evans-Methuen, Working Paper 57. **83**

Schools Council (1977) *All About Me* and *Think Well* (Sunbury-on-Thames: Nelson). **75**

Schools Council (1978) *Planning for Home and Family Education* and five teacher's guides (London: Forbes Publications). **75**

Schools Council (1982) *Health Education 13–18* (London: Forbes Publications). **84**

Scottish Education Department (1979) *Health Education in Primary, Secondary and Special Schools in Scotland.* Report by HM Inspectors of Schools, Edinburgh (London: HMSO). **67**

Scottish Pre-school Playgroups Association (1976) *Teenagers in Playgroups* (Edinburgh). **78**

Scribbins, J. (1983) *Parent Education and Mothering* (University of London Department of Extra Mural Studies). **151**

Searing, H. (1980) *Eastland House Group: an account of the formation of a group of mothers and young children in Thornbury* (Bristol: Thornbury Hospital) mimeo. **158**

Select Committee on Violence in the Family (1977) *First Report from the Select Committee on Violence to Children*, vol. 1 (London: HMSO). **41, 68**

Shaw, H. and Matthews, D. (1981) *Working Together, A Handbook for Parents of Teenagers.* 2nd edition (Christchurch, New Zealand: Burnside High School). (Available from Lifeskills Associates, Leeds). **189**

Shepperdson, B. (1980) *Mothers' Attitudes to Future Home Deliveries* (Swansea: Medical Sociology Research Centre). **130**

Shinman, S. (1981) *A Chance for Every Child? Access and Response to Pre-school Provision* (London: Tavistock Publications). **160**

Simms, M. and Smith, C. (1980) 'Ten schoolgirl mothers', *Youth in Society*, December, 49, 16–18. **112**

Simms, M. and Smith, C. (1981) 'Ten schoolgirl mothers revisited', *Youth in Society*, December, 61, 18–20. **112**

Simms, M. and Smith, C. (1983) 'Separated teenage mothers', *Marriage Guidance Journal*, Summer, 2–9. **105, 111**

Simpson, R. (1978) *Day Care for School Age Children* (Manchester: Equal Opportunities Commission). **170**

Smith, M. (1980) *Creators not Consumers* (London: NAYC Publications). **97**

Smith, T. (1980) *Parents and Preschool* (London: Grant McIntyre). **143, 154**

Social Development Council (1977) *Bringing up Children in New Zealand: Can we do better?* (New Zealand: SDC). **145**

Somerset County Council (1980) *Health and Social Education* (Taunton: Somerset CC). **72, 75, 81**

Spastics Society (1981) *A Charter for the Eighties.* **122**

Spock, B. (1979) *Baby and Child Care* (London: W. H. Allen). **20**

Stacey, M. (1983) 'Home visiting and the pre-school centre in Haringey', in Aplin and Pugh (1983). **155**

Stern, H. H. (1960) *Parent Education: An international survey* (University of Hull/UNESCO). **39, 50, 59, 66–7, 145, 173**

Strathclyde Regional Council (1978) *Understanding Children* (Glasgow: SRC). **79**

The Times (1981) 'Some surprises in the new Gallup Poll on European attitudes', 9 December. **186**

Thomas, S. (1982) 'I understood then how parents feel', *Times Educational Supplement*, 18 June, 43. **78**

Thornes, B. and Collard, J. (1979) *Who Divorces?* (London: Routledge and Kegan Paul). **111**

Tizard, B. *et al.* (1981) *Involving Parents in Nursery and Infant Schools* (London: Grant McIntyre). **172, 176, 178, 182**

Tizard, J. *et al.* (1982) 'Collaboration between teachers and parents in assisting children's reading'. *British Journal of Educational Psychology*, 52, 1–15. **177**

Torkington, K. (1981) 'Whether to marry and whether to have children?', in *Education for Family Life*, Source book, (Milton Keynes: Open University Press) P532. **51, 116**

Torkington, K. (1982) 'Parenthood education – a life-cycle approach', in Pugh, G. (1982e). **148**

Troth, D. (1982) 'Bull in a baby shop', *Times Educational Supplement*, 31 December, 14. **79**

Tucker, B. (1907) *Notes on the Care of Babies and Young Children* (London: Longman). **66**

Turner, P. (1983) 'IT for girls – a recipe for success', *Youth in Society*, 77, 16–18.

Tyerman, E. (1982) 'Teenage sexual activity', *Marriage Guidance*, 20, 1, 18–22.

Van der Eyken, W. (1982) *Home Start. A four-year evaluation* (Leicester: Home Start Consultancy). **120, 161, 162**

Verdon, F. (1980) 'Some reflections', in Pugh, G. (1980). **65**

Voluntary Council for Handicapped Children (1984) *Help Starts Here* (London).

Wallerstein, J. and Kelly, J. (1980) *Surviving the Break-up: How Children and Parents Cope with Divorce* (Grant McIntyre). **14**

Waltham Forest Education Department/Redbridge and Waltham Forest Area Health Authority (1980) *Health Education.* **72**

Wedge, P. and Essen, J. (1982) *Children in Adversity* (London: Pan Books). **34–5**

Weikart, D. (1980) 'Organising delivery of parent education', in Fantini, M. D. and Cardenas, R. (1980). **43**

Wellings, A. (1981) 'Parent education', in Hayes, M. (ed.) *Papers on Adult Basic Education* (University of Southampton). **154**

Wells, N. (1983) *Teenage Mothers* (Liverpool: European Collaborative Community for Child Health, Children's Research Fund). **109**

Westmacott, E. and Cameron, R. (1981) *Behaviour Can Change* (Basingstoke: Globe Education). **52**

White, B. L. (1975) *The First Years of Life* (New York: Avon Books). **136**

White, B. (1979) 'Preliminary results of our survey of education for parenthood programmes', *Centre for Parent Education Newsletter*, II, 1, December (Newton, Mass.: Centre for Parent Education). **144**

Whitfield, R. C. (1980) *Education for Family Life* (London: Hodder and Stoughton). **86**

Wilkinson, E. *et al.* (1978) *Strathclyde Experiment in Education: Govan Project* (Glasgow University), mimeo. **180**

Wilson, H. (1980) 'Parental supervision: a neglected aspect of delinquency', *British Journal of Criminology*, 20, 3, 203–35. **184**

Wiltshire County Council Education Committee (1978) *Social and Personal Education* (Trowbridge: Wiltshire CC) **72, 81**

Winnicott, D. W. (1964) *The Child, the Family and the Outside World* (Harmondsworth: Penguin). **12**

Wolfendale, S. (1979) 'Preschool development surveillance'. *Remedial Education*, 14, 4. **138**

Wolfson, J. (1982) 'Tools for teaching parenting skills', in Pugh, G. (1982d). **51**

Wood, A. and Simpkins, L. (1982) *Involving Parents in the Curriculum*. 3rd edition (Gravesend: Home and School Council). **177**

Wynn, M. and Wynn, A. (1981) *The Prevention of Handicap of Early Pregnancy Origin: Some evidence for the value of good health before conception* (London: Foundation for Education and Research in Childbearing). **48, 117**

Youth Service Development Council (1967) *Immigrants and the Youth Services; report* (Hunt report) (London: HMSO).

Youth Service Development Council (1969) *Youth and Community Work in the 70s; proposals* (Milson-Fairbairn report) (London: HMSO). **93**

Yule, W. (1975) 'Training psychological principles to non-psychologists: training parents in child management', *AEP Journal*, 3, 10, 5–16. **52**

Zander, L. *et al.* (1978) 'Integration of general practitioners and specialist antenatal care', *Journal of the Royal College of General Practitioners*, 28, 455–8. **123**

Index